DØ583935

THE
HISTORY OF
PERU

ADVISORY BOARD

THE HISTORY OF PERU

Daniel Masterson

The Greenwood Histories of the Modern Nations
Frank W. Thackeray and John E. Findling, Series Editors

Greenwood Press
Westport, Connecticut • London

Library of Congress Cataloging-in-Publication Data

Masterson, Daniel M.
    The history of Peru / Daniel Masterson.
        p. cm. — (The Greenwood histories of the modern nations, ISSN 1096–2905)
    Includes bibliographical references and index.
    ISBN 978–0–313–34072–7 (alk. paper)
  1. Peru—History. I. Title.
    F3431.M38   2009
    985—dc22   2009010348

British Library Cataloguing in Publication Data is available.

Library of Congress Catalog Card Number: 2009010348
ISBN: 978–0–313–34072–7
ISSN: 1096–2905

First published in 2009

Greenwood Publishing, 88 Post Road West, Westport, CT 06881
An imprint of Greenwood Publishing Group, Inc.
www.greenwood.com

Printed in the United States of America

The paper used in this book complies with the
Permanent Paper Standard issued by the National
Information Standards Organization (Z39.48–1984).

10 9 8 7 6 5 4 3 2 1

Contents

Photo essay follows page 94

Peru in Profile

GEOGRAPHY

Location: western South America; borders on Ecuador, Colombia, Brazil, Bolivia, and Chile

Area: 1,285,220 square kilometers, slightly smaller in size than Alaska

Coastline on Pacific Ocean: 2,414 kilometers

Maritime claims: 200 mile offshore resource zone

Climate: varies widely from humid rainforest in the east to temperate and frigid in the high Andes to extremely dry in the coastal desert. Local or mini-climates characterize much of the Andes. All of these climates can be significantly modified by the El Niño, which can strike Peru every four to six years

Highest elevation: Mount Huascarán at 22,205 feet, fifth highest mountain in South America

Main river systems: Amazon (to Iquitos), Marañón, Ucayali, Napo, Urubamba, Madre de Dios

Primary natural resources: copper, silver, gold, iron ore, petroleum, fish and marine animals, coal, phosphate, potash, natural gas

Environmental hazards: El Niño (flooding), earthquakes, tsunamis, volcanic activity, landslides, drought

Plant and animal diversity: total known species of plants, 17,144 (269 threatened); 460 mammals (49 threatened); breeding birds 695 (76 threatened); reptiles 347 (6 threatened); amphibians 352 (1 threatened); fish 166 (1 threatened)

PEOPLE

Population: 29,180,900 (July 2008)

Largest cities: Lima 7.8 million; Arequipa 841,130; Callao (Lima's port city) 813,264; Trujillo 747,450; Chiclayo 577,375; Iquitos 437,620

Median age: 25.8 years; male 25.5 years; female 26.1 years

Population growth rate: 1.264%

Life expectancy at birth: 70.44 years; males 68.61 years; females 72.37 years

Ethnic groups: indigenous (Amerindian) 45%; mestizo 37%; white, 15%; Afro Peruvian, Japanese, and Chinese, 3%

Languages: Spanish, Quechua, Aymara, Japanese, nearly 100 Amerindian dialects among the Amazon regions indigenous population

Literacy (can read and write at age 15): 87.7%

ECONOMY

Gross domestic product (GDP): $109.1 billion (2007)

GDP by economic sector: agriculture 8.4%; industry 25.6%; services 66%

GDP as defined by real growth: 9%

GDP per capita: $3,855

Labor by occupation: agriculture 9%; industry 18%; services, 73%

Population below poverty line: 44.5%

Inflation: 3.9 % (2008)

Foreign debt: $28 billion, principal and interest repayments $5.734 billion (2007)

Export partners: United States 15.5%; China 9.6%; Switzerland 7.1%; Canada 6.8%; Chile 6.0%; Japan 5.2%

Import partners: United States 16.5%; China 10.3%; Brazil 10.3%; Ecuador 7.2%; Colombia 6.1%

Oil proven reserves: 430.8 million barrels

Natural gas proven reserves: 236.9 billion cubic meters

Monetary unit: *Nuevo sol* 2.83 to U.S. dollar (July 2008)

GOVERNMENT

Government form: constitutional republic

Capital: Lima

Federated system: in 25 regions and one province (Amazonas), but in effect a strongly centralized government

Constitution: ratified December 29, 1993
Suffrage: universal and compulsory under penalty of substantial fine from 18
    to 70 years of age. Spanish literacy is not required
Chief of State: President of the Republic with one vice president
Legislative branch: unicameral legislature is known as the Congress of Peru.
    There are 120 seats elected in popular manner to five-year terms

EDUCATION

Governed by: the General Law of Education, 1982, and significant reforms in
    1992
Duration of compulsory education: 12 years
Age of entry: 5 years (1 year pre-primary)
Age of exit: 16 years.
Rate of grade repetition: rural areas (26%); urban areas (17%)
Class attendance hours: 40% higher in urban than rural areas
Funding and supervision: lack of funding for both primary and secondary
    schooling; and supervision and assessment of teaching is not strong
Higher education: dramatic expansion in the 20th century with over 50 insti-
    tutions serving nearly every Peruvian province
Types of higher educational institutions: public universities, private universi-
    ties, technical higher institute, teacher training schools, and higher post-
    graduate centers
Diploma requirements: includes a pass-fail compulsory national undergradu-
    ate exam

MILITARY

Main branches: army, air force, and navy, includes naval air, naval infantry
    (marines), and coast guard
Service: open to male and female volunteers 18 to 30 years of age; no conscrip-
    tion; term of service is two years
Army force levels: commissioned officers, 6,231; noncommissioned officers,
    13,600; enlisted personnel, 54,300
Enrollment at Chorillos Military Academy: 1,090
Air force levels: commissioned officers, 1,909; noncommissioned officers,
    7,559; enlisted personnel, 7,880
Air Force Academy enrollment: 325
Navy force levels: commission officers, 2,107; noncommissioned officers,
    18,396; enlisted 5,079
Naval Academy enrollment: 620

Series Foreword

The Greenwood Histories of the Modern Nations series is intended to provide students and interested laypeople with up-to-date, concise, and analytical histories of many of the nations of the contemporary world. Not since the 1960s has there been a systematic attempt to publish a series of national histories, and as series advisors, we believe that this series will prove to be a valuable contribution to our understanding of other countries in our increasingly interdependent world.

Some 40 years ago, at the end of the 1960s, the Cold War was an accepted reality of global politics. The process of decolonization was still in progress, the idea of a unified Europe with a single currency was unheard of, the United States was mired in a war in Vietnam, and the economic boom in Asia was still years in the future. Richard Nixon was president of the United States, Mao Tse-tung (not yet Mao Zedong) ruled China, Leonid Brezhnev guided the Soviet Union, and Harold Wilson was prime minister of the United Kingdom. Authoritarian dictators still controlled most of Latin America, the Middle East was reeling in the wake of the Six-Day War, and Shah Mohammad Reza Pahlavi was at the height of his power in Iran.

Since then, the Cold War has ended, the Soviet Union has vanished, leaving 16 independent republics in its wake, the advent of the computer age has radically transformed global communications, the rising demand for oil makes the Middle East still a dangerous flashpoint, and the rise of new economic powers like the People's Republic of China and India threatens to bring about a new world order. All of these developments have had a dramatic impact on the recent history of every nation of the world.

For this series, which was launched in 1998, we first selected nations whose political, economic, and socio-cultural affairs marked them as among the most important of our time. For each nation, we found an author who was recognized as a specialist in the history of that nation. These authors worked cooperatively with us and with Greenwood Press to produce volumes that reflected current research on their nations and that are interesting and informative to their readers. In the first decade of the series, more than 40 volumes were published, and as of 2008, some are moving into second editions.

The success of the series has encouraged us to broaden our scope to include additional nations, whose histories have had significant effects on their regions, if not on the entire world. In addition, geopolitical changes have elevated other nations into positions of greater importance in world affairs and, so, we have chosen to include them in this series as well. The importance of a series such as this cannot be underestimated. As a superpower whose influence is felt all over the world, the United States can claim a "special" relationship with almost every other nation. Yet many Americans know very little about the histories of nations with which the United States relates. How did they get to be the way they are? What kind of political systems have evolved there? What kind of influence do they have on their own regions? What are the dominant political, religious, and cultural forces that move their leaders? These and many other questions are answered in the volumes of this series.

The authors who contribute to this series write comprehensive histories of their nations, dating back, in some instances, to prehistoric times. Each of them, however, has devoted a significant portion of their book to events of the past 40 years because the modern era has contributed the most to contemporary issues that have an impact on U.S. policy. Authors make every effort to be as up-to-date as possible so that readers can benefit from discussion and analysis of recent events.

In addition to the historical narrative, each volume contains an introductory chapter giving an overview of that country's geography, political institutions, economic structure, and cultural attributes. This is meant to give readers a snapshot of the nation as it exists in the contemporary world. Each history also includes supplementary information following the narrative, which may include a timeline that represents a succinct chronology of the nation's historical evolution, biographical sketches of the nation's most important historical figures, and a glossary of important terms or concepts that are usually expressed in a foreign language. Finally, each author prepares a comprehensive bibliography for readers who wish to pursue the subject further.

Readers of these volumes will find them fascinating and well-written. More importantly, they will come away with a better understanding of the contemporary world and the nations that comprise it. As series advisors, we hope that this series will contribute to a heightened sense of global understanding as we move through the early years of the twenty-first century.

Frank W. Thackeray and John E. Findling
Indiana University Southeast

Acknowledgments

This work owes much to the scholarship of Peruvian and non Peruvian historians who have addressed so many key aspects of the Andean experience. Of course, Jorge Basadre's multivolume history of Peru to the 1930s is the standard reference for all historians of Peru. Previous high quality surveys by Peter Klarén and Christine Hunefeldt have served as valuable references for students of Peru. Víctor Villanueva Valencia, army officer, rebel, and consummate historian, guided my early work on the military with much gracious patience many years ago. I have included only some aspects of my previous work on the Japanese experience in Peru. Still, the assistance of Emilia Morimoto and Alejandro Sakuda in that area of research must be noted. Felix Denegri Luna kindly gave me the use of his wonderful library in Lima. My discussions with him about a range of issues in Peruvian history were very useful. Steve Hirsch, student of labor and gender issues as related to the American Popular Revolutionary Alliance (APRA), helped review some of the earlier chapters of this study with a careful and unsparing eye. My daughter Erin and Ros Rice tried to clarify my prose as I ran up against deadlines that always seemed to be bearing down on me. Cathy Higgins was always there with the technical help when it was needed.

My compadre for nearly a quarter century, Jorge Ortíz Sotelo has been a constant source of support, insight, and balance in my scholarship. To now have him as a colleague at the U.S. Naval Academy is a special delight and privilege. Lorena Toledo has been an gracious sounding board for a number of important historical issues of 20th-century Peru, particularly the impact of the agrarian reform program of the 1970s. Fellow scholar of Peru Larry Clayton made this project possible for me and I thank him for confidence and friendship.

Over the many years I have been working in Peru I have come to understand how much strength and resilience marks the character of the Peruvian people. From the repeated devastation of Los Niños throughout the millennia, to deadly earthquakes such as the Callejon de Huaylas disaster in 1970, Peru's environment is often harsh and demanding. Still, its landscapes are beautiful beyond compare. And in the end, Peruvians rebuild. They have also endured violence and hardship begot by revolutionaries who rarely understood the true nature of the Quechua and Aymara peoples of the highlands or the natives of the Amazon. Although Peruvians have struggled with long and difficult periods poverty, in the past decade Peru has enjoyed peace and growth. Hopefully, the nation is finally fulfilling the promise articulated by Peru renowned historian Jorge Basadre who claimed that Peru's hopes for the future have never fully taken shape because of our nations consistent inability to do what we must do. Peru's people, who have endured so much throughout the modern history of this nation, deserve a better future. Their continued struggles in the face of nearly constant adversity have always been an inspiration to me.

Timeline of Historical Events

Pre-Columbian Cultures

3200–2500 B.C.	Coastal cultures in Norte Chico regions thrive on combined fishing and farming
1500–1800 B.C.	Coastal irrigation is perfected and maize becomes a staple crop
500–800 B.C.	Chavín culture's period of influence
500 B.C.–A.D. 100	Nazca (south) and Moche (north) dominate regional coastal areas with elaborate irrigation systems
A.D. 500–750	Huari and Tihuanaco cultures flourish in the southern Andes
800–900	Chimor, a north coast settlement, builds elaborate capital at Chan Chan
1200–1400	Inca expansion and conquest occurs in the valley of Cuzco and beyond
1438–1525	Formal period of pan-Andean Inca conquest

1525–1530	European-based diseases reach the Andes with devastating consequences. Civil war divides the Inca Empire
1490s	In Spain, Muslims are finally expelled from the peninsula. Jews must convert to Catholicism or be expelled. The Inquisition is established. Columbus encounters the Caribbean and establishes permanent colonies

The Encounter

1530–1650	Ravaged by diseases from the old world the population of Peru declines from an estimated 16 million to 3.03 million during this period
1532	Pizarro ambushes Inca emperor Atahualpa's entourage at Cajamarca and takes the emperor hostage. Atahualpa is later executed after a ransom is collected
1533	Spaniards capture Cuzco with Indian allies
1535	Lima is established as the coastal stronghold of Spanish power in Peru
1536	Inca resistance continues under Manco Capac
1537–1538	Almargo rebellion divides Spanish conquistador ranks
1540–1548	Both Francisco Pizarro and his brother Gonzalo die in power struggles to control the new Peruvian empire
1545	A "Mountain of Silver" is discovered at Potosí in present-day Bolivia

Spanish Colonial Era

1550s	Spanish Empire in Peru is consolidated; University of San Marcos established; second viceroy Mendoza arrives
1555	Taki Onqoy millenarian movement emerges in the Andes
1570s	Viceroy Toledo's administrative reforms are enacted; *mita* labor system begins; "Indian reductions" are implemented
1572	Tupac Amaru rebellion challenges Spanish rule in Peru; it is suppressed with great bloodshed

1580–1700	Silver mines at Potosí and Cerro de Pasco provide the bulk of Spanish revenue from its Peru colony. Patio process increases silver yields
1600	Most major religious orders, Franciscan, Dominicans, Jesuits are well established at this time
1633	Beginning of the sale of imperial offices in Peru; sales will eventually undermine tax base and royal revenues
1700	The Spanish Crown passes to the French Bourbons from the Habsburgs
1739	Bourbon administrative reforms begin as the new Viceroyalty of Nueva Granada (Colombia and Venezuela) is created
1767	Jesuit religious order is expelled from Latin America
1776	Vice Royalty of Rio de la Plata (Argentina) is created to curb smuggling and safeguard revenues
1770–1800	"Free trade" among Spanish colonies is decreed; new taxes and other revenue measures are enacted by Spanish Bourbons
1780–1782	Tupac Amaru II rebellion is pan-Andean in scope and nearly defeats Spanish power until its leader is captured and executed
1782	System of intendancies for greater administrative control is created in colonies by the Bourbons. Peru has seven of these districts
1780–1789	American Independence movement succeeds; French Revolution begins
1799–1815	Napoleonic Wars; Spain is occupied by French armies; Spanish king is held hostage

Early Independence Era

| 1808 | Latin American independence movements begin in the Rio de la Plata region |
| 1814 | Cuzco rebels against Spanish authority |

1815	Napoleon defeated at Waterloo; Spanish forces regroup to resist Latin American independence movements
1820–1821	Campaign from the South by General José San Martín liberates Peru
1821–1845	Age of *caudiillos* see little political stability in Peru and little economic progress to rebuild the nation from the destructive independence wars
1822	Meeting of Simón Bolívar and San Martín in Guayaquil (Ecuador); San Martín retires from the battlefield
1824	Last royalist forces in Peru are defeated at Ayacucho by troops led by General Sucre

Early Nation Building

1836–1839	Era of the failed Peru-Bolivia Confederation
1839–1874	Guano age wherein huge state revenues do not promote national development or a native middle class. Chinese immigrants supply the labor for the terrible task of "mining" the guano on Peru's Chincha Islands
1845–1862	General Ramón Castilla brings a measures of stability to Peru bolstered by guano revenues. African slavery is abolished in 1854 with compensation to the owners.
1850s	Valuable nitrate deposits are discovered in Peru's Atacama desert
1868–1877	U.S. entrepreneur Henry Meiggs builds Peru's internal railroad infrastructure with state guano revenues
1872	Manuel Pardo elected Peru's first civilian president; founds the Civilista Party
1876–1879	Guano age ends and Peru is forced to default on its external debt

Defeat and Reconstruction

| 1879–1883 | Peru loses nitrate-laden provinces of Tarapacá and Arica to Chile in the War of the Pacific. War settlement exacerbates rivalry between two nations |

1885	Indian rebellion in southern sierra has roots in the War of the Pacific
1886	Peru assigns foreign debt to European lenders against future state revenues
1895	Civil war won by Nicolás Piérola, known as the "democratic caudillo"; Piérola leads Peru into a era of republican government ruled by a small oligarchy
1896	Piérola signs contract with the French army for a training mission; he will have a lasting influence on Peruvian military and developmentalist thinking

In Search of National Identity

1899	First Japanese immigrants arrive in Peru from southern Japan to work in work on sugar and cotton plantations
1912–1914	Short-term populist rule by Guillermo Billinghurst. Oligarchy calls on the army led by Oscar Benavides to restore order. First coup d'état of the 20th century
1914–1919	World War and the Russian Revolution encourage radical student and worker politics
1919–1930	*Oncenio* of Augusto Leguía. Close ties with the United States economically and militarily. Major U.S. corporations (Grace, International Petroleum Company [I.P.C.], Cerro de Pasco) establish dominance in key sectors of the economy
1924	APRA party is formed in Mexico by Haya de la Torre and followers
1929	Tacna and Arica settlement is widely unpopular in Peru
1930	Marxist writer Mariátegui dies. Peru's left will drift ideologically for decades in his absence

Populism and Violence

1930	Nationalist coup led by *cholo* Lieutenant Colonel Sánchez Cerro ushers in a period of violence and intrigue pitting the new *caudillo* against the emergent APRA

1932	Elections return Sánchez Cerro to power. APRA uprising in Trujillo is suppressed with much loss of life. Feud between APRA and the army begins
1932–1933	Border conflict with Colombia in the Leticia region highlights Peru's "national defense" problems
1933	Sánchez Cerro is assassinated by a young *Aprista*. Benavides is given control of Peru's government against the terms of 1933 constitution
1933	Leticia dispute is resolved peacefully by Benavides
1935–1939	Benavides turns to fascist Italy and Germany for weapons and advisors
1939	Conservative Manuel Prado is elected president with APRA support
1940	Massive anti-Japanese riots in Lima destroy most of their businesses
1941	Two-month border war with Ecuador. Peace terms are resolved at January 1942 Inter-American conference in Rio de Janeiro
1942	Peru breaks relations with the Axis
1942–1945	Peru deports Japanese, Italian, and German nationals to the United States as "enemy aliens"
1945	Peru declares war on the Axis

Old Solutions to Old Problems

1945–1948	APRA is again legalized and forms coalition with Bustamante y Rivero. Troubled three-year alliance
1948	APRA–affiliated Callao Naval revolt fails, splitting the party into factions and weakening Bustamante
1948–1956	Anti-APRA general Manuel Odría overthrows Bustamante and establishes an eight-year dictatorship
1950–1954	Peru's economy benefits from the Korea War. Surplus World War II equipment arms the Peruvian military

1950s	Massive Indian migration from the sierra to Lima. Odría establishes a housing program for the poor. Land invasions in the highlands begin
1956–1962	Manuel Prado is again elected president with APRA support. The party's left wing is badly alienated
1959	Castro's revolutionary victory in Cuba awakens Peruvian military to the potential of rural insurgency
1962	Prado is overthrown by military coup in July.
1962–1963	Military junta rules Peru for one year to attempt pilot reforms and pave the way for Belaúnde's election in June 1963
1963–1968	Fernando Belaúnde Terry elected president with military's support. He is a visionary technocrat who lacks political acumen and support from the United States to initiate necessary reforms.
	I.P.C. expropriation issue
1965	Suppression of guerrilla campaign by Peruvian army and air force in the Cuzco region
1967	French Mirage jet controversy

The Military Modernizers

1968	Belaúnde deposed by a coup led by army General Juan Velasco Alvarado. Leaders intend long-term reformist rule
1968	I.P.C. is expropriated, the first of many seizures of foreign properties by the junta
1969	Massive agrarian reform is enacted. Peru recognized Cuba, China, Soviet Union
1970	Deadly earthquake and subsequent mudslides kills 70,000 in the Callejón de Huaylas in the Department of Ancash
1972–1976	Major weapons purchases from the Soviet Union
1974	Economic reforms of military government begin to falter

1975	Police strike in Lima causes widespread violence. Velasco is deposed by fellow generals in August
1975–1980	Conservative shift of the military government led by General Morales Bermúdez Transition to civilian rule. Difficult economic times
1979	New Peruvian constitution is enacted

Peru in Turmoil

1980–1985	Belaúnde again is elected president. Is burdened with large foreign debt and the Sendero Luminoso insurgency
1985–1990	First APRA president Alan García Pérez is elected. Economy badly deteriorates, and Sendero war widens to Lima
1990–2000	The "Fujimori Tsunami" Japanese Peruvian is elected as a man of color and immediately establishes the basis for economic, reform, national, and his own long-term rule
1992	Fujimori suspends congress in order to rule by decree
1992	Abimael Gúzman Reynoso captured in a Lima suburb with important associates; the insurgency is badly crippled
1993	New Constitution is enacted allowing Fujimori to be reelected
1995	Fujimori is reelected for a second five-year term
1995–1998	Alta Cenepa conflict with Ecuador is resolved by 1998 treaty
1995–1997	Destructive El Niño floods north coast Peru and causes severe damage
2000	Fujimori wins questionable presidential victory; international community condemns the election and violent riots break out in Peru's major cities

Old Faces with Better Results

2000	Vladimir Montesinos, Fujmori's intelligence chief, flees country after a bribery scandal breaks. Fujimori resigns the presidency from Japan and goes into self exile there

2001–2006	Fernando Toledo, a "child of the Andes" and educated at Stanford, leads a period of substantial economic growth and social peace
2003	Peru's Truth and Reconciliation Commission issues its report claiming 69,000 victims of the 1980–1995 insurgency
2005	Fujimori seeks to return to Peru by way of Japan, is arrested and eventually returned to Peru
2006	Alan García is again elected Peru's president. He promises a continuation of Toledo's free trade policies
2007	Serious earthquake in Pisco
2007–2008	Fujimori is tried in Peru for alleged crimes during his presidency
2008	U.S. Congress approves free trade agreement with Peru

Map of Peru. Cartography by Bookcomp, Inc.

1

The Three Worlds of Peru

THE COSTA

For thousands of years Peru's people have met the challenges of one of the most demanding environments in the world. Of the world's 40 distinct environmental zones, Peru has more than half. Three of these are most apparent, each with its own cultural patterns. These regions are the *costa* (coastal region), the sierra (Andean mountain chain), and the *selva* (Peru's vast Eastern rain forest). Peru is situated on the west coast of South America, with Ecuador to the north and Chile bordering on the Atacama desert to the south. Peru shares common control of Lake Titicaca, the world's highest navigable lake, with Bolivia, to the southeast. Colombia and Brazil border Peru's Amazon rain forest region to the north and east respectively. Peru effectively exploits the navigable waters of the Amazon through its port at Iquitos deep within the eastern Amazon basin.

Peru is the third largest nation in South America, behind Brazil and Argentina; it covers a total area of 496,222 square miles, slightly smaller than Alaska. Integrating disparate regions into a modern nation has been difficult for a country of Peru's size to accomplish. Economic interchange may well have been most successfully conducted by the Incas before the arrival of the Europeans. But even the Inca, who centered their empire at Cusco in the southern sierra, were fully aware of the difficulties of life on Peru's coast and jungle region.

Peru's coastal region is an area of very sparse rainfall that extends 1,477 miles from Ecuador to Chile. Thus for many centuries it has been watered by some of the most elaborate irrigation networks found anywhere in the world. As barren as the lands of the coastal desert are, the offshore Peru current contains a rich variety of marine life. Under normal conditions, the current carries huge stocks of anchovies and sardines, as well as Jack Mackerel and other species. The Peru Current system, otherwise known as the Humboldt Current, moves northward along South America's coastline from central Chile to the Gulf of Guayaquil in Ecuador. These waters then flow westward, where they join the South Equatorial Current in a long passage across the Pacific Ocean to eventually return in a cyclical pattern to South America's coastal region.[1]

The Peru Current forms one of the most productive fisheries in the world and by the 1960s Peru was the world's leading fishing nation, despite harvesting only in its home waters. Millions of tons of anchovies were being harvested from the shallow offshore shoals. Fishmeal sold as animal feed was one of Peru's primary exports into the early 1970s. As one would imagine fishing has been prominent in Peru for thousands of years.

Now regarded by many as the oldest urban site in the Americas, Caral is located on the coastal desert about 130 miles north of Lima. Substantial quantities of fish bones at the site give strong evidence that this community was in large measure marine-based in its diet. The early cultivation of cotton in Peru is linked to the need for larger and stronger nets for fishing. In the south the great civilizations at Paracas and Nazca, noted for their exquisite textiles and the famous Nazca geoglyphs, were possibly fashioned by fisher folk as well. A number of the more than 30 geoglyphs on the desert floor that depict animals are devoted to fish patterns and one to an abstract representation of a killer whale.[2]

Inland from the Pacific Ocean, the desert peoples of Peru made their arid setting come alive with very elaborate irrigation systems dating at least as far back as 1800 B.C. Drawing water from more than 20 short river systems and streams flowing with abundant snow melt from the high Andes, irrigation created the fertile, well-watered settings that permitted the rise of powerful desert cultures such as the Moche and Chimú of northern Peru and the Paracas and Nazca societies in the South. The Inca made the most effective use of these irrigation networks by integrating them into a highly productive regional systems of agriculture, distribution, and storage. Over the past 500 years many of these irrigation canals have fallen into disrepair, but recently some have been restored on an experimental basis and have proven to be more efficient than modern systems. Still, there are ominous signs for the future of Peru's water supply. An Ohio State University geologist who has studied Peru's glaciers since 1974 notes that they are shrinking rapidly. This is one aspect of a world-wide global warming trend. For example, the Quelccaya glacier north of Lake Titicaca has diminished in size by more than 700 meters in the first two years of the new century.[3]

Other key elements in the desert ecology of Peru are guano and nitrates. Guano, the droppings from millions of seabirds that have fed for thousands of years on the rich marine life of the Peru current, has accumulated in huge deposits on the arid offshore islands of Chincha and Ballestas and in Peru's coastal desert. Nitrates (saltpeter) also were exposed and readily accessible. These deposits were of great commercial value as fertilizer and explosives.

Peru's coastal lands have also produced commercial crops of great value. Cotton has been cultivated in Peru for thousands of years and continues to be one of the nation's most important commercial crops today. Revitalized in some measure by Japanese immigrant farmers in the 1930s, the Peruvian cotton industry served the Allied War effort well during World War II, even while a number of Peru's leading Japanese Peruvian cotton growers were deported and interned in the United States, purportedly for security reasons. Sugar production on Peru's north coast was the most important agricultural activity through the mid 20th century. African slaves, Chinese contract laborers, and Japanese free labor harvested sugar cane for the world market. Peru's coastal elite was intimately tied to sugar production.

Coastal peoples nearly everywhere must confront the ravages of typhoons, and tsunamis. The regularity of the powerful environmental phenomenon known as El Niño (the baby Jesus), so called because it often appears during the Christmas season, is a burden that Peru's coastal people have endured since the beginning of human habitation. Although not completely understood, El Niño is manifested by a warming of the ocean waters off the coasts of Peru and Ecuador for about 1,000 kilometers. Excessively strong southeast trade winds are frequent in the central Pacific for two years in advance of the onset of El Niño, thus strengthening the southern equatorial currents. This pattern seems to hold the warmer waters of the central Pacific until released by a lessening of the trade winds to flow east, they eventually reach the coasts of Peru and Ecuador. With increased scientific attention devoted to El Niño in the past half century, we know now that its cycle of occurrence is about every three years, with a major event happening every six.

One of the immediate effects of the El Niño is the interruption of the flow of the Peru Current, which often results in a dramatic lowering of fish stocks.[4] When warmer water replaces the nutrient-rich colder water of the Peru current, the fishing industries of Peru and the other Andean nations are confronted with very hard times. After climbing to world leadership in metric tons harvested in the late 1960s, Peru's fishing industry experienced a near-collapse with the highly destructive El Niño event of 1972–73 and overfishing.

When major El Niño events occur the damage can be catastrophic as fragile coral reefs are often badly damaged by warmer waters and related turbidity. By one estimate, 95 percent of the coral reefs off the Galapagos Islands were destroyed by the El Niño event of 1982–83.[5] Historically, torrential rains and subsequent flooding in primarily arid northern Peru have destroyed crops and severely damaged coastal villages and towns, irrigation networks, and road systems. The dreaded partner effect of El Niño's flooding in northern Peru are droughts in southern Peru and elsewhere in the Andes. Indeed, as research on the El Niño phenomenon continues, the worldwide impact of this oceanographic occurrence is now more fully understood. In this vein, the characteristics of the so-called La Niña event were first identified only in 1985, by a Princeton University oceanographer. El Niño is often linked directly to La Niña conditions, which are said to exist when very cold surface temperatures in the central and eastern Pacific along the equator are coupled with strong westward blowing prevailing winds, and sea levels in the Western Pacific drop and those in the Eastern Pacific rise.[6] Causing great extremes in the amount of precipitation in Australia, Indonesia, and the Philippines, La Niña is thought to bring excessively arid conditions to northern Peru while El Niño can produce not only rain but disastrous flooding.

What can be said about the impact of these two environmental conditions on the peoples of Peru throughout history? Clearly, the periodic devastation in the coastal regions and drought in the highland have made life very difficult for at least several millennia. Through the study of ice core samples, scientists are now reasonably certain that significant El Niño events have been influencing the climate on a regular basis over the past 1,500 years in the Cusco area in Peru's south central sierra. Around 500 B.C., El Niño–related storms and flooding nearly destroyed the irrigation networks, agricultural fields, and coastal housing of the Moche civilization situated on Peru's north coast. Most of the Moche people were forced to resettle in the foothills of the Andes. Their faith in their rulers was then badly shaken. The El Niño of 1591–92 was a weather disaster of worldwide significance, with nations as distant as Denmark and Mali being buffeted by severe storms. These patterns of severe weather events associated with El Niño have been occurring as often as four times a century during the past three hundred years. El Niño incurred severe damage to the Peruvian economy during 1972 to 1973 and again during 1997 to 1998.

Another natural disaster that has had devastating consequences for Peru are earthquakes. Often these seismic events have their epicenters at sea, deep within the earth. But the effect of these tremors is often most devastating in the highlands where landslides have buried entire towns with very high death tolls.

Peru's costa region is a long narrow ribbon of abundance during favorable environmental conditions, and yet a land of misery and deprivation when the waters of the Pacific periodically warm and El Niño conditions prevail. As with other regions of Peru, the costa is a domain of contrasts that present great challenges to its inhabitants. Still, the peoples of the Peruvian coast have made marvelous achievements in their difficult environments. This can also be said of the inhabitants of Peru's highlands or the sierra.

THE SIERRA

The Peruvian Andes are part of the second highest mountain range in the world but are the longest, spanning 4,400 miles from Venezuela to Southern Chile. At their widest point in the Peruvian/Bolivia Altiplano, the Andes reach a width of 300 miles. As part of the mountain system extending along the western part of South America, Peruvian Andes are formed by three main mountain chains, with many mountain summits which rise above 18,000 feet. Of these, Huascaran is Peru's highest (22,205 feet). Alpamayo, which is perpetually snow clad, has been judged the "world's most beautiful mountain" by UNESCO. These ranges are separated from one another by deep intermountain valleys and smaller mountain chains; the combination of mountain chains and deep valleys creates an extremely rugged topography. This geological reality results in significant differences in temperature and rainfall at various locales within the Andes region. An exception is the Altiplano plateau, second only in size to the Tibetan plateau. Lake Titicaca, the world's highest navigable lake is located in the Altiplano plateau. Here the topography is more constant and the lake influences the local climate. Only the Himalayas are higher than the Andes, and like the Himalayas, the Andes are still rising. The Andes were uplifted relatively recently, during the Cretaceous and the Tertiary periods, and are thus still quite unstable geologically. *Serranos,* as residents of the sierra are called frequently, must confront as common occurrences the earthquakes and resulting land and mudslides that have buried entire villages, as recently as 1970. Peru also has several volcanoes, a number of which have been active recently. The best known is El Misti, which towers majestically over the southern city of Arequipa, known as the "white city" because of the white volcanic pumice called *sillar* from which many of its buildings are constructed. El Misti last erupted in 1948, but it stands as a deceptively serene reminder of Peru's volatile geological makeup.

Produced by the uplifting, faulting, and folding of ancient geological structures, the Andes are still in motion. Tectonic forces along the west coast of South America have caused the Nazca plate and part of the Antarctic plate to slide under the South American plate. The shifting of these plates have caused numerous and sometimes catastrophic earthquakes in the Peruvian Andes and coastal regions. A brief look at two of these earthquakes (*terremotos*) will illustrate their potential for disruptive change. The earthquake of 1746 was the most destructive event in Lima's and Callao's history. Nearly all of Lima's homes and public structures were damaged and the dead were estimated as high as 6,000 from a population of 55,000. The death toll in Lima's port city of Callao, however, was far worse. A tsunami spawned by the earthquake nearly obliterated the town and most of its inhabitants drowned. In the aftermath of the earthquake there were months of social upheaval, eventually leading the viceroy to rebuild Peru's capital in the style of the Bourbon architectural reformers who later redesigned Lisbon after its massive earthquake of 1755.[7]

The deadliest earthquake ever to occur in the western hemisphere struck at 3:23 p.m., May 31, 1970, with an epicenter offshore of Peru's department of Ancash in the central sector of the nation. Towns in the valley called the Callejón de Huaylas were devastated and in particular the towns Yungay and Huaraz suffered the highest loss of life. Yungay was buried under an avalanche of mud, ice, and rock from Peru's highest mountain, Huascarán. Many of Yungay's residents were buried alive only to succumb hours and even days after "the mountain fell on them." By some estimates, 1 in every 4 of the 300,000 residents of the Callejón de Huaylas lost their lives.

These same mountains that are so threatening are also laden with some of the world's richest mineral deposits. There are six major components to Peru's mining industry, dating from the early years of the Spanish colonial era. In order of prominence they are: iron ore, copper, zinc, lead, silver, and gold. The Chinese mining corporation *Shougang* purchased Peru's Marcona iron ore firm in 1992. Since then, much of the nation's mining sector has welcomed foreign investment enthusiastically. However, a major issue that has never been resolved in the mining industry since its inception in the 16th century. Damage to Peru's environment, particularly to its rivers and streams, continues.

Some of this is due to the use of mining techniques that are not regulated by the government. Progress has been made since the 1990s when stricter regulations were imposed on mining operations. The shift to open pit mining since World War I has significantly changed the conditions of mining operations. More will be said about these issues when Spanish colonial mining operations are discussed later, but for now it is interesting to note that Peru's mining industry has established a partnership with China, which has perhaps the worst record of mine safety in the world; however, Canadian and Australian mining interests, whose record of concern for environmental and safety issues is considerably better than the Chinese, are also present in Peru. Today, only about 2.5 percent of Peru's labor force is engaged in mining despite the fact that this industry accounts for nearly half of state revenue. This can be explained largely by the highly mechanized nature of mining operations, particularly in the huge open pit mines that have dominated the extractive industries in Peru for most of the past 75 years.

Typical of these huge open pit mines is the Toquepala copper mine in Southern Peru about 60 miles inland from the port of Ilo. One of the world's largest mines, Toquepala is nearly four miles across and almost two miles deep. Owned by a consortium of Mexican and U.S. investors, Toquepala was opened in 1960 and has been on a regular production schedule ever since.

When one imagines the rugged Andean ecosystems, it is not easy to envision a rich history of agricultural in this region. But that is in fact the case. Today less than three percent of Peru's land is considered arable, and yet highly crea-tive and labor intensive systems such as irrigation, terracing, and raised field agriculture have been practiced in the Andes for thousands of year. Peru has not only survived but thrived by means of what Cornell anthropologist John Murra termed "vertical archipelagos." Few villages could sustain themselves in the high Andes with their short growing seasons, unpredictable rainfall, and damaging frosts. Improving on previous Andean patterns of production, the Incas brought seafood and cotton from the sea and coast, and the main food staples of maize, potatoes, and quinoa from their irrigated and terraced fields, which were cultivated on land below 10,000 feet elevation. Finally, their sources of wool, meat transport, namely their domesticated llama and alpaca, were herded on the high *puna* above 12,000 to 14,000 feet elevation. The Inca, with their genius for organization turned this form of vertical integration of differing ecosystems into an art form with their elaborate system of roads. In the modern era, villages such as Qeros in the south central Andes near Cuzco maintain the practice of verticality to this day. The Qeros villagers, who have now drawn the attention of Cuzco tourist agencies as "direct descendents of the Incas," live in stone homes and pasture their llamas and alpacas at 14,000 feet elevation. Living there on the eastern slope of the Andes, Qeros villag-ers have access to the high rain forest of the Amazon basin. At least twice a year, they build temporary timber bridges above the mountain streams that become swollen during the rainy season. Descending to 8,000 feet with their llamas, used as pack animals, they gather their corn raised in the high selva (jungle) that will be used as a staple food and for *chicha* (corn beer). Amid fields and temporary lodgings at 12,000 feet, the Qeros villagers plant their potato sets with an ancient digging stick used in the Andes. The men work at this "station" and in the high selva tending the crops, while the women and children stay with the herds near the top of the mountain. When the potatoes are harvested, some of them will be preserved in a freeze-dried form known as *chuñu*, which can remain edible for a very long time and has been used as a surplus food in the Andes for centuries. Most agriculture in Qeros and in the Andes is performed in common or *ayllu* (kinship groups), which have existed for thousands of years.

SELVA

Peru's Eastern rainforest region occupies nearly 60 percent of its total area but contains less than 10 percent of the nation's people. Divided into the high selva, and lower vast expanse of rain forest. The selva long has been viewed optimistically by Spaniards and Peruvians alike as the key to a prosperous future for their land. Jesuits established a mission at present-day Iquitos in the 1750s but the town grew slowly until the Department of Loreto, in which Iquitos is located, was created by the new Peruvian republic in 1864. A short-lived rubber boom in the late 19th and early 20th centuries sparked renewed interest in this rainforest region, and drew European and U.S. investors and immigrants from Japan and other nations to live the remote and lonely existence of rubber tappers deep within the rain forest. With the emergence of powerful British-financed East Asian competition, the Amazonian rubber boom ended before World War I. During Peru's rubber boom, many Indian peoples were enslaved and frequently abused by the rubber companies, and the search for rubber created border tensions with Colombia, which eventually erupted into war in 1911 and again in 1932.

Still, those with a vision of a developed Amazon to which Peru's land-hungry poor could migrate remained. Fernando Belaúnde Terry, Peru's architect-president (1963–68 and 1980–85), advocated a scheme called the Marginal Jungle Highway, which would run along Peru's high selva and open Peru's eastern rainforest region to colonization and development.

Belaúnde's dream was never realized but the hopes of a selva bonanza were rekindled by preliminary reports of large oil reserves in the region in the late 1960s. Again, after substantial foreign investment in the search for increasingly valuable petroleum deposits, the results were disappointing, with only enough reserves being found to provide Peru with petroleum self-sufficiency. Instead, Peru's northern neighbor Ecuador has been exploiting the bulk of the oil reserves in the selva. Peru has been forced to utilize other economic resources from the region, among which are timber, coffee, and fruit. Much of the labor that produces these commodities is supplied by migrants from the high Andes who have been moving into the area since the late 1940s. Today, these selva inhabitants compose about 20 percent of the population of the region who struggle to meet their needs by cultivating undersized coffee plots and fruit groves. It is easy to understand therefore why the economic appeal of coca production in the selva become so strong when the demand for cocaine soared in the U.S. and European markets, beginning in the early 1980s.

For more than three decades, Peru's Upper Huallaga Valley, extending 200 miles in north central Peru in the Department of San Martín, has been the center of the world's coca trade. Historically, that valley, along with production in the Apurímac and in the La Convención Valley in the south, supplies between 60 and 70 percent of the world's dried coca leaves that are processed into cocaine. Despite determined efforts by the Peruvian government with the support of the United States since the 1980s to eradicate coca production in

Peru, the effort has largely failed, primarily because of the economic benefits that accrue to the coca-producing peasant.

Peru's selva is very lightly populated. Its largest city, Iquitos with approximately 400,000 inhabitants, is located about 80 miles downstream from the confluence of the Ucayali and Marañón rivers, generally considered to be the beginning of the mighty Amazon. Ocean-going vessels can reach Iquitos from the mouth of the Amazon where it flows into the Atlantic nearly 2,000 miles downriver. Other cities of consequence in the selva are Pucallpa in the province of Ucayali, Puerto Maldonado in the Department of Madre de Dios and Tingo María in the Department of Huánuco. Iquitos is thought to be the largest city in the world that cannot be reached by road. The city is served instead by air and river transport. Despite its isolated location, Iquitos supports a thriving tourist trade, boasts two universities and is the base of operations for continually expanding scientific programs dedicated to learning more about the rain forest. Pharmaceutical companies are also now exploiting the selva's widely diverse flora and fauna for natural sources for new drugs as they follow the footsteps of native healers, who have done so for centuries.

The Peruvian government is making a strong effort to ensure that the biodiversity of the selva is protected. There are 24 national parks in the region, the largest and best known of which is the Manu National Park. Considered the most biodiverse rain forest in the world and encompassing over 4.5 million acres, the park contains more than 800 species of birds and other forms of rare wildlife such as giant otters and armadillos, as well as a large population of jaguars.

The indigenous population living in the lower Amazon rain forest are Peru's most forgotten peoples. Living along the region's river systems they number only about 250,000 of a nation of 29 million. Gathered in approximately 50 distinct cultural groups, they are scattered among the Departments of Loreto, Ucayali, Amazonas, Huánuco, Ayacucho, Cuzco Puno, and Madre de Dios. Still subject to the devastation of modern diseases and the stress of contact with modern society, these people of the rain forest have been vulnerable since the Spanish conquest. Since the 1960s, the menaces of logging, oil exploration, colonization, and guerilla warfare have confronted Peru's indigenous peoples of the Amazon region nearly continuously, not only threatening their way of life but even their very existence. Representative of these Amazon peoples are the Campa Asháninka. One of the larger tribes within the selva, the Asháninka have had their territory reduced substantially since the Spanish colonial era. But their greatest test came from the Sendero Luminoso guerillas who assaulted their villages on a regular basis. With Sendero Luminoso largely disabled, the Asháninka face continuing difficulty from land invasions by displaced coca producers and even evangelical missionaries who are seeking to make radical changes in their belief systems. In response to these problems, the Asháninka's leaders have become politically engaged with the government in Lima in an often frustrating attempt to protect their home territories, which are now effectively limited to the Ene and Tambo river basin.

Today there is growing evidence that some of the original indigenous cultures of the Amazon basin developed somewhat complex societies that were far different from the simple migrating hunters and gatherers of today's Peruvian selva. That these complex cultures were likely reduced to their present state by the impact of disease and by destructive incursions into their very fragile ecosystems over the past 500 years is becoming increasingly evident.[8]

PERUVIAN SOCIETY

Modern Peruvian society is marked by racial and cultural diversity and rich ethnic traditions that have survived for centuries. Even in this age of advanced genetic research regarding the notion of race, cultural issues are still of fundamental importance in determining one's place in Peruvian society. Peru's population is approximately 29 million, of which nearly a third is 14 years old or under. The median age of 25 is a relatively young, and the population growth rate is a modest 1.3 percent. Peruvians can expect to live, on average, 70 years, a substantial improvement over the past three decades. Still, the infant mortality rate is high, primarily because of a lack of medical care in remote areas of the sierra and the selva and poor health conditions in urban squatter settlements known as *barriadas.*

The primary racial groups in Peru are the native Amerindian composing 45 percent of the population; the mestizo, mixed Amerindian and white European (37%), and white European (12%). Relatively small numbers of Afro-Peruvians and Asians complete the racial mosaic of Peruvian society. Mestizos, are, the product of the admixture of native and Spanish peoples after the conquest. Today, they compose the bulk of the middle sectors of Peruvian society, attested to by an increased presence in the professions, commerce, and education. Peru has never been a substantial recipient of immigrants and today is actually experiencing substantial out-migration to Japan, the United States, and Europe. Chinese workers were lured to Peru to work in the guano fields in the mid-19th century. Between 1899 and World War II the Japanese immigrant population in Peru grew to nearly 30,000. Additionally, relatively small groups of Italians, Germans, and some Eastern Europeans settled in Lima and Arequipa after the 1880s. Peru's early Italian immigrants were particularly successful in banking and commerce, while the Japanese Peruvians came to dominate the urban retail trade. Peru's Japanese descendents ranks second in number in Latin America behind Japanese Brazilians and is estimated to be about 55,000. Many of the younger *Nikkei* (people of Japanese heritage overseas) have migrated to Japan for work since 1990. Among Peru's Nikkei, the most prominent representative is former president Alberto Fujimori (1990–2000).[9]

Beginning with the war against Sendero Luminoso and the hard economic times of the last two decades of the 20th century, Peruvians began emigrating in substantial numbers. Key destinations for these emigrants have been Brazil, Italy, Spain, Miami, Washington, D.C., and the suburbs of New York City (especially Paterson, New Jersey), as well as Chile and Argentina. Many Japanese Peruvians have gone to Japan in search of highly paid industrial jobs The Peruvian emigrant communities in the United States and Spain have become well established and are marked by a thriving cultural scene, particularly in the fine arts in the New York City and Miami areas.

The key demographic trend to note about Peru's population in the last half century is the nation's rapid urbanization. Lima's population, for example, increased from 645,000 in 1940 to more than 8 million in 2006. Overall, the percentage of Peruvians living in cities has risen dramatically from 36 percent in 1950 to a projected 79 percent in 2010. Not surprisingly, housing and urban services have not kept pace with this growth and today about 2 million *Limeños* are living without municipal water service. Some of the former squatter settlements in the Lima metropolitan area such as Villa El Salvador have become largely self-sustaining communities unto themselves. Villa El Salvador was founded by settlers in the desert near Lima in May 1971. Today it has a population of 230,000 with sewage, water, and electrical services mainly supplied by the hard work of its inhabitants. During the very hard times between 1980 and 1995 important needs of the community such as fresh milk for the children were supplied by the government and administered by women's groups under a program known as *vaso de leche* (glass of milk). At this time Peru's feminist movement began to burgeon as the inequities in Peruvian society with regard to gender were spotlighted. Peru's women did not receive the right to vote until 1952, but by the 1980s they were a fundamental component of Peruvian politics. With the active participation of women leaders, and the great sacrifice of a few very brave ones, Villa El Salvador steadily grew into a viable community. The Prince of Asturias Award, awarded annually by the Spanish people, was given to Villa El Salvador in 1987 for its outstanding community achievements. More recently women's groups have been actively involved in the human rights organizations that have responded to the alleged abuses committed during the Fujimori regime (1990–2000). The agency given responsibility for investigating human rights issues was know as the Truth and Reconciliation Commission, consisting of 12 members included only 2 women. But one of these women was Sofia Macher Batanero, a sociologist and former executive secretary of one of Peru's leading human rights coordinating groups. Macher Batanero was one of the most vocal members of the commission, especially on issues involving women. She was joined on the panel by former congresswomen and lawyer Beatriz Alva Hart.

Efforts are quietly being made to resolve the divide between human rights groups and the military. For instance, there is a group of retired armed forces officers and human rights activists, a number of whom are women, who meet monthly at the Circulo Militar in Lima to discuss pertinent security issues and human rights. I had an opportunity to attend one of these meetings in August 2006 and found it to be cordial, frank, and open-ended. The one institution that is most active in sustaining the initiative of the Truth and Reconciliation Commission is the *Instituto de Defensa Legal* (Legal Defense Institute). If Peru's human rights issues relating to the troubles of the Sendero war are to move toward resolution, this group will likely be responsible.

POLITICAL ADMINISTRATION

Peru is a constitutional republic that gained its independence from Spain on July 28, 1821. The country is divided into 24 departments and the constitutional province of Callao, the port city of Lima. Peruvians must be age 18 to vote, and literacy in Spanish is not required. This has expanded the electorate significantly since the early 1970s. The president is elected by popular vote for a five-year term and may not be reelected. A preliminary election round is held in April of the presidential election year, and if no candidate receives a majority of the vote, a runoff between the top two candidates is held in June. The Peruvian Congress is unicameral, with 120 seats, and congressmen serve for a five-year term with the president. This structure is relatively recent as a result of reform, and Peru remains heavily centralized with an executive who retains an inordinate amount of political power. This may change if Congress can demonstrate a greater degree of effective autonomy. During the recent Toledo Administration (2001–2006), steps were taken to extend more decision making and funding to regional and local authorities.

Even taking into account the brief suspension of Congress by Alberto Fujimori in 1992, Peru has enjoyed one of its longest periods of constitutional government since independence in the 1820s. Since the election of Fernando Belaúnde Terry in 1980, national elections have occurred as scheduled. Manipulation of the constitutional process has occurred, however. The most blatant example happened during the Alberto Fujimori administration in 1992, when the president suspended the National Congress on the grounds of a national emergency. Since then, the National legislature has struggled to establish a balance between the executive and legislative branches of government. Slowing the development of democratic process in Peru is the weakness of its political parties.

PERU'S ECONOMY

Over the past 15 years, Peru's economy has stabilized while experiencing moderate but sustained growth. During the past six years the growth rate has been quite substantial. The runaway inflation of the late 1980s is now well under control at less than 4 percent annual rate. The recent moderate inflation is keeping with global trends reflecting higher prices for petroleum and mineral resources. The GDP growth rate is a healthy 8 percent and new export sectors, such as natural gas, are now being exploited. Like much of Latin America, Peru has privatized much of the state-owned industries particularly during the decade-long Fujimori regime. Spanish, Chilean, Brazilian, Mexican, Japanese, German, Chinese, Canadian, and other investors have stepped in to dominate significant sectors of the Peruvian economy. Yet Peru's continuing problem is persistent poverty. Fifty-three percent of Peruvians live in poverty. Although unemployment is listed at 9.7 percent, far more than that subsist through marginal employment such as street vendors and day laborers. Peru's export sector is now as strong as it has been in many decades. Led by mining, fisheries, metals, and textiles, these sectors have recently come to dominate the economic picture. Still, coffee and cotton have remained important staples of the agricultural sector. Constraining Peru's public spending in the domestic sector is its sizeable external debt of $30 billion. This amounted to nearly half of the value of Peru's GDP in 2004.

Although the economic picture in Peru is far better than in decades past, fundamental structural problems remain. The heavy dependence on metals and minerals forces Peru to tolerate wide fluctuations in the world market price for these products. Peru's fishing industry has taken care not to overexploit its fishing stocks as was done during the 1960s and is now diversifying its fish exports. Nevertheless, potential ravages of future El Niños can not be known. Also plaguing Peru is its poor infrastructure, as the cost of building modern roads, bridges, rural water systems, and electrical grids in Peru's terrain is enormous. Moreover, a good deal of the country's infrastructure was damaged by Sendero Luminoso's sabotage in the period from 1980 to 1992. A telling fact about Peru's labor force is that only 6 percent are now engaged in agriculture. What this reflects is the massive migration from rural areas to Lima and other cities since World War II. It is unlikely that this pattern of migration will be even partially reversed unless the rural infrastructure such as schools, roads, and communications are dramatically improved. However, new forms of agricultural activity that hold the possibility of future agricultural employment are being attempted in the southern coastal regions. For a nation whose primary exports for more than a century were drawn from this area of the economy, it is vitally important that this area of the economy remain stable.

Peru's primary trading partner is the United States, with which it exchanges more than a quarter of its imports and exports, and China is becoming an increasingly important customer for Peru. Despite Fujimori's close ties with Japan, that nation remains a cautious consumer of Peru's exports, taking less than 5 percent of exports. At present, the most promising prospect on Peru's economic horizon is its potential for natural gas revenue. Though smaller than the reserves of its neighbor Bolivia, Peru's known proved natural gas reserves are 245 billion cubic meters. Potential customers for natural gas could be Chile and for natural gas in liquefied form, the United States. Potential revenue from these reserves are the long-awaited solace for those who hoped in vain for the oil boom in the 1970s. Another economic sector that is prospering is Peru's burgeoning tourist industry. With the end of terrorism in the sierra by the mid 1990s, travel to Cusco and Machu Picchu became one of the focal points of a trip to Peru. European tourists especially were attracted to these world-renowned attractions. Tourism at these sites has been facilitated by the construction of better hotel and rail accommodations in the past decade. Also of great interest are Amazon River tours based in Iquitos and eco-based tours, which are centered in Peru's immense Manu National Park and others parks such as Pacaya-Samiria national reserve near Iquitos. PromPeru, the national tourism agency, has done a wonderful job of promoting Peruvian tourism and has led to substantially improved financial gains from this industry. Much of Peru's tourist industry is foreign owned, however. The operations of Lima's Jorge Chavez airport, for example, are controlled primarily by European investors.

Tourist revenues will not have great meaning to the mass of the Peruvian people unless job creation across nearly all economic sectors can improve dramatically. At present, the lowest 10 percent of Peru's income level share a mere 1.6 percent of consumer income while the highest 10 percent hold 35 percent of the spending capability. This distribution has changed little over the past 50 years. Improvements in education, health care, and employment hold the key to a better economic future for Peru.

PERU'S MILITARY AND POLICE

Peru's military is composed of the standard three services, army, navy, and air force. Military service begins at age 18. The annual military budget is approximately $850 million, which represents only 1.4 percent of the nation's GDP. The army is led by 6,231 commissioned officers, nearly all of whom are graduates of the Chorrillos Military College. The ranks of the noncommissioned officers has grown over the past two decades to nearly 13,600. Rank and file recruits serve for two years and number approximately 54,300. The military academy at Chorillos enrolls a cadet corps of 1,090. Entrance for

Chorillos and all military academies is decided by an entrance exam and personal recommendations. Great strains were placed upon the armed forces during the decade-long combat against Sendero Luminoso. Historically oriented more to border defense, the armed forces were not well-suited to fighting an irregular war in some of the most difficult terrains in the world. There also existed significant inter-service tension between the navy, a more conservative institution trained primarily by the United States during the early decades of the 20th century, and the army, which draws primarily from the lower middle class and mestizo social strata and in reality is a class apart from the navy and air force. Moreover, the army has been at times one of the most radical reformist military institutions in Latin America. Since 1895, the army has been trained and equipped by first French, then U.S., and until the mid-1980s, Soviet military sponsors. With its mission often vacillating between border defense and domestic counterinsurgency over the past 50 years, the army has suffered internal dissension.[10] The air force since its creation as a separate institution in 1945 has gone the way of the army in aligning itself first with the United States and then the Soviet Union, beginning with the regime of General Juan Velasco Alvarado (1968–75). Today, its personnel number nearly 18,000 with 1,909 commissioned officers, 7,559 noncommissioned officers, and 7,880 enlisted personnel. The corps of cadets at the air force academy is relatively small, numbering only 325.

The U.S. navy and Peruvian navy have maintained a strong professional bond since a retired U.S. naval officer was President of the Peruvian naval academy at La Punta in Callao from 1921 to 1930. Since then, top students from Peru's naval academy have consistently attended the U.S. Naval Academy at Annapolis. U.S. Naval training missions, called UNITAS, regularly make Callao one of their ports of call. Historically, Peru's naval strength has rested with its submarine force, but it responsibilities now include interdiction of drug traffickers on the high seas and in the Amazon basin, with its river flotilla. Despite its close ties with the U.S. navy, Peru's navy has looked to Europe for its major ships purchases since the Korean War. Another critical element of the navy's mission has become counterinsurgency. Front line troops in the war against Sendero Luminoso were taken from the ranks of Peru's marines. Fulfilling a similar role to U.S. marines' in conflicts such as Vietnam and Iraq, Peru's marines were often assigned to the areas of the greatest military activity, such as the Ayacucho region.

PERUVIAN POPULAR CULTURE

The internet and globalization have influenced the direction and content of Peru's mainstream culture. Yet traditional folk music and dance, the nearly universal enthusiasm for soccer as the country's main sport, and a continued appreciation by Peruvians for the classical arts and literature still characterize the nation's cultural milieu.

Huaynos, yaravies, kashuas, huaylas, tuntuna, and others are the traditional folk songs of the Andes remained popular in Peru's cities largely because of the huge influx of serranos in the aftermath of World War II. The pioneer in promoting Peruvian folk music to an urban audience was Luiz Pizarro, who began broadcasting his folk music show *El Sol de los Andes* (The Andean Sun) in 1951. The program had an immediate following, and today songs billed as "Super Huaynos" by popular artists like Alegres del Peru are widely available and popular. Most recently Andean music played with modern instruments and rock music played in the medium of Andean instruments has created a form of fusion of modern and traditional music played often in a disco setting. Peruvian folk dances such as the *Marinera* and *Tondero,* classical dances of the coast, are still performed and taught in Peru and overseas where Peruvians have emigrated. The Ballet Folklorico Peru, for example, is based in New Jersey and offers performances and classes in nearly all forms of Peruvian folk dance. The Ballet Folklorico has performed to large and appreciative audiences in the New York city area. Afro Peruvian dancers have also made a mark with U.S. audiences with performances of *festejo* and traditional Afro Peruvian routines.

Unquestionably the best known Peruvian vocalist of the last half century has been Yma Sumac. With a great vocal range, this native Peruvian became known throughout South America in the 1940s as rich and powerful renditions of Peruvian folk music. By the early 1950s Sumac brought her vocal prowess to the United States where her recording "Voice of Xtabay" reached number one on the LP charts, where it remained for six weeks. Born Zoila Augusta Emperatriz Chavarri del Castillo in Peru probably during the mid 1920s, Sumac continued to tour and sing to welcoming audiences until 1997 when she was in her 70s.

Today, Susana Baca, an Afro Peruvian singer from the Lima district of Chorrillos has become an internationally acclaimed singer of songs grounded in Peru's African culture. Her song "Maria Lando," a track from her CD *The Soul of Black Peru* released in 1995, drew the attention of audiences in Europe and the United States. Since then she has enjoyed acclaim in both these settings on numerous concert tours. Baca has been a student of Afro Peruvian music most of her adult life and is determined to promote its revival and broader appeal in Peru and elsewhere. To accomplish this, she has traveled throughout Peru to listen to aging singers and composers and gathered material for her songs. In a Seattle interview she explained her motives by noting that she wanted to bring credit to Afro-Peruvian culture. To some extent Baca was following the path of Nicomedes Santa Cruz, a pioneer in this genre.

Peru's young serrano migrants have maintained their devotion to the nation's traditional music and a good number of these Andean bands have entertained audiences off the beaten path in the United States and Europe in recent years. Young people in Peru's largest cities tend to have eclectic tastes in music. Many listen to U.S. and European mainstream rock and roll, rap, and hip hop, but they prefer to dance to salsa and meringue. Many still maintain an active interest in Peruvian and Latin American folk music. Jazz in Peru is performed primarily in Lima where a small but vibrant club scene is quite active. Many of Peru's jazz musicians have a classical music background and have studied and played in Europe and the United States. A young musician who is equally at home playing both jazz and classical selections is the young guitarist Andres Prado. He has acquired a good fan base in South America and Europe and his now beginning to do the same in the United States. In the realm of opera, Peru has one of the world's great talents in Juan Diego Flores, who is often said to be the assumed successor to Pavarotti. All Peruvian humanistic literature owes a great debt to the work of Garcilaso de la Vega. Born in Peru, the son of one of the first conquistadores, Garcilaso's mother was a high-ranking member of the Inca nobility. Thus, Garcilaso was one of Peru first mestizos. He quickly learned what it meant to be from another caste than that of the Spanish ruling class in Peru or the *peninsulares,* who were Spaniards born in Spain. Educated in both Quechua (the language of the Inca) and the Spanish classics, he soon became an accomplished scholar and literary figure. After 1560, he lived in Spain. His most important works were the *Royal Commentaries of the Incas* (1609) and the *General History of Peru,* which was published after his death in 1617. Drawing upon his own experience in Peru and firsthand accounts from his many contacts in his native land, Garcilaso wrote one the first histories of the early Spanish colonies. While praising some aspects of Spanish rule he stressed that the Inca should be treated with dignity and respect and that the Andean traditions that the Inca represented would add, not detract, from the course of Spanish rule. From his point of view, the mestizo was to be viewed as a positive amalgam of Spanish and Inca cultural traditions, not denigrated as the half caste that mestizos quickly became in Spanish America. Although not necessarily balanced or completely accurate in his historical perspective, in important ways Garcilaso de la Vega established the framework of critical social commentary used by key modern Peruvians such as César Vallejo, Ciro Alegría, José Maria Arguedas, Mario Vargas Llosa, and José Carlos Mariátegui.

The most heralded poetic voice of the 20th century Peru is César Vallejo (1892–1938). Born in the northern Peru to a large middle-class mestizo family, Vallejo's work reflects a keen understanding of the suffering of Peru's poor *casta*s (castes). His poetry is original, complex, and full of powerful imagery. Like a number of Peru's prominent men of letters, Vallejo spent a good portion of his most productive artistic years in self-imposed exile in Europe. His best work was written in France and Spain during the era of the Spanish Civil War.

Vallejo's major work was his *Poemas Humanos (Human Poems)* (1939), which reflects on the uncertain fate of mankind in a seemingly irrational world tortured by depression and rampant militarism.

Taught by Cesar Vallejo during his early school years, Ciro Alegría (1909–67) who, by the estimate of Mario Vargas Llosa, was Peru's "first classic novelist." Raised in close contact with Peru's *castas,* Alegría developed a deep sympathy for their plight. As a member of the leftist American Popular Revolutionary Alliance (APRA), he was in prison or in exile from 1932 to 1960. Most of that time in exile was spent in Chile, where Alegría wrote his most important novels *La serpiente de oro* (*The Golden Serpent;* 1935) and *El mundo es ancho y ajeno* (*Broad and Alien is the World;* 1941).

The latter novel confronts Peru's exploitive social system head-on by depicting the nearly impossible struggle of highland Indian villages against the campaign of a land-hungry *hacendado* (large landowner) to usurp their communal holdings. This novel depicts the serranos as hard working, peaceful people who only want to live in harmony with the land. In the end, government troops overwhelm the villagers and their struggle is lost. Alegría's use of anthropological principles to the develop this novel was a harbinger of future literary mannerism. Alegría spent most of his life outside Peru in Chile and the United States. However, he died in Peru in 1967, only one year before Peru's military government began to enact the social reforms he had called for in his powerful novels.

José Maria Arguedas (1911–69) was a anthropologist, poet, and a novelist. Born to parents of European heritage Arguedas was raised among the Quechua-speaking Indians of Peru's sierra. Arguedas admired many of the aspects of the Spanish and Quechua heritage. He sought a kind of fusion or *mestizaje* of the best qualities of both cultures. In his unfinished manuscript entitled *El zorro de arriba y el zorro abajo* (The Fox Above and the Fox Below), he pondered the difficulties confronting cultural integration even while Peru's military government was taking important strides toward that goal. Arguedas career was delayed by poverty, and he did not publish his first novel until 1944. His work as an anthropologist and administrator complemented his scholarship and literary contributions. By the end of his life in 1969 he was one of Peru's most respected men of letters.

One of the most renowned writers of the past 40 years in Latin America is Mario Vargas Llosa. Born in the Southern city of Arequipa in 1936, Vargas Llosa spent his early years in middle-class comfort in Bolivia and in northern Peru. After his parents moved to Lima and then separated, he was sent to the military prep school Leoncio Prado. His experience at the school was his inspiration for his first novel *La ciudad de los Perros* (*The Time of the Hero*). Vargas Llosa's saw Leoncio Prado as the embodiment of most of what was wrong with Peru, including deep class prejudices, overweening machismo, and hypocrisy. Very much in the tradition of literary social criticism among Peru's and Latin America's most formative writers, Vargas Llosa's work is represented by an untiring attack on what he perceives as ignorance and exploitation. It also at times is titillating, as with his *Elogio de la madrasta* (*In Praise of the Stepmother*; 1990). Like the work of the work of the Latin America boom movement of the past 50 years, his writings involve a good deal of experimentation regarding the structure of the narrative. As his literary reputation grew, so did Vargas Llosa's interest in politics. In 1990 he entered the race for the Peruvian presidency. His unexpected defeat by Alberto Fujimori led to an estrangement from his native Peru, and in 1993 Vargas Llosa became a citizen of Spain and has lived primarily in Europe since then. Few historians have contributed more to their nation than Peru's Jorge Basadre Grobman (1903–1980). Educated at Lima's National University of San Marcos, Basadre later taught history and law at the University and directed its library. He served terms as the director of Peru's National Library and was also Minister of Education. Basadre worked tirelessly to facilitate access for foreign scholars to Peruvian archives and other key historical resources. But his most important legacy is his grand *Historia de la Republica del Peru, 1822–1933* (*History of the Peruvian Republic*). It remains the single most important source for Peru's early republican history. It would not be unusual for the visitor to a large urban center in Peru to see a street named after Jorge Basadre. That is how much this historian is respected in Peru.

Beyond the life of letters, a major aspect of Peruvian culture is sports. As is true with most Latin American nations except those in the Caribbean basin, soccer dominates Peru's sports scene. The team that is most widely identified with excellence in Peruvian soccer is Alianza Lima (Lima Alliance). Formed in 1901 and composed mainly of Afro Peruvian players, Alianza Lima dominated Peruvian soccer for most of the past century. The club's only true rival after World War II was Universitario de Deportes (University Sports). Poorly funded, generally lacking in corporate sponsors, and without good facilities, Alianza Lima still produced Peru's greatest soccer players. Peru's Pele was Teofilo "Nene" Cubillas. Born in March 1949 in Lima of Afro Peruvian parents, Cubillas became Alianza Lima's most legendary player and one of the most prolific scorers from South American in World Cup history. In both the 1970 and 1974 World Cups, Cubillas scored five goals, helping Peru reach the quarterfinals in 1970. He was named "South American Footballer of the Year" in 1972 and eventually went on to play for European teams and in the North American Soccer League for five seasons.

Nearly as popular to soccer in Lima's poor neighborhoods is women's volleyball. Peru's team finished second at the 1982 World Championships. It is the only sport in Peru at present that offers significant economic mobility to talented women athletes. Not yet on a par with soccer, women's volleyball is beginning to draw the necessary corporate sponsors so critical in developing world-class talent. Some of Peru's distinct ethnic groups have maintained an affinity for their own sporting activity. Among the Japanese Peruvians, for example, baseball still remains very popular as it has been since the Japanese arrived in significant numbers in the early 1900s. Older Japanese Peruvians commonly relax by playing gate ball or croquet. For young Peruvians of means, surfing has became very popular. The best surfing is during Peru's winter (June through August), off Peru's north coast. Of the few golf courses in Peru, by far the best is the Lima Golf club in the Lima suburb of San Isidro.

Peru has a rich tradition in international tennis. Its best player was Alex Olmedo, who bested tennis greats Neal Fraser and Rod Laver to win the 1959 Australian and Wimbledon Championships respectively. In 1959, Olmedo was also runner-up for the U.S. Open Championships. Luis (Lucho) Horna, now 26 years old, is highly ranked on the international tennis circuit and has won two major singles titles in his career. One of the best-recognized Peruvian women tennis players is Laura Gildemeister, who won four important tennis matches during the 1980s before her retirement. Her highest finish in a Grand Slam event was the quarterfinals of the 1991 Wimbledon. Tennis remains a sport of the economically advantaged in Peru because of the cost of equipment and facilities. This does not appear likely to change substantially in the foreseeable future.

Chess is a Peruvian passion, and its best player is generally recognized to be Estaban Canal. Born in 1896 in Chiclayo, his best tournaments were in the 1930s in Europe. He was made an Honorary International Grand Master in 1977, four years before his death in Varese, Italy. It is common for young Peruvians to play chess as the game has a long and respected tradition in Peru.

Increasingly, foreign tourists are coming to Peru to take part in some of the most challenging mountain climbing and trekking found anywhere in the world. In recent years, marathons have been run on the original Inca trail near Cuzco. Tourist packages of all types are available for these types of challenging excursions. This type of tourism undoubtedly has been the most beneficial for Peru since the sierra became much safer and the decline of Sendero Luminoso in the mid 1990s. Along with increased tourism in the Andes has come a greater concern for environmental issues, particularly in the past decade.

Accessibility to sports activities in Peru is directly dependent upon state and private funding for facilities, travel, equipment, and other essentials. Until now, these funds have been relatively meager. The absence of sufficient track and field facilities is particularly noticeable in Peru. Clearly, Peruvian athletes have the talent to compete at high levels if the funding and infrastructure becomes available. Anyone who has traveled the Inca trail knows this from having watched in amazement as the serrano porters run the paths while carrying their heavy loads at more than 11,000 feet in altitude.

CONCLUSION

Peru's three separate worlds have been merging steadily over the past century. Modernization has brought the Indians of the sierra to the cities of the coast. With the migration of the serrano have come their food, music, dance, and other fundamental components of their lifestyles. The Afro Peruvian tradition tracing back to the age of slavery is reflected in the working classes of Lima and other large coastal cities. Peru's remote selva regions are isolated no longer. Ecotourism has brought a certain cosmopolitanism to Iquitos and to other sites in the selva. But it must be stressed again that modern Peru must greatly reduce the endemic poverty that has limited security and opportunity for its people since the Spanish Conquest. For this reason it is useful to look at the pre-Columbian foundations of modern Peru. The often-breathtaking accomplishments of Andean civilizations before the arrival of Pizarro can offer hope for the future. These cultures also provide a useful context for better understanding present-day Peru.

NOTES

1. Michael H. Glantz, *Currents of Change: Impacts of El Niño and La Niña on Climate and Society* (Cambridge: Cambridge University Press, 2001), 15–29.

2. Michael E. Moseley, *The Incas and their Ancestors: The Archaeology of Peru* (London: Thames and Hudson, 2001), 131–144.

3. *Washington Post,* July 29, 2006, 1, 12.

4. Glantz, *Currents of Change,* 67–83.

5. César N. Caviedes, *El Niño in History: Storming Through the Ages* (Gainesville: University of Florida Press, 2001), 24.

6. Glantz, *Currents of Change,* 72–74.

7. Charles Walker, "The Upper Classes and Upper Stories: Architecture and the Lima Earthquake of 1746," *Hispanic American Historical Review* 83, 1 (2003): 53–80.

8. See Charles C. Mann, *1491: New Revelations of the Americas Before Columbus* (New York: Knopf, 2006).

9. See Daniel M. Masterson with Sayaka Funada Classen, *The Japanese in Latin America* (Urbana: University of Illinois Press, 2004).

10. See Daniel M. Masterson, *Militarism and Politics in Latin America: Peru from Sánchez Cerro to Sendero Luminoso* (Westport, CT: Greenwood Press, 1991).

2

Empires of the Andes

EARLY CULTURES OF COASTAL PERU

Are the ancient urban civilizations of Peru as old as those of ancient Egypt? Only four decades ago this notion would not have received recognition in most college or high school textbooks. But as a result of pioneering work by archeologists Michael Moseley of the University of Florida and Ruth Shady Solis of the University of San Marcos in Lima and subsequent discoveries by other archeologists in the Norte Chico region of the valley north of Lima, coastal Peru has joined the Tigris-Euphrates River valley, the Indus River valley, Egypt's Nile Delta, the Yellow River valley in China, and Mesoamerica's Olmecs as the earliest centers of civilizations. In the past decade archeologists have uncovered evidence that inhabitants of the Peruvian desert coast were building sophisticated cities as early as 3200–2500 B.C.[1] Well-accepted archeological findings have established that from as early as 11000 B.C., cave dwelling hunters and gatherers lived in temporary encampments, hunted deer and vicuña, fished in coastal rivers and the Pacific Ocean, and ate a variety of fruits, tubers, and squash. But the Norte Chico findings affirm ancient Peru as one of the world's most formative centers of cultural development well before the emergence of far better known societies such as the Moche and the Inca.

At least 25 ceremonial and residential sites have been identified in the Norte Chico region, which contains the valleys of the Huaura, Supe, Pativilca, and Fortaleza rivers. Little substantive archeological work was done in the Norte Chico region after the first efforts, begun in 1941, were slowed by World War II. But now the remains of these urban centers are being studied systematically, with some extraordinary findings being unearthed. These cities were built without fortified defenses, which suggests a level of peaceful communality that was rare in the ancient world. Just as remarkably, these cities situated on Peru's arid coast developed sophisticated irrigation networks that greatly benefited from the hydrologic power of the short rivers plunging from the steep foothills of the Cordillera La Viuda. One of the key products of the irrigated fields in the Norte Chico was cotton, which was employed in this coastal region of Peru for uses as diverse as weaving textiles and fashioning fishing nets. After years of work in the Aspero region of coastal Peru, with particular attention to the sites in the Supe Valley, Moseley proposed the concept of the "maritime foundations" of Andean culture. Immense numbers of fish bones from sardines, anchovies, shellfish, and other species, and minimal evidence of food agriculture led Moseley to surmise that coastal Peru cultures were born and sustained by the sea and not by traditional agriculture as was true everywhere else in the world. Even highland-based cultures such as the Inca hundreds of years later were still dependent on the sea for important resources. In fact, Moseley estimated that coastal societies, with access to the rich supply of anchovies alone, could have reached populations of six million or more long before the Inca.[2]

The site at Caral in the Supe Valley has become the centerpiece of archeological attention since Shady Solis' article in the journal *Science* in 2001 reported her extensive discoveries there. Caral is 14 miles inland and nearly 150 acres in size. In 2700 B.C. Caral likely had a population of 3,000, thus making it the oldest city in the Americas. The city may have arisen as its inhabitants developed irrigation-based agriculture with such staples as squash, beans, guava, and cotton (for fishing nets, trade, and clothing). Caral is dominated by six stone platforms in the shape of mounds that rise to a height of almost eight feet. A large amphitheater provided a venue for Caral's public activities. Engravings in the vicinity of the mounds show birds and monkeys native to the rainforest region. These suggest long-distance trade or communication. Caral is a pre-ceramic society, with its containers being fashioned from gourds, twine, and reeds. But most significantly, skilled weavers in Caral produced representational and abstract cotton textiles that presage the exquisite cloth products that the Peruvian people continued to weave for the ensuing 4,700 years. During more than half of this time period, coastal settlements advanced through the development of more sophisticated irrigation networks. As these cultures moved away from the sea and into the foothills of the Andes, more foodstuffs were domesticated such as potatoes, sweet potatoes, avocados, and peanuts. Cotton continued to grow in significance and the Peruvian culture of cloth became a dominant component of peoples lives. The introduction of ceramics around 1800 B.C. profoundly influenced the course of cultural development in Peru. Not only could food be transported and stored more securely now but the pottery itself became an elaborate art form. With the Moche, for example, the most intimate aspects of their lives were portrayed in their pottery. Thus, the peoples of Peru told their stories in their ceramics and exquisitely woven textiles, which often were representational, without the benefit of writing as we know it today.

CHAVÍN AND THE SOUTHERN CULTURES DURING THE EARLY HORIZON

Peru's highland cultures developed more slowly than did the coastal settlements. Relying on a tripartite approach to subsistence involving agriculture, pastoralism, and hunting, the peoples of the sierra were applying the system of vertical integration that was discussed in chapter 1. The first truly prominent ceremonial center to emerge beyond the coastal regions became known as Chavín de Huantar and was clearly the religious center for the culture known as Chavín. Located at the confluence of two small rivers that are part of the Marañón river watershed in north central Peru, Chavín de Huantar was situated at an elevation of 10,500 feet in the Cordillera Blanca. This religious center flourished between 800 and 200 B.C. The site, once thought to be the birthplace of Andean civilization, is now believed to have it origins in the Amazon basin. At its apex, the site housed as many as 3,000 inhabitants. A U-shaped ceremonial center known as the *Castillo* (castle) is the central architectural feature of the Chavín center. Finely constructed canals were built under the site to provide an acoustic effect for the ceremonies that took place in the Castillo. The artistic and spiritual focus of the Castillo is a striking stela known as the *Lanzón* (goading stick) with both human and feline characteristics. The Lanzón exhibits both a seemingly smiling face while also displaying fierce canine teeth. Thus the deity is seen as both a beneficent and threatening god.[3]

Dating from approximately 1400 to 850 B.C., the Chiripa culture was located on the southern shore of the great Lake Titicaca. The Chiripas were fisher folk who drew on the rich resources of the great lake, using their totora reed boats, much as the fisherman of Lake Titicaca do today. But the people of Chiripa were more varied than the earliest inhabitants of coastal Peru, as they likely planted potatoes and quinoa, and hunted and possibly herded alpaca and llama.

The Paracas culture (800 B.C.–A.D. 100) was located on the seacoast between the Pisco River in the north and the Nazca River to the south, with the modern city of Ica being the principal urban center of the region. First systematically examined by the famed Peruvian archeologist Julio C. Tello in the 1940s, Paracas is famed for its very well-preserved ceramics and textiles. Paracas necropolis also contained a good number of mummy "bundles" who were entombed in a seated position. Clearly these were persons of high prestige because of the rich fabrics in which they were dressed. The Huari-Kayan necropolis located here was one of the richest sites explored in the Paracas region as it produced a substantial number of the mummy bundles and an abundance of textiles. Cloth fabrics made from both wool and cotton were decorated with feathers, tie-dyed, embroidered, and braided, thus establishing a legacy of fine cloth for later Andean peoples to follow.[4]

MOCHE AND NAZCA DESERT CULTURES

As Andean civilization evolved into what archeologists call the Early Intermediate period (A.D. 250–600), the societies began to take on the characteristics of fully developed states. Social structures became more clearly stratified, with elites known as *curacas* playing central leadership roles. Territorial control beyond their own immediate valley location became common. This meant that there was a greater emphasis on the building of fortifications and the establishment of military groups to defend and expand a state's territory and power. During the previous epochs, particularly in the case of the Chavín culture, monumental architecture had been mainly for ceremonial and religious purposes. During the Early Intermediate period, building tended to be for civic activities and habitation within the centers themselves, and societies organized labor very efficiently for agricultural and related irrigation projects. As became the case with later Andean societies, particularly the Inca, agricultural labor and state projects such as irrigation canal construction and maintenance were likely performed as a tax obligation by the peasantry. The culture that best represented these tendencies during this period were the Moche.

Centered in the Moche and Chicama river valleys on Peru's north coastal plain, the Moche were a formative presence from 100 B.C. to A.D. 750. At its height, the Moche realm extended more than 300 miles, from Lambayeque to the north and Nepeña in the south. It is not certain whether the Moche represented a true empire or rather a culturally unified set of communities sharing common technologies and art styles. Noted for their highly realistic ceramics, fine textiles. and great feats of engineering with their vast irrigation networks, the Moche left an archeological record that is richly informative. Moche ceramics are the most expressive of any peoples in the Americas. Depicting nearly every aspect of everyday life, Moche pottery is truly a window on their daily lives. A predominant motif of Moche ceramics was the stirrup spout libation vessels. Molded in three-dimensional styles, these pieces represented themes from mythology to the most mundane aspects of everyday life including tools, pets, weapons, clothing, and work activities like metallurgy. These ceramics were often painted with fine line drawings that elaborated on the theme of the vessel itself. Most representative of this art style were the Moche "portrait heads," which are exquisitely detailed molded depictions of the curaca nobility. The erotic pottery produced by the Moche has also drawn significant attention. Because the Moche depicted nearly every aspect of their lives in their ceramics, pottery representing their diverse sexual activities is not out of character with the rest of their art.

One of the largest adobe structures built in the Americas is found in the Moche realm and is known as the *Huaca del Sol* (Temple of the Sun). A principal burial site, as was the nearby *Huaca de la Luna* (Temple of the Moon), Huaca del Sol was partially destroyed by Spanish looters after the conquest and by subsequent El Niño flooding. Nonetheless, both structures reflect sophisticated skills in organization of labor and engineering on the part of the Moche, who were primarily a nation of farmers and fisher folk. There is little question that there was a military component to Moche life as well. Man-to-man combat involving curaca nobility, with ritual sacrifice following the contest, was certainly practiced, as is evident from archeological study.

Whether this evolved into more extensive combat in the late Moche period as was the case with the Maya is not clear. However, Peruvian archeologist Walter Alva has termed the nobleman interred in the grave of the Lord of Sipan a *warrior-priest*. Alva bases his view on the rich array of objects found in the tomb. The Lord of Sipan was called the King Tutankhamen of the Americas by many journalists when his tomb was discovered. He had been buried in a site located in the *Huaca Rajada,* a burial site on Peru's north coast region in the Lambayeque Valley, 22 miles east of the city of Chiclayo. Alva was tipped to the tomb's location by the appearance on the black market in northern Peru of objects of exceptional craftsmanship. Fortunately, the grave robbers had not destroyed four incredibly rich tombs dedicated to the Moche nobility. Alva and his workers discovered an untouched tomb that revealed a nobleman who was about 40 years old and about 5 feet 4 inches tall. He had been interred in a wooden coffin and adorned with gold necklaces of exquisite workmanship, ear spools inlaid with turquoise, and many ceremonial utensils and everyday objects. Interred with the Lord of Sipan were six other individuals: a child, placed at the head of his coffin; three young women; and two strong men, one of whom had had his feet removed. These may well have been warriors who were sacrificed as guardians of the tomb. Also sacrificed and placed near the Lord's tomb were a dog and two llamas. The Lord of Sipan was clearly a man of great importance who ruled in the Lambayeque Valley between A.D. 200 and 300. His tomb shows evidence of long-distance trade practiced by the Moche. It also suggested the importance of a warrior ethic that played a central role in the status of the Moche elite. The Sipan tomb was a glorious discovery but many of significant archaeological discoveries have been made in this area in the last few years. The wondrous artifacts of the Huaca Rajada site are now housed in a museum administered by Dr. Alva and located near the city of Lambayeque in northern Peru.

Three centuries after the reign of the Lord of Sipan, coastal Peru began to suffer one of its most profoundly disruptive environmental periods in the past two thousand years. Severe drought conditions lasted for most of the final third of the seventh century. This disaster coupled with major earthquakes and a number of highly destructive El Niño events, severely damaged irrigation works and well-established housing. Once again, Peru's harsh environment produced the end of an era. Later termed the Middle Horizon, this period lasted from A.D. 600 to 900.

The decline of the Moche due to the environmental shocks of the seventh and eighth centuries did not lead to their complete demise. They were still able to harvest the sea, and these clever people also benefited from the availability of a new variety of maize with larger cobs. This maize was introduced into fields relocated farther from the sea because of encroaching sand dunes created by the El Niño. Still, the Moche had to abandon their urban center at Cerro Blanco and with it the upper canyon lands and southern valleys that were in close proximity.[5]

Also confronting the same environmental challenges in Peru's south central coast were the Nazca. Contemporary with the Moche (100B.C. to A.D. 600), the Nazca culture was centered in the Ica and Nazca River drainage systems. The populations of these various drainage systems were heavily influenced by local topography. Despite supporting a population that probably never numbered more than 50,000, the people of the Nazca region produced elegant pottery and textiles in addition to world-famous desert geoglyphs, which have generated much scholarly attention as well as poorly informed speculation. The various phases of Nazca pottery retained mythical aspects of the earlier Paracas art styles. Its own stylistic components were added, such as common objects from the everyday world as well as demonic figures holding severed heads as trophies. Later ceramics had militaristic themes and may have reflected similar trends in Moche society about the same period. Nazca textiles were woven from highly prized Alpaca wool, which was very likely obtained through long-distance trade with herders in the Ayacucho region.[6]

Cahuachi, the Nazca urban center, was located 31 miles upriver from the sea. The site appears to be more of a ceremonial than a residential capital as archeological evidence does not point to significant numbers of permanent inhabitants. Archeologist Helaine Silverman has theorized that the Nazca people did not reside in Cahuachi but rather visited it on a cyclical timetable to perform rituals and conduct other common affairs. As such, Cahuachi can not compare to the more elaborate monumental architecture of Moche. But the Nazca geoglyphs are indeed a wonder that has fascinated the world.[7]

Modern investigators have concluded that the geoglyphs could easily have been created by a small crew of workers sweeping away the upper layer of material on the bone dry desert floor. Pioneering work by Paul Kosok and Maria Reiche as well as Anthony Aveni have determined that geoglyphs on the hillsides could be viewed by the local population, akin to signboards on a highway. Drawing the most attention are the markings of animals (hummingbirds, killer whales, spiders, and monkeys), long straight lines, and geometrical figures. More than 3.5 million square feet of the desert floor are covered with these figures. Of the many theories presented for the purpose of the Nazca geoglyphs, the most plausible seem to be related to both agricultural and cosmological purposes. Aveni and his colleagues determined that there was indeed a link between the markings and water flow necessary for irrigation. Most of the animal geoglyphs are located next to what were populated areas. Moseley suggested that these figures were likely constructed by individuals in that locale as a reflection of their own cosmological beliefs.[8] This would be consistent with the somewhat disparate lifestyles of the residents of Nazca, who by way of their particular geography, may well have lived more individualized lives than did the other peoples of coastal Peru. Indeed, Silverman argues persuasively that the "pilgrimage" function of Cahuachi is mirrored today in similar ritual visits by locals to the shrine of the Virgin of Yauca located 17 miles east of the city of Ica. The white church on this site is located next to a desolate plain and is abandoned throughout the year except for the week of the festival, which occurs on the first Sunday in October. Striking similarities in the ancient ceremonies by the Nazca peoples and those of the present day are noted by Silverman. Most of all, it appears that the Nazca cosmological references are rooted more in the household than in the community.[9]

HUARI AND TIAHUANCO

Coinciding with the environmental shocks of the sixth through eighth centuries in coastal Peru, new and important civilizations began to emerge in the highlands. These centers differed from the model of intensive state domination of outlying regions such as we have seen with the Moche. The peoples of this region were known as the Huari. Their capital was situated near the present city of Ayacucho in the south-central Andes. Tiahunaco was located in the Lake Titicaca basin. Moseley considers the Huari and Tiahuanaco peoples examples of civilizations that dispersed nodes of authority and ideology throughout local as well as distant populations.[10] Archeologist William Isbell suggests the possibility of a centralized state structure, pointing to the existence of administrative-style buildings, a road system, and Huari settlements that bear clear similarities to later Inca sites. Their capital, known as Huari, was located at about 8,600 feet, 16 miles north of the city of Ayacucho. Investigated primarily by archeologists Luis Lumbreras and William Isbell, the city may have housed as many as 35,000 inhabitants for much of the four centuries of its cultural and possibly political and military dominance. In some ways, the Huari were important precursors of the Inca. They developed an architecture of control by constructing state edifices in outlying areas. They also began to implement the concept of agricultural and pastoral verticality (see chapter 1), which became so critical to the expansion of the Inca empire.

Potatoes and maize were their principal foods, as would be the case with later Andean highland cultures. The Huari began to initiate terrace farming, which also would be a fundamental component of the Inca agricultural system. The Huari's terracing was so intensive that perhaps as much as a million acres of farmland were hewn out of the rugged Cordillera mountainsides by a highly disciplined labor force.

With these abundant resources and the extended influence of the Huari culture that dominated the central Andes for hundreds of miles, it seems logical to assume that these people were militarized. But there is little evidence to support this assumption. Rather, Huari dominance seems to have been intellectual, commercial, and perhaps spiritual in ways similar to that of the Chavín culture.[11]

One of the more striking features of Huari settlement patterns is the site located on top of a mesa known as *Cerro Baúl* near the present city of Moquegua, near the river valley of the same name. The mesa was little more than a quarter mile long and only 62 acres in area. Towering 2,000 feet above the valley floor, it was an impregnable site that marked the southernmost advance of Huari civilization. Yet it had a water supply and sufficient acreage to grow enough food for the city. Thus the Huari settlers, who were very likely to be members of the elite, were supplied with food, water, and other necessaries by a labor force that toiled daily to up the steep slopes of Cerro Baúl to keep the city functioning. Even with all these logistical drawbacks, Cerro Baúl remained occupied until 1475. The key to Cerro Baúl's longevity may not have been its strategic location, but rather the willingness of the Huari to live in relative harmony with the other dominant power in the region, Tiahuanaco.[12]

The site that became the center of Tiahuanaco's grand culture was occupied as early as 800 B.C. Much of substantial archaeological sites are today located in Bolivia. Nevertheless, it did not begin to expand its influence beyond the region of Lake Titicaca until more than 600 years later. Two of the key elements in Tiahuanaco's prominence in the Lake Titicaca region and beyond were its raised field agricultural systems and the marine bounty from the lake. The agricultural technique known today by the local inhabitants near Lake Titicaca as *raised field* may well have begun to be used at approximately the time that Tiahuanaco began its rise to cultural dominance. Watered by irrigation canals, elevated rows approximately three feet high are constructed above the fields themselves and planted in the traditional Andean crops. These systems have been reconstructed by archeologist Alan Kolata and his assistants with impressive results.[13] These experimental fields, constructed to emulate those of ancient Tiahuanaco, tripled production over contemporary methods employing modern fertilizers and machinery. Raised field agriculture retained nutrients in the soils where potatoes and quinoa were grown. The standing water in the fields also seemed to warm the climate of the Tiahuanaco region, harshly cold at the more than 12,000 foot altitude. There is evidence that as much as 250,000 acres may have been planted during the dominant period of Tiahuanaco. Supplementing the high yields of the raised fields were the marine life of the vast Lake Titicaca. With a surface area of 3,204 square miles (about half that of Lake Ontario), Lake Titicaca is the world's highest commercially navigable lake at 12,532 feet. The ancient Tiahuanaco peoples successfully exploited the resources of the lake to add to an already bountiful agricultural production system. Fisherman today still use the large reed boats known as *totoras* to fish Lake Titicaca's waters in a time-honored fashion that can be traced back two millennia.[14] With these resources at hand Tiahuanaco became, in the words of the archeologist Kolata, a "predatory state," not in the sense of the Incas' military power but rather as an awe-inspiring, commercial, ideological, and spiritual force in the Lake Titicaca region.

Given the power of Tiahuanaco and Huari, and their close proximity, it is amazing that these two cultures lived in peace. The Huari and Tiahuanaco peoples continued to live their different lives, with little commercial or ideological interchange. Even at Cerro Baúl, where frontier elements of both cultures intermingled in the same valleys, the cultures remained separate and peaceful. Little artistic mingling is seen in their pottery. Their textiles and other aspects of their daily lives appear distinct. Only an extended drought after 800 A.D. brought this curious kind of neighborliness to an end, as Huari and Tiahuanaco plunged into decline. Even the raised fields of the Lake Titicaca basin had to be abandoned.

As we have seen thus far, Andean settlement patterns from the earliest time have followed two models; the "lowland maritime oasis" pattern and the "highland arid montane" model.[15] The highland model was best exemplified by the Inca empire and the lowland oasis pattern by the immediate precursors of the Inca, the Kingdom of Chimor.

CHIMOR

Second only to the Inca empire in its expanse in South America, the empire of Chimor (A.D. 850–1470) of the Late Intermediate period covered nearly 700 miles along Peru's coast from Ecuador to approximately present-day Pisco in the south. The Chimú were able to control nearly 70 percent of the population and irrigation works of coastal Peru for more than half a millennium. Such longevity was never matched by the Inca as their imperial rule was cut short by disease, civil war, and ultimately the Spanish invasion. The foundations of kingdom of Chimor were diverse. The Chimú occupied the desert landscapes once inhabited so successfully by the Moche. Indeed, the Chimú clearly drew on past irrigation techniques as they were able to farm 50 thousand acres of desert adjacent to the Moche river in cotton, maize, and other crops.[16] The corporate-style art of Chimor was both impressive and widespread, strongly suggesting the commercial and military power of their empire. Chimú artisans excelled in metal work and produced fine ceramics, textiles, and carved wooden items as well. Chimú metallurgists were so skilled that when the Inca overran their territory in the 1470s, many of the best were deported to Cuzco, where their skills were soon incorporated into the fine art of Inca metalworking. Much of the Chimú metalwork was done in highly specialized workplaces in Batan Grande. Copper and bronze stamped sheets called *naipes* by the Spanish were frequently found in bundles and were apparently used as a form of currency.

In Chimor's thousands of burial sites, the dead were found often in the flexed positions reminiscent of the Huari burial tradition. These tombs were often rich in artifacts such as gold and silver necklaces, gold *keros* (ceremonial cups), and large caches of copper naipes. The artifacts were presumably made for the use of the mummified corpses that the Chimú venerated. Human sacrifice was also practiced by the people of Chimor and one grave contains the remains of 17 victims. However, the practice of human sacrifice occurred on a far more limited scale than was case among the Mesoamerican peoples.

Geoffrey Conrad argues that there were three main areas of conjunction between the empires of Chimor and the Inca. Both states used military conquest through varying stages and with differing degrees of success, depending on the leadership skills of their respective rulers. Each empire tried to conciliate and then consolidate its foes into its empire rather than annihilating the enemy. Both Chimor and Cuzco justified their imperial wars on the grounds that they were spreading their superior civilization and religion. Their religions had clear similarities as both the Chimú and the Inca believed in creator gods and worshipped celestial bodies as their principal deity.

The kingdom of Chimor and the Inca empire were ruled by dynasties based upon a hereditary elite whose rulers were descended from celestial deities. From these dynasties came dominant militaristic emperors who succeeded in conquering large portions of their empires and consolidating their rule. Tradition has Chimor established by Tacainamo, who arrived from the sea in balsa rafts. He and his sons then built the first settlement and move on to establish more in the surrounding region. In Inca lore the central ruler/deity is Pacha-cuti Inca (Worldshaker), who came to power in 1438, initiated the Inca con-quests, and established Cuzco as the metropolis of the empire. The kingdom of Chimor's marvelous capital at Chan Chan near present-day Trujillo may well have been the inspiration for the luxurious capital that Cuzco was soon to become. Theoretically, the Chimor and Inca dynasties were constructed on the principle of reciprocity. In each imperium the state required labor from its people as a form of tax. In return, the state would assure that the people were fed and housed by a careful division of labor, distribution, and storage sys-tems. As each state became more oppressively hierarchical and demanding, this system of reciprocity became very strained. Nevertheless, Chimor and the Inca empire were sustained through prolonged drought and El Niño events that had doomed earlier cultures.

Chan Chan, Chimor's capital, boasted a population of 100,000 at the time of its surrender to Inca armies in 1470. Divided into a series of compounds or *ciudadelas* as they were called by the Spaniards, Chan Chan was a working city, as well as an administrative and religious capital. Estimates are that as many as 10,000 craftsmen and metallurgists labored in Chan Chan during its peak years of activity. Some of these ciudadelas were very substantial, with the one known as Rivero occupying an area over six acres in size.[17] These compounds housed the higher and lesser nobility of Chimor and their burial sites as well. A constant problem for the city was the securing of sufficient amounts of potable water. Prolonged drought forced the excavation of deeper wells and even a failed attempt to build a nearly 50-mile long irrigation canal in the Chicama river valley. Like some great metropolises in the Americas such as the Mayan city of Copán in Honduras, Chan Chan outstripped the capability of its surrounding environment to support its dense population. The Chimú responded to this environmental challenge with intelligence and discipline. Expansive sunken gardens, dug closer to the depleted water table, were constructed in the environs of the city. Nevertheless, these extraordinary measures were not enough and Chan Chan's population steadily declined in the 15th century. After the arrival of the Spanish, the city was abandoned, and Chan Chan was then battered and eroded by time and the elements in the ensuing centuries. One of the most tragic events in Peru's history took place in the Chimor capital long after 1500. When an abortive revolution launched in the nearby city of Trujillo was put down in July 1932, Peruvian government forces used the cover of Chan Chan's intricate maze of streets and passage-ways to execute hundreds of suspected rebels in reprisal for the revolt. For Peruvians with a sense of the past, the mighty city of Chan Chan thus presents two very different visions of its history.

THE EMPIRE OF THE INCAS

Like the Aztecs (Mixeca) of Mexico, the Inca Empire embodied many key aspects of the cultures that came before it. In this sense the Inca were capstone cultures that often assimilated much more than they innovated. The Inca were master administrators who forged a realm geographically larger than any previous peoples in the Americas. *Tahuantinsuyu* (Realm of the Four Quarters) occupied nearly a third of the South American continent and had a population of between 9 and 16 million people. These lands were conquered in less than a century with conscripted armies that were often drawn from the manpower of their defeated enemies. Organizing labor and soldiering were what the Inca did best. Indeed, labor was viewed with the highest regard. Labor specialization within the Inca empire produced an infrastructure, architecture, and fine arts of the highest quality. Most importantly, the Inca, by employing the concept of verticality to near perfection, came closer than any society in the Americas, and perhaps in the world, to eliminating chronic hunger among its subjects. The onslaughts of El Niño, earthquakes, and droughts notwithstanding, the Inca adapted to the harsh Andean environment with consummate skill. This security came at a price for the people of *Tahuantinsuyu*. The increasingly authoritarian Inca rulers sought to weaken or completely obliterate ethnic identities within the empire in order to create a conforming populace that would simply do what it was told in the context of the Inca reciprocal system. So rather than the idealized socialist utopia mistakenly praised by Voltaire, the Inca were never completely free of internal resistance by subject peoples who opposed ethnic subjugation.

We know far more about the Inca than we do about their Andean ancestors because the sources are not exclusively archeological; however, as Peter Klarén has noted, the sources are problematic.[18] The Inca did not have a written language akin to those of the Mesoamerican peoples. Nevertheless, the highly expressive nature of their pottery, metal work, and particularly their textiles is quite revealing. Gary Urton, Robert Ascher, and Elizabeth Hill Boone, among others, have also shown that the *quipu* system, a method of retaining quantitative data on knotted cords, was crucial not only in recordkeeping but also as a device for retaining syntactic and semantic information. The complexity of the *quipu* system has been known for a long time. Computer-based analysis has begun to be used to further understand how to quipu system works.[19] Of course, the Inca chronicles and their rich mythologies have to be regarded with care. However, they do give us significant insights into the cosmologies of the Andean peoples long after the arrival of the Spanish.

Garcilaso de la Vega's early 17th-century histories are central to our understanding of the Inca past but inevitably they do not primarily reflect the Andean cosmological view. Garcilaso was a mestizo with ties to the Inca royalty. He sought to portray the Inca in the most positive light possible. He was certainly seeking to recreate a vision of a benevolent Inca empire that would sharply contrast with that created by the Spanish. More in touch with the Andean worldview was Guaman Poma de Ayala (ca. 1535–ca. 1615), who knew both Quechua and Spanish and penned a prodigious 1,188 page illustrated history of Andean and early Spanish rule that was completed in 1615. However, it was not available to the public until 1978, when it was published in a translated and abridged version entitled *Letter to the King*. This book was the earliest, most literate, and certainly most militant expression of pride in the Andean past, and it was certainly a protest against conditions fostered by Spanish rule. Our understanding of everyday life in the Inca empire and the intricacies of its cosmology have occupied the attention of scholars for much of the past 50 years. Thomas Zuidema, for example, argued that Andean peoples viewed themselves in a temporal and spacial context far different from that of the European peoples.[20] John Murra explained complex vertical integrated agricultural colonies in Andean America.[21] He also made clear the overwhelming importance of cloth in the material and spiritual life of the Inca. Recent scholarship, such as that by John Hyslop has shed new light on Inca settlement patterns, road systems, and fortifications.[22] As a result of this scholarship we are far more aware today of the rapid evolution of Inca power and its impact upon Andean peoples from the mid 14th century onward.

CONQUEST AND EXPANSION

Most scholars today believe that the Inca originated in the Altiplano and then moved to Cuzco Valley around the 12th century. Like the Aztecs in the Valley of Mexico at about the same time, the Inca began to conquer and assimilate other ethnic groups in the valley by incorporating the rulers of these conquered peoples into a system of royal *ayllus* (kinship group). They thus became known as "Incas by privilege."[23] This strategy of conquest and incorporation would be the model by which the Inca would dominate the Andean regions in the centuries to come. Clearly, Inca expansion was prompted, in some degree, by the desire to spread their ideology throughout the Andes. Others have also suggested the "split inheritance" theory, wherein deceased Inca emperors retained all their lands and earthly possessions and forced new emperors to engage in conquest to establish their own realms. After 1200, Inca leadership was firmly centered in the emperor, whose lineage was hereditary. Opening the succession process to great intrigue was the practice of choosing a successor not from the emperor's eldest male heir but from his most "worthy of sons."[24] Of the 13 emperors before the Spanish invasion, by far the most dynamic was Pachacuti (1438–1471). Considered by some to be on a par with Alexander the Great, Pachacuti shaped the Inca realm through conquest and innovative administration that stressed reciprocity rather than repression. His vision of Inca grandeur was unmatched by any Andean ruler.

Pachacuti's military conquests are all the more impressive given that his armies were largely drawn from the ranks of conquered peoples and through the *mita* system, in which the most able males of a conquered people were quickly given the opportunity to serve as "mercenaries" in the amorphous Inca armies, with promises of the spoils taken from future defeated peoples. Often battles were undertaken against traditional enemies of the newly conquered to ensure greater fervor by the new rank and file. This complex military strategy required frequent warfare. Still, sound military strategies are rarely successful if they are not matched by appropriate tactics. The Inca did not fight to annihilate their enemies. Instead their foes were first offered diplomatic alternatives to warfare. Inca generals gave the enemy's elite the chance to be integrated into the Inca empire with significant social status. If initial diplomatic offers were refused, intelligence was gathered regarding the enemy's strength, weak points in their fortifications, and the likelihood of aid from nearby allies. Even scales models of the enemy's fortifications were made to facilitate planning. In this aspect, the Inca military leadership foreshadowed modern armies such as the Russians in counterattacks against the Germans in World War II. Attacks would usually begin with archers drawn from the selva regions. Dressed in cloth armor that was layered and quilted for extra protection, the infantry then attacked. Armed with the mace, spears, and their most effective weapon, the sling, the infantry would conduct the main assault. Campaigns against some formidable opponents such as Chimor in the 1470s apparently were planned very carefully well in advance by the Inca leadership. Spies and scouts provided intelligence regarding fortifications, troop strength, and food supplies before the Inca armies entered the field. Mobility was one of the great advantages of the Inca military. The Inca highways and suspension bridges over cavernous gorges aided Inca military operations enormously. Because the Americas lacked the modern horse and the modern concept of the wheel before 1492, these roads were designed for commercial foot travel and for travel by the swift Inca messengers known as *Chasquis*. Sure-footed llamas, carrying loads up to 80 pounds, also traversed these roads with ease.

The Inca were master builders and were also very practical. Their military installations were not simply fortresses, as John Hyslop has shown, but often served other purposes such as storehouses. The extensive Inca road system allowing rapid movement of troops might explain the lack of fortifications, in parts of the empire. Also, minimal resistance from the Chilean and Argentine frontiers could also be an explanation. The northern frontier into Ecuador, however, offers ample archeological evidence of fortifications that were constructed during the protracted wars in this region. Additionally, the Inca concentrated fortifications in the Bolivia *oriente* (eastern region), in anticipation of possible attack from the nomadic Amazonian and Chaco peoples. The Inca built a good number of what today are called squad outposts, which were occupied by less than 15 men who were housed in installations a few miles away. These forts likely served as surveillance posts or guarded strategic transit areas.[25]

One of the larger military structures was Incawasi, in the Cañete Valley, south of Lima on the Pacific coast. A huge installation, Incawasi housed 800 separate rooms. As imagined, the site contained some residential areas, but it also served as a major storage site. Significantly, it had a large plaza for ritual purposes. From the configuration of the buildings Hyslop argues that Incawasi functioned as a launching site for major attacks from its higher location down into the river valley. Troops did not appear to be housed within the confines of Incawasi, but rather camped outside temporarily as they prepared for battle. This site was built in haste, very likely with *mita* labor. The main Inca fortress in Cuzco, Sacsyhuman, was built with expert Inca masons to endure for the ages.[26]

INCA COSMOLOGY AND ADMINISTRATION

Cuzco was designed to be not only the imperial center of Inca power but to demonstrate its cosmological supremacy as well. As Zuidema's work has suggested, *Tahuantinsuyu*'s integral connection to the great order of the heavens was most clearly reflected in the Milky Way or *Mayu* (Celestial River).[27] This view argues that a series of 41 spiritually charged lines connected the central plaza in Cuzco with holy objects or places in the surrounding landscapes. Known as *huacas*, these holy places were caves, mountain peaks, the junction of two rivers, and special shrines linking the Inca and other Andean peoples to *Pachamama* or mother earth. Indeed, for the Inca Pachamama had supreme importance in the Inca world view for, as with the Maya, who believed they evolved from maize, the Inca claimed their origins lay with Pachamama herself. It is interesting then that the Inca, who professed such reverence for the land, altered it more than any peoples in the Americas before the arrival of the Spaniards. Terracing, vast irrigation networks, a road system spanning 25,000 miles, and even the redirection of river systems all reflected a pragmatic approach to their relations with Pachamama that seems to indicate that agricultural production was a higher priority for the Inca than a pristine landscape. Still, as Irene Silverblatt and Moseley have noted, female and male forces within Andean cosmology worked together to create gender duality, balance, and equality. All may worship the sun but women in the Andean world have a special kinship with the moon and Pachamama. In a fundamental sense the Inca and their descendants retain a most intimate relationship with their environment, regarding much of it as sacred. These cosmological beliefs are reflected in their textiles, ceramics, and their spiritual life, which was intimately tied to their labor, kinship groups, and the landscape on which they worked and lived.[28]

Among the Inca pantheon of gods, the creator god, *Viracocha*, was a central deity. *Inti*, the sun god, and *Mamaquilla*, the moon deity, held special significance based upon gender. Of course, Pachamama, the feminine earth deity, was intimately tied to the Andean people's responses to their unstable landscape. Huacas, the sacred places of the Andean peoples, could be sites for the location of local shrines. Cuzco was replete with religion sites and the city was, in fact, created in the shape of the sacred puma. The massive fortress of *Sacsayhuaman* formed the head of the great cat's body. Sacrifice was an important component of Inca religion. The ubiquitous *cuy* (guinea pig) was frequently kept in the household, along with llamas (for special rituals), coca leaves, chicha corn beer, and other everyday commodities, which also were offered in ritual form. Ritual offerings could be as simple as offering roasted corn to Inti as the day began or as complex as the ritual sacrifice of children such as the famed "Ice Maiden" found at Nevado Amato Volcano in 1995, 500 years after she gave her life to satisfy the Inca belief system. Human sacrifice was not nearly as frequent in the Andean world as it was in Mesoamerica. Nevertheless, it was an integral component of Inca religion.

For many centuries before the Inca, ancestor worship loomed large as an aspect of Andean belief systems. As we have seen, the Inca and their ancestors marshaled scarce resources by means of ayllus, or kinship groups. The forebears of the original ayllu were highly venerated because they gathered its original resources and established the primary identity and autonomy of the ayllu. Among the Inca, the nobility were considered immortal. When they died their bodies were mummified. Known by their Quechua name, *Mallquis*, these royal mummies, and those of lesser status were granted lands and llama herds and were often consulted on important matters of state, local, and ayllu affairs. As one can imagine, the *panacas* (royal lineages) associated with the royal mummies, could retain significant influence. Most importantly, those deceased Inca emperors retained their wealth and holdings as immortal deities. This led to the split inheritance concept, fostered primarily by the eminent Peruvian scholar Maria Rostworoski de Diez Canseco, that new emperors were compelled to acquire their own lands and resources through expansion of the empire if they were to achieve the status of their predecessors.[29] Among the sacred Inca emperors, few could compare with the military prowess of Pachacuti. Despite all his accomplishments, however, it would be simplistic to attribute the expansion of the Inca empire to him alone. The two social and economic building blocks that served as the foundation of the empire were the ayllu and the closely related system of reciprocity that governed nearly all work in the Andes. The Inca were able to harness these social systems very effectively, enabling them to organize labor with great efficiency. The ayllu has a very long history in the Andes. Because of the harsh Andean environment, many basic tasks, such as house construction, planting and harvesting of potatoes, and herding cannot be accomplished by the labor of a single family. Thus arose the ayllu, defined by Moseley as an "autonomous unit of production and reproduction (that) is an alliance of households and kindred that exchange labor and jointly own land and other resources."[30] The obligation within an ayllu is labor, the most valuable commodity in the Andean world. Labor is provided with the highly secure anticipation that it will be returned in kind when needed or will be repaid in goods of equal value.

Labor reciprocity, of course was extended beyond the ayllu. In this context a family may call upon labor temporarily beyond the ayllu for large tasks such as house building. The amount of work given is carefully determined with the expectation that it will be returned in kind. The Inca expanded the existing *mita* system on a grand scale as a form of labor tax to recruit a labor force for its empire. Every male in the Inca realm was obligated to provide a period of service. Males could work as weavers, soldiers, miners, herders, road builders, or any other work that was required of them. Relocation from their home communities must have been difficult for those called away for distant tasks. But some scholars argue that the *mitayos* (mita workers) were provided with substantial food and drink, and carried out their work in ritualistic and festive manner.[31] How then did the Inca state reciprocate to the workers it so successfully organized?

The Inca met their reciprocal responsibilities in some measure through highly developed systems of storage and distribution. Lacking a market economy, except at the local level, the Inca would store massive quantities of foodstuffs, textiles, building materials, ceramics, military supplies, and a variety of other items in storehouses called *qollqas*. Located close to roads and in major administrative centers, these qollqas were often placed on hillsides where they were constant reminders of the immense wealth of the empire. The contents of these qollqas were used to clothe, feed, and arm the mitayos and the Inca armies. Indeed, without these qollqas, the range of the Inca armies would have been very limited, as they never were able to sustain long supply trains in the rugged Andean landscape. Ritual feasting for the Inca elite seemed also to be facilitated by the vast storage systems. One Spanish commentator noted, for example, that in just one storehouse in Cuzco, 100,000 dead birds were stored for the purpose of making luxury textiles in the future for the Inca elite.[32]

Inca society was very stratified and power was fixed in the very small nobility (*orejones*). Perhaps no more than 1,500 carried the "pure blood" of the original Inca leaders in Cuzco. All high administrative posts, especially in the army, were held by this nobility. People from areas bordering on Cuzco who had lived and cooperated with the Inca empire for an extended time were known as *Hahua* or Inca by adoption. More distant members of the provincial nobilities under Inca rule then held some limited governance power. Finally, as Gordon McEwan has summarized, the *Hatun runa* were the common heads of families that were integrated in the ayllu. For administrative purposes, the Inca organized the *Hatun runa* in to groups of 10 (*chuncha*), 50 (*piscachuncha*), 100 (*pachaca*), 500 (*piscapachaca*), 1,000 (*huaranca*), 5,000 (*piscahuaranca*), and 10,000 (*hunu*). This system worked very well for organizing the complex tax and labor obligations, which allowed the Inca empire to expand and function. During the early decades of the 16th century, however, problems of succession within the Inca empire and the silent and deadly mantle of disease shattered the unity of the once proud realm and resulted in devastation of the Spanish invasion.

CIVIL WAR, PLAGUE, AND THE SPANISH INVASION

Some early scholars of the Inca likened their rule to a form of beneficent socialism. It was hardly that. As we have seen, Inca rule was strictly hierarchical. In a highly efficient manner, labor and tribute were gathered from peoples who were placated by assimilation, relocation, and reciprocity. Still, the system was exploitive. It was harmful to the different ethnic groups within a monolithic empire. *Mitmae* (forced relocation of subject peoples) was perhaps the best example of how ethnic groups were subjugated. In many ways this *mitmae* system was effective in reducing dissent and settling new agricultural lands. But it never completely quelled opposition to the Inca in the northern regions of the empire. There the Cañari resisted Inca armies for a protracted period. Increasingly, because of a greater military presence in the north, that part of the empire began to acquire greater significance.

Inca royal succession also became problematic. The right of the Sapa Inca to choose the next emperor from among his "most worthy sons" caused intrigue within the ranks of the nobility. The various interest groups represented by the royal lineages and their power also complicated the question of succession. After a troubled accession to the Inca throne involving the bloody elimination of his competitors, Huayna Capac took the throne in 1520 and soon proceeded to lead a protracted series of military campaigns in Ecuador. He established a magnificent palace in Tomebamba far away from the affairs of state in Cuzco. Commanding the bulk of the Inca armies, Huayna Capac's protracted presence in the north upset the balance of power in the empire. When he died in 1525, the question of his successor was unsettled. It is probable that Huayna Capac and many close to him, including relatives, military leaders, and members of his entourage, died of smallpox that may have entered the empire from Panama as early as 1524.

In the aftermath of Huayna Capac's death, two of his sons, Huascar and Atahualpa, contested the throne. Huáscar, based in Cuzco, was Huayna Capac's choice and was backed by most of the powerful royal lineage in Cuzco. Atahualpa drew his support from key commanders of the Inca armies stationed in the north where they had long been contesting rebellion against the empire. As might be expected, control of the Inca armies was critical in a protracted and brutal civil war made even more horrific by the terrible toll of disease. Initially, Huáscar fared well in the conflict as he relied heavily on an alliance with the Cañari armies, who readily fought their hated enemy Atahualpa. Eventually, however, the full weight of the Inca armies with their experienced leadership drove Huáscar's forces from the field. Tens of thousands of soldiers were engaged in this conflict and the casualties were very heavy. An initial epidemic of smallpox that raced through the Inca empire from 1524 to 1526 and another plague of smallpox and measles that struck from 1530 to 1532 may well have reduced the population of the empire by half before the arrival of the Spaniards. Scholars are divided on the totality of the demographic catastrophe that occurred when these two epidemics struck Peru even before the appearance of the European. But with the arrival of two more waves of plague in 1533 and 1535, the ability of the Inca empire to resist the Spanish invasion greatly diminished. There is no consensus on the population of the Inca empire before the arrival of Pizarro's contingent. Estimates range from 4 to 15 million. Less than a century after the first epidemic in 1524, David Noble Cook's careful estimate places the Indian population of Peru at only 700,000.[33] Francisco Pizarro, like his predecessor Cortés in Mexico, expertly exploited the advantages of disease, divisions between the Andean peoples, the horse, and the broadsword, along with utter ruthlessness and a sense of reckless desperation surmounted long odds to defeat the Inca armies. But Pizarro's victory was not easy, nor was it as immediate as many shallow textbook versions imply.

Francisco Pizarro is thought to have been born in 1478 in Trujillo, in Spain's barren province of Extremadura in the southwest. Migrants and adventurers fleeing the poverty of Extremadura filled the ranks of those Spaniards seeking opportunity in the Americas in the 16th century. Men like Pizarro and Cortes were continuing the tradition of the centuries old *Reconquista* (Reconquest) that the *hidalgos* (lesser nobility) of Catholic Spain waged against Islam. For centuries these "men of lesser means" fought not just for the return of Spain to the Catholic faith but for their own validation as men of status bolstered by the spoils of war. Pizarro was but one of the most successful of the conquistadores.

As the illegitimate son of a hidalgo, Pizarro received no formal education or possibility of inheritance. As a young man he attained some military experience with Spanish forces in Italy. In 1502 he arrived in the Caribbean and subsequently took part in a number of expeditions including Balboa's trek across Panama to the Pacific Ocean in 1513. By 1519 Pizarro was one of the leading figures in the founding of Spain's colony in Panama. From there, the adventurer conducted two maritime explorations off the west coast of South America south to the present day site of Tumbés in northern Peru. Pizarro's third and final foray brought him to within marching distance of the Inca city of Cajamarca in September 1532. In early November his force of 62 cavalry and 102 foot soldiers entered the nearly abandoned city. As he planned his ambush of Atahualpa, Pizarro confidently held the mandate of Charles V that awarded him the title of governor and captain general of northern Peru. More important, he also possessed valuable intelligence detailing the ravages of the civil war and disease within the Inca realm. Perhaps understanding the rigid hierarchy of the Inca command structure, Pizarro planned to replicate Cortes's strategy and capture Atahualpa. He could then exploit the divisions with the Inca empire and even the overwhelming odds he faced.

Atahualpa, suspecting little danger from a small force of strangers reported by his scouts, arrived in the central plaza of Cajamarca on November 16, 1532. A Spanish friar read the "requirement" in Spanish, which demanded the Inca ruler submit to the authority of the Spanish Crown. When Atahualpa responded to this demand with contempt, Pizarro's men attacked the Inca's retinue from their places of ambush.

With the advantages of complete surprise, a battle plan, gunpowder, and the deadly use of mounted fighters and swordsmen, Pizarro's force cut a deadly swath through the Inca ranks and captured Atahualpa as planned. The emperor was then ransomed for vast sums of gold and silver objects crafted by the empire's artisans. Soon, however, Atahualpa was executed by Pizarro for plotting against the new government of Peru.

The capture of Atahualpa by no means ended Inca resistance to the Spanish. When Pizarro marched south to occupy Cuzco he was assisted by the former enemies of Atahualpa, which included the Cañaris, Huancas, and the Chachapoyas. Just as Cortés had done in Mexico, Pizarro named a new puppet emperor, Tupac Huallpa or Toparpa , to legitimize his rule. The new ruler died soon thereafter and Pizarro replaced him with Manco Inca. The Andean peoples initially rejected Manco Inca as Pizarro's puppet and focused much of their opposition toward the "false Inca" and not Pizarro himself. Although the Spaniards entered Cuzco one year after their victory at Cajamarca, their dominance in Cuzco was short-lived. In early May 1536, a force of 100,000 Inca fighters, commanded by an angry and humiliated Manco Inca, rebelled against the Spanish and lay siege to Cuzco. Against great odds, the Spanish endured a fiery siege and broke out of their entrapment to take the great fortress of Sacsyhuaman. Manco Inca was forced to retreat to a mountain redoubt in Villacamba where he was slain eventually by Spanish assassins in 1545. During his first years of rule in Peru, Pizarro established coastal centers of Spanish power to maintain better communication with the outside world. Lima, situated on the Rimac River, soon became the administrative capital of Spanish colonial Peru. Even there, during the Manco Inca rebellion, the Spanish barely withstood an Inca siege. Andean resistance to Spanish rule took many forms during the next two centuries of Spanish dominance in the Andes. Despite the social and economic pressures applied by the Spanish and caused by disease, the Andean sense of community, work ethic, and spiritual relationship with their environment helped the Andean people to endure.

CONCLUSION

The early cultures of Peru were wondrously expressive in artistic forms, engineering, agricultural techniques, and astronomy, among their many accomplishments. Andean metallurgists drew upon the rich deposits of gold and silver to create marvelous tributes to their leaders and deities that have only been hinted at by such treasures as those found in the tomb of the Lord of Sipan. Agricultural techniques such as the raised field technique used on the shores of Lake Titicaca were as productive as any used to this very day. The irrigation networks of the coastal peoples and the intricate road network constructed by the Inca sustained the agriculture and commerce of millions of peoples before the arrival of the European. These accomplishments were achieved in one of the most challenging environmental settings in the world. What was the key to the stunning accomplishments of these Andean peoples? Certainly one of the foremost achievements was the effective management of labor through a system of reciprocity, which endures to the present day among Andean peoples. Also, it was the ability of the Andean peoples to adapt to the demand of their environmental setting. Verticality, as explained by John Murra, is but one significant facet of this success. In the end, however, it is the imagination and the creativity of the Andean peoples that was their greatest strength. That imagination is seen in the ceramics of the Moche, the ancient textiles of Paracas, the desert lines of Nazca, and the architecture of the Inca. Andean history before the Europeans includes many rich civilizations that have made Peru the home of cultural diversity that is only now being fully appreciated.

NOTES

1. Charles C. Mann, *1491: New Revelations of the Americas Before Columbus* (New York: Knopf, 2006), 176–178.

2. Michael E. Moseley, *The Incas and their Ancestors: The Archeology of Peru* (London: Thames and Hudson, 2001), 110. This book is an excellent survey of pre-Columbian peoples from an archeological perspective.

3. Ibid., 163–168.

4. Ibid., 160–163.

5. Ibid., 225.

6. Ibid., 198.

7. See Helaine Silverman, *Cahuachi in the Ancient Nazca World* (Iowa City: University of Iowa Press, 1993).

8. Moseley, *Incas and their Ancestors*, 202.

9. Helaine Silverman, "The Archeological Identification of an Ancient Peruvian Peruvian Pilgrimage Center," *World Archeology* 26, no. 1 (1994), 1–18.

10. Moseley, *Incas and their Ancestors*, 230.

11. Mann, *1491*, 231.

12. Ibid., 234–235.

13. See Alan Kolata, *Tiwanaku and its Hinterland: Archaeology and Paleoecology of Andean Civilization* (Washington, DC: Smithsonian Books, 1996).

14. Jorge Ortíz Sotelo, "Embarcaciones aborígenes en el Area Andina," en *Historia y Cultura*, Revista del Museo Nacional de Historia No. 20, (1990), pp. 49–79.

15. Moseley, *Incas and their Ancestors*, 275.

16. Mann, *1491*, 235.

17. Moseley, *Incas and their Ancestors*, 272.

18. Peter F. Klarén, *Peru: Society and Nationhood in the Andes* (Oxford: Oxford University Press, 2000), 12.

19. Gary Urton, *Signs of the Inka Khipu: Binary Coding in the Inka Knot String Records* (Austin: University of Texas Press, 2003).

20. R. Tom Zuidema, *Inca Civilization in Cuzco* (Austin: University of Texas Press, 1990).

21. John Murra, *The Economic Organization of the Inca State* (Greenwich, CT: JAI Press, 1988).

22. John Hyslop, *Inca Settlement Planning* (Austin: University of Texas Press, 1990).

23. Klarén, *Peru*, 14.

24. Irene Silverblatt, *Moon, Sun and Witches: Gender, Ideology and Class in Inca and Colonial Peru* (Princeton: Princeton University Press, 1987).

25. Maria Rostworoski de Diez Canseco, with Harry Iceland. *History of the Inca Realm* (Cambridge: Cambridge University Press, 1999).

26. Hyslop, *Inca Settlement Planning*, 147–175.

27. See among his many works, R. Thomas Zuidema's early work on the ceque system of Cusco, *The Ceque System of Cuzco*, Leiden, International Archives of Ethnography, Supplement to Volume 50, 1964.

28. Silverblatt, *Moon, Sun and Witches; Moseley, Inca and their Ancestors*, 51–52.

29. For this concept see particularly the work of Peruvian scholars Maria Rostworski de Diez Canseco and Franklin Pease García-Yrogoyen.

30. Moseley, *Incas and their Ancestors*, 53.

31. Klarén, *Peru*, 23–24.

32. Terry LeVine, editor, *Inca Storage Systems* (Norman: University of Oklahoma Press, 1992), IX, X.

33. David Noble Cook, *Demographic Collapse: Indian Peru, 1520–1620* (Cambridge: Cambridge University Press, 1981), 247–256.

3

Spanish Colonial Peru

After the military suppression of the native Andean peoples in the late 1500s, Spanish colonial power in South America became centered in Lima, capital of the Viceroyalty of Peru. Spanish administrators would not leave Peru for nearly 300 years, until their expulsion after the battle of Ayacucho in December 1824. In examining the impact of Spanish colonialism on Peru we will focus on five key issues: (1) the nature and consequences of the indigenous population's demographic collapse as a result of disease and exploitation; (2) Peru's native people's efforts to retain their cultural identity; (3) the Andean people's modes of resistance to Spanish rule; (4) the design and function of the Spanish colonial state and its economy; and (5) the makeup of Spanish colonial society in Peru. We will begin with a review of population decline and its consequences.

THE ORDEAL OF SURVIVAL

The overwhelming reality of the first century of Spanish rule in Peru was the devastating decline of the indigenous population due to disease and related factors. This demographic collapse bore drastic consequences for Spanish labor and tribute policy. It also affected the ability of the Andean people to retain their social systems and confront the new Spanish order. As we have seen in the previous chapter, plague had entered the Andes even before the arrival of the Spanish. As Cook notes, Peru's indigenous population likely declined from the time of the conquest by more than 50 percent to 1.3 million in 1570.[1] A half century later, it had plunged further to only 700,000. The decline would continue, albeit less rapidly, well into the 17th century. The south coast experienced the most pronounced decline in the Indian population through the end of the 1600s.[2] Already a harsh environment due to eruptions from the chain of volcanoes extending nearly 100 miles north of the city of Arequipa, this region also endured a series of deadly earthquakes during the early colonial period. El Niño-related droughts also accelerated the decline of the native peoples in this region.

The earthquake of January 1582 nearly destroyed Arequipa, and the ensuing tsunami badly damaged most of the coastal farm land. By this time, Spanish settlers were occupying many of the coastal valleys that the Indian peoples had once cultivated; the lands were often unoccupied because many of the Indians had died from disease or fled to escape the onerous tribute taxes imposed by the Spanish. Estimates are that the Indian population decline in Peru's south coast exceeded three percent annually from 1570 until the early 1600s. By the end of the 17th century, agriculture in the region was completely dominated by the Spanish, with the cultivation of grapes for wine being the predominant activity.

Of Peru's highland regions, Cook concludes that the northern sierra regions of Huaraz, Cajamarca, and Jaén saw the most marked decline among the native peoples, from 210,000 in 1570 to approximately 120,000 in 1620. Mita, the state labor requirement that the Spanish imposed upon the Indian population, may have increased the death rate by concentrating the Indians in work crews in the mines of this region. This was certainly true in the central sierra, including in the regions of Tarma, Jauja, and Lucanas. The Huancavelica mercury mine in this region was essential for the processing of high-grade silver. Indian laborers in the mercury mines were subject to quick deaths from accidents, cave-ins, and rapid onset of pulmonary diseases such as pneumonia. Slower deaths resulted from *mala de mina,* or mine sickness, due to poisoning from mercury, arsenic, and cinnabar dust that the workers inhaled constantly during their work deep in the shafts. Actual death rates for mine workers in the Huancavelica mines are not available. But Cook notes an interesting anomaly: as dangerous as work in these mines was, the death rate for the Indian population in the central sierra was less than half that of the coastal region. Here again, environmental factors are of primary importance. The warm climate of Peru's coastal regions clearly provided better conditions for the spread of disease than the frigid atmosphere of the Peruvian sierra.[3] Nevertheless, Peru's desperate Indian peoples, forced to work in the deadly mines that produced enormous wealth for Spain, resisted by fleeing their villages during the worst demographic collapse in recorded human history.

One of the key consequences of demographic collapse during the early colonial period was the both voluntary and forced migration of much of the Indian population. The high death rate from disease in Peru's south coastal region prompted significant migration out of that area. The labor demands for the mines by the mita uprooted many males from their home villages for long periods. Finally, the program of the Spanish viceroy Francisco de Toledo y Figueroa (1569–1581) of resettling Andean villagers from their ancestral homes to Spanish towns (*reducciones*) weakened ayllu relations, which had endured for hundreds of years. As the Andean people were forced to leave their homes, their intricate reciprocal relationships within their communities and with the environment often were broken. Toledo sought to increase Spanish revenue by more closely monitoring and collecting tribute within the reducciones. This set in motion a migration as native peoples who fled the Spanish settlements in an effort to escape the onerous tribute system. For reasons of either death or flight as Cook notes, Peru's tributary population declined from 260,544 in 1670 to 136,235 in 1620, a decrease of nearly 50 percent. In human terms, the implications were far more important than just questions of revenue for the Spanish crown. Kenneth Andrien, among others, makes clear that the resettlement of Peru's indigenous peoples by Viceroy Toledo not only separated them from their homes, *huacas* (sacred places), and the ayllu but also weakened their relationships with their long-recognized leaders, the curacas. This made resistance to Spanish rule much more difficult but by no means did the Andean people capitulate to Spanish rule.[4]

RESISTANCE AND REBELLION

In 1560 a primarily spiritual resistance movement confronting the Spanish invaders became known as *Taki Ongoy* (dancing sickness). The Quechua name refers to the seizures reported experienced by followers of this messianic movement at the moment of their conversion. Mainly confined to the Huamanga region, Taki Ongoy believers envisioned that their gods, bound by the cyclical nature of the Andean universe, would soon turn against the Spaniards and destroy their empire in Peru. In its place would emerge a more pure form of Andean belief systems. In a pattern that foreshadowed the passive resistance practiced by 20th-century revolutionaries, Taki Ongoy leaders called for their followers to sever contact with all things Spanish in an effort to end Spain's domination. Authorities eventually suppressed Taki Ongoy through arrests, imprisonment, and exile of its leaders. At least in one area of the old Inca empire, peoples were desperately clinging to their beliefs in an effort to cope with Spanish suppression and plague, which were making their existence nearly intolerable.

In the midst of their terrible troubles the Inca leadership continued to oppose Spanish domination. The last Inca emperor, Túpac Amaru the third son of Manco Capac, led the fight against the Spanish from his mountain redoubt at Vilacabamba, in Eastern Peru. Holding out for decades against the Spanish, Inca fighters used guerrilla tactics to wage war from Vilacabamba. Viceroy Francisco de Toledo dispatched military units to this remote stronghold in 1572, eventually defeating the Inca defenders and capturing their leader. Túpac Amaru was beheaded in a public execution in the public square in Cuzco before thousands of Andeans. Although with this public execution Viceroy Toledo formally ended the Inca empire, the death of the last Inca by no means ended Andean resistance to Spanish rule.

Population decline and Toledo's policy of establishing reducciones made organized resistance by the Andeans very difficult throughout the 17th century. Instead, flight from the Spanish towns by Andeans was one of the most common acts of resistance against the authorities, particularly those who sought to enforce the mita and tribute taxes. These refugees fled to the remote countryside and hid, much like runaways slaves. Others placed their fates in the hands of mine owners or *hacendados*, who needed them as wage laborers because of the declining Indian population.[5] Indians in the Huamanga region through the early 17th century became adept at using the newly established Spanish colonial courts to contest the terms of Spanish exploitation. Legal resistance did not just become a refuge for individuals but also a broadly based strategy for the Andean community in Huamanga. Even as some of their leaders were being co-opted by the Spanish into abandoning their economic and social roots in the Andean communities, the indigenous people of Huamanga used both legal and illegal means in an effort to retain their dignity. Stern argues, however, that "the European ruling class, despite moments of near crisis and failure, succeeded in establishing an exploitive society which lasted for centuries."[6] This was made possible by those Andeans who allowed kinship rivalries to undermine resistance to Spanish authority. In the end, the willingness of many Indians to enter the marketplace in an effort to better their economic lot solidified their dependency upon the Spanish economic system and distanced them even more from the more intimate work relationships of the ancient ayllu system. This was certainly true in the Ayacucho region and very likely so in other parts of the Viceroyalty of Peru.

Open rebellion in Peru did not flare up again until the mid-18th century, after Bourbon economic reforms placed an even heavier tax burden than previously on the Andean population. The first of these revolts began in May 1742, led by an Indian from Cuzco with a Jesuit education and a mixed Andean and Christian message. Juan Santos Atahualpa, as he called himself, claimed Inca lineage. He settled in the low jungle region east of the provinces of Tarma and Jauja. There he gathered forces among the lowland Indians of the region for the purpose of creating a pan-Andean messianic movement whose goal was to expel Spaniards from the selva and then eventually from all of Peru. Far from Spanish power, Santos Atahualpa was opposed initially only by the well-established Franciscan missionaries in the region, and for more than a decade Spanish authorities were unable to defeat the jungle rebels. Santos Atahualpa was even able to lead an expedition into the highlands and capture the town of Andamarca. At this crucial juncture, however, he was unable to attract the local serranos to his cause. Andrien argues that influential Andean kin networks that favored the status quo opposed the rebel leader as an outsider and thus undermined his cause.[7] In any event, the rebellion never gained firm footing outside the lowlands, and when Santos Atahualpa died sometime in the mid-1750s, the rebellion subsided. However, resistance movements in this region of the selva known as the *Cerro de Sal* remained a problem for the Spanish for several decades thereafter.

The same phenomenon that was being experienced by the British, whose major changes in colonial policy produced resistance and ultimately rebellion in North America, was also occurring in the Viceroyalty of Peru and throughout the Spanish American colonies. The Bourbon leadership in Spain sought to make their colonies more efficiently administered in order to collect more revenue. With the implementation of the Bourbon reforms in the mid-18th century the condition of Peru's Indian masses actually worsened. The primary reason for this was *repartimiento de comercio* (*reparto*) enacted in 1751. This measure obligated the indigenous population to purchase, through cash, labor services or goods, products that they often neither desired or needed. The reparto was an obvious attempt by the Spanish authorities to revitalize a sluggish commercial situation at the expense of the native population. The effect of the reparto was to force many Indians to work in the mines and to deplete their communities' resources as they struggled to meet their new economic obligations. Debt peonage labor obligations increased, and, as might be expected, the reparto prompted a deep resentment that fueled indigenous resistance throughout the later decades of the 18th century. This will be discussed in more detail later, but for now it is important to note that the reparto and the *alcabala* (sales tax) were the most objectionable to the Andeans. The Spanish increased the alcabala progressively, and it had reached by 1775 a rate of 6 percent on most goods traded in Peru and elsewhere in the Spanish American colonies. Spanish revenues from the alcabala were significant and in Peru had reached 600,000 pesos at the end of the 18th century.

When faced with crises such as these, many Andeans sought relief through curacas who would negotiate with the Spanish government officials on their behalf. But by the mid-18th century many of these curacas had been suborned by corrupt Spanish officials or were compromised by a system that rarely worked as it was intended. The Indians, using the Spanish legal system as best they could, contested much of the reparto legislation in the colonial courts. When these efforts met with poor results, the final recourse was widespread rebellion.

The massive revolt led by José Gabriel Condorcanqui, who adopted the name Túpac Amaru II, stands out among the numerous uprisings in the Andes in the 20 years after 1770 as having been the greatest threat to Spanish hegemony in Peru since the conquest. Like his predecessor, Túpac Amaru II claimed lineage from Inca nobility through the original Túpac Amaru. He had been born in Surimana in the province of Canas, Cuzco. Educated in the best Jesuit school in Cuzco, the would-be rebel had a strong sense of his nobility. Still, he made a humble living traveling the difficult roads around Tinta, trading goods from the mules he had inherited from his father. His travels showed him firsthand the plight of the Indians as their lives worsened under the burdens of the mita, reparto, and the alcabala. José Gabriel was very ambitious and tried repeatedly but unsuccessfully to persuade the Spanish to grant him the title of *cacique* or local chieftain. Finally, after a long period of planning, José Gabriel and his followers seized the corrupt and hated corregidor Antonio de Arriaga of Tinta on November 4, 1780. After forcing his captive to turn over arms and tribute monies, the self-declared Túpac Amaru II tried the captive official and quickly hanged him. With this bold action Túpac Amaru II instigated the most serious challenge to Spanish rule in the Americas up to that time.

Starting with a force of about 6,000, Túpac Amaru II won a significant victory against Spanish and Andean troops in the town of Sangarará after only one week in the field. This victory quickly raised his standing as a revolutionary leader. He augmented his status when he characterized the Cuzco militias contemptuously as "useless individuals fit only to kill sparrows and eat cornmeal mush."[8] Soon thousands of Andeans were joining the rebel army. The rebellion directly challenged Spanish rule in Peru because it was situated along the main roads in the highland and directly threatened the former Inca capital of Cuzco. Additionally, the rich silver mining region of Potosí in Upper Peru (present-day Bolivia) also stood in the path of the rebels. Adding to the difficulties of the Spanish army was the ongoing war for the American Revolution, which was occupying the Madrid government. Troops were needed to guard coastal installations against possible attacks by the British navy. The Viceroyalty's newly created militia was both poorly trained and poorly financed, and was not up to the task of fighting against a rebellion.

Despite the obvious weaknesses of Spanish colonial officials in confronting the Túpac Amaru II rebellion, the rebel leader himself faced genuine difficulties in unifying the diverse social and political elements present in the

Andes. He tried to cultivate the image of a messianic leader who was seeking to recreate the Incari myth of a resurrected Inca emperor by using the name of his martyred ancestor, Túpac Amaru. To appeal to mestizo and other castas, however, he blended traditional and Christian imagery by proclaiming himself, "God's chosen instrument on Earth."[9] These approaches still did not convince many of the region's powerful Indian caciques to join his movement. Most were afraid of losing their influence and relative wealth to a rebel leader whose intentions were never really clear. In one instance, a cacique with royal Inca lineage rejected Túpac Amaru II's letter requesting his support for the revolt from the Spanish authorities, calling him a "bastard and usurper."[10] In the end, Túpac Amaru II was never able to gain the support of the Cuzco region's caciques, and the lack of this crucial support proved to be a critical failing of his movement. Indeed, when shaping his army's command structure, he had to rely heavily on creoles and mestizos who had technical or military experience; he organized his units along ethnic lines, paying Indian soldiers half of what creole and mestizo soldiers were receiving. This appeared be a pragmatic response to the need to retain people with some military experience and literacy. Most of all, it reflected the diverse nature of Túpac Amaru's army and the complex objectives his movement sought to attain.[11] The rebel leader seems never to have advocated a class-based peasant uprising to overthrow the existing social order. He realized that a caste war would cost him the support of creoles and most mestizos. However, he lost creole support anyway as fears of a blood bath in the Andes caused creoles to turn away from the rebellion. Túpac Amaru II may have hoped that substantial military success in Peru's central highlands would enable him to negotiate with the Spanish Crown for the repeal of the reparto, alcabala, and the mita. Such a negotiation would have allowed him to retain a position of authority, with his Inca lineage formally recognized. If this was his hope, it proved a lofty but vain ambition.

At the urging of his wife, Micaela Bastidas, Túpac Amaru II launched a long-delayed attack on Cuzco on January 8, 1781, with a force of 30,000 men. After two days of futile attempts to take the city, the rebel leader withdrew his forces, claiming the need to regroup and supply his army. On the contrary, the retreat was devastating to the rebels' morale and the rebel army began to disintegrate. Withdrawing to his home base at Tinta, Túpac Amaru II was soon surrounded by a Spanish force and was captured in early April. In a fierce show of retribution meant as a lesson to the Indian masses, Spanish authorities in Cuzco tried and condemned to death Túpac Amaru II, his wife Bastidas, and eight other rebel leaders. The eight leaders were hanged, but Micaela Bastidas was tortured and beheaded before her husband's eyes. His fate was even more gruesome: his limbs were pulled from his body by four stout horses, and his body beheaded. His body parts were put on display in prominent places in Cuzco as a lesson to potential rebels.

Tellingly, these extreme measures did not quell resistance to Spanish authority. After Túpac Amaru II's death, leadership of the revolt passed to his cousin Diego Cristóbal Túpac Amaru. Regaining the initiative, Diego Cristóbal led his contingent south to Puno in Upper Peru, where he captured the city in May 1781. There he tried to join with the Aymara forces that had been resisting the Spanish since the late 1770s. Tomás Katari became the leader of these protests. He sought desperately through legal means to rid the Aymara peasants of the corrupt Spanish officials who had abused the mita and tribute payments as well as the particularly despised repartimiento de comercio. After traveling to Buenos Aires to plead his case before the viceroy, Katari returned eventually to Upper Peru. There he was arrested and later murdered by the Spanish while he was in captivity, in December 1780. Peasants throughout the Chayanta region of Upper Peru engaged in widespread violence in retribution for the murder. Subsequently, they were able to raise an army that laid siege to the distant city of La Plata in the Viceroyalty of Rio de la Plata.

Another significant resistance movement was led by a former merchant Julián Apasa Túpac Katari, who recruited Aymaras to his cause and laid siege to La Paz twice in 1781. Like Túpac Amaru II, Túpac Katari's movement was undermined by fears of caste war. He also died at the hands of Spanish executioners in November 1781.[12]

From the time of Atahualpa's defeat at Cajamarca until the beginning of the Independence movements in the early 19th century, the Andean peoples asserted their rights as outlined by the Spanish crown. This was done most often by legal petition, but this approach rarely provided redress as underpaid Spanish officials frequently abused their positions for personal gain. In response, the Andeans of the viceroyalty frequently resorted to resistance. Often their goals were limited to ending the abuses associated with the mita, repartimiento de comercio, and the ever-present tribute payments, without seeking to overthrow the Spanish crown's authority. Ethnic differences, fear of caste struggle between creole and indigenous peoples, and the more efficient tax collection by the Spanish Bourbons combined to weaken these resistance movements at nearly every turn. Ironically, it was the Bourbons and not their predecessors on the Spanish throne that achieved the level of centralized Spanish power in Peru that Isabella, Ferdinand, and their Habsburg successors so actively desired.

THE IMPERIAL STATE AND ECONOMY

The eminent historian Charles Gibson characterized early Spanish policy in Peru as an attempt to implement "thoroughgoing, meticulous, Hispanic absolutism."[13] The Viceroyalty of Peru was created in 1545 in the midst of civil unrest in Spain's South American colony. The viceroyalty included Panama and all of present-day South America, with the exception of Portuguese Brazil. Thus its territory was immense, geographically diverse, and exceedingly difficult to govern uniformly. Viceroys, also known at the time as "the shadows of the King," held substantial administrative, military, and economic power. But their terms of office were usually limited to less than seven years. Their tenure was also subject to administrative reviews known as the *visita* and the *residencia*. The viceroys in Peru and the other viceroyalties in New Spain (Mexico, Central America, and the U.S. Southwest), which was founded in 1535, ruled in conjunction with *Audiencias*. Audiencias served as regional high courts in the Spanish colonies. These were the supreme judicial tribunals in Spanish America but they also had legislative powers and ruled in the viceroy's stead when he was absent. Viceroys were nearly always *peninsulares* (native Spaniards) until the 18th century, when creoles were appointed. In contrast, members of the Audiencia were frequently native Americans and were often well-educated lawyers who served for life. These entities were the most stable institutions of Spanish American government. Among the administrative subdivisions that answered to the Viceroy were corregidores, *alcaldes mayores*, and *gobernadores*. Some of these bodies, such as the *cabildos*, or town councils, were appointed and not elected. By appointing officials, Spain was able to maintain royal absolutism in Peru until the independence wars. In reality, however, Peru's royal officials dealt with the Andeans much as the British would do later in India, through curaca intermediaries who bridged the Indian and Hispanic worlds.

The first Spanish viceroy, Blasco Núñez Vela, arrived in May 1544 in the wake of civil war and insurrection among the original conquistadores. Francisco Pizarro was assassinated in 1541 by the followers of his former partner in conquest, Diego de Almagro. Pizarro's cadre, however, was still able to hold on to power in Peru until Viceroy Núñez Vela arrived. The viceroy was fully intent on subjecting the Pizarro clan to the "Hispanic absolutism." The first obstacle the viceroy confronted was the Crown's effort to abolish encomienda. In keeping with the principles of the Reconquista in Spain, encomienda originally gave the Spanish conquerors the right to require taxes and labor from Indian communities in return for military protection and instruction in the Catholic faith. The crown soon realized, however, that encomienda was thinly disguised slavery and that this system potentially gave Peru's early settlers enormous power to challenge Spanish authority. Consequently, Viceroy Núñez Vela was tasked with implementing the New Laws of 1541, which abolished Indian slavery, all but prevented the use of Indian labor in the mines, and asserted that all encomienda grants would revert to the crown upon the death of the original holder. The Crown was indeed seeking to protect the Andean peoples from further abuses. But more importantly, royal officials were trying to regain control over a colony that had sunk into near chaos as its soldiers of fortune struggled to gain control over the spoils of conquest. In the view of James Lockhart, "*Encomenderos* in Peru could live as lords and be the center of all things to an extent impossible to all but dukes and counts in Spain."[14]

Clearly, Gonzalo Pizarro, having endured the trials of the conquest and the death of his brother, Francisco, was not prepared to forfeit his hard-won gains to the new viceroy, who had little military support of his own. Rising in direct challenge to the Crown, Gonzalo Pizarro defeated the meager forces of Viceroy Núñez Vela near Quito in January 1546. After this defeat, royal authority in Peru then reached its low ebb. The reign of the Pizarros in Peru was short-lived, however, as Gonzalo Pizarro was defeated by a royalist military force some two years later, and then executed. In the aftermath of this violence it became quite clear to royalist officials that only a strong and efficient viceroy could bring the fractured colony under control. This would not occur, however, until 1569 when Viceroy Francisco de Toledo was sent to Peru by King Phillip II. In the intervening years, the basic structure of Spanish civil government in Peru remained in limbo as questions relating to encomienda and the sharply declining indigenous population were confronted.

Viceroy Toledo was an experienced and able administrator, but he faced a daunting task in the Andes. As Andrien notes, he viewed his mission as having three main objectives: to relocate the indigenous population in settled towns known as reducciones, to regularize and increase the efficiency of tax collecting, and to provide more stable Indian labor sources for Peru's silver mines.[15] In sum, what Toledo sought to accomplish was the strengthening of royal rule in the colonies and an increase in its revenue base. Toledo was unconcerned about the welfare of the indigenous population even as their numbers continued to rapidly decline. Possibly as many as 1.5 million Andeans were resettled in towns designed on the Spanish grid pattern. The concentration of the Indians undoubtedly helped spread disease. It certainly caused dramatic social and cultural trauma as the Andeans were forced to abandon the lands of their ancestors, weaken ties with their ayllus, and leave behind their huacas. Taxes in Peru were levied at varying rates according to social classes, but all adult Indian males were subject to tribute. Data for tax collecting were derived from regular census figures gathered by colonial administrators.

Draft labor for the great mining operation at Potosí was organized by Toledo under the same name as the Inca corvee system: the mita. Each year more than 13,000 laborers were obliged to travel from all over the Viceroyalty of Peru to work in the mines. The mita obligation came due every seven years for Indian males. It was augmented by voluntary wage laborers (*mingas*). Although the mitayos earned wages, they were hardly just compensation for the terrible disruption and the dangerous hardships mine labor imposed on their lives. Mita labor often extended beyond the legal time prescribed, and conditions in both the silver mines and the mercury mine at Huancavelica were hazardous to the extreme. Toxic air, poorly constructed tunnels, and the tremendous physical demands of the mine labor broke many a young male mitayo. Additionally, their meager wages did not cover the cost of extensive travel the mitayos were forced to make from their home villages. Many potential draft laborers fled their village to avoid the mita and became rootless migrants (*forasteros*) in a land were community was everything.[16]

Viceroy's Toledo's reforms had important consequences for Peru's future. Indian labor was the foundation, and tax revenue redirected the mineral wealth of the Andes to the Spanish state. When the rich silver veins at the Potosí mine were exhausted, the patio process that employed mercury to extract the silver ore was installed. The result was a nearly continuous flow of silver to Spain during the first two centuries of Spanish rule. Although this flow ebbed in the 16th and 17th centuries, Habsburg power in Europe could be said to have been based in some measure on the backs of Indian laborers in Peru and Mexico. Agricultural product to feed the population at Potosí, which reached 160,000 in the late 16th century, came from all parts of the viceroyalty. These included wheat from Chile's central valley, maize and *chicha* (corn beer) from the high eastern Andes. Coarse woolen clothing for the workers in the mines was fashioned from the Andean llama herds by Indian workers in the *obrajes* (textile workshops), which arose to meet the clothing needs of the mitayos. A mercantilist patrimonial economic system was thus instituted by the dynamic administration of Viceroy Toledo. The Andean peoples however, responded in intelligent and adaptive ways to protect themselves from the worst ravages of a fully exploitive system. As historians Steve Stern and Karen Spaulding have shown, Andean villagers began raising cash groups for the local market to mitigate their dependence on the Spanish state and its financial and labor obligations. Indians began to acquire land, raise cattle, and enter into new barter arrangements with different communities than they had done in the past. Some communities with a cash surplus were even able to "rent" laborers from other villages to transfer the onerous mita obligation from their own community.[17] What resulted from this mercantilist engine driving a highly diverse economic train was a system that could not consistently sustain itself without resorting to coercive economic measures such as the *repartimiento de mercancías*.

Simply put, the repartimiento de mercancías was another obligation imposed upon native serranos to buy goods they did not desire nor could afford. Usually, local merchants, some crown officials, and even caciques profited from this hated obligation. Lacking cash, the Indians often met this requirement with further labor service or land. As increasingly larger amounts of smuggled goods entered Peru during the late 17th and 18th centuries, the surpluses grew larger and the obligations under this system grew more onerous. Much of the abuse of the late colonial era can be attributed, at least in part, to the repartimiento de mercancías. A good deal of the Andean peoples' resources were drained by this system. Debt peonage expanded in some measure because of it. Even the sweeping Bourbon reforms of the 18th century in Spanish America were not sufficient to end this oppressive obligation on Peru's indigenous peoples.

Within the pre-capitalist economic system in Spanish Peru, the Catholic Church was the principal purveyor of credit. Accumulating wealth from many sources including rents, indulgences, bequests, and dowries, the church funded a good deal of colonial enterprises without a larger vision of the economic development of the colony. Thus, funding for the colony's infrastructure, roads, irrigation networks, and port facilities was rarely sufficient. Funding for such projects never remotely approached the wealth extracted from Peru's mines. But even the mines at Potosí and Huancavelica could not underwrite Spanish mercantilism in Peru indefinitely. By the early 17th century, the quality and quantity of the silver ore extracted at Potosí substantially declined. This decline, coupled with raids on Spanish treasure fleets and the high price of goods sold to Lima merchants from inflation-ridden Spain, forced a major adjustment in Peru's colonial economy.

Andrien argues convincingly that Peru's economy became more diversified in the face of declining silver exports.[18] As the Indian population dramatically declined by 1630, lands in the coastal regions became available to Spanish immigrants and soon wide-scale commercial agriculture developed. Coastal crops of sugar and cotton as well as a flourishing wine industry, fruits, and vegetables for the Lima and Arequipa markets trace their origins to the decline in the mining industry. This economic diversification also extended to the highland, where cattle raising and crops of potatoes, quinoa, and even tobacco flourished. These goods found welcome markets in Peru's coastal cities. Indeed, many of the same products were imported from the far reaches of the empire such as Chile's central valley, highland Ecuador, and the western provinces of Argentina. It was in the 18th century that the demographic patterns of modern Peru were first established. Lima tripled in population during this period, and soon the Europeanized coastal pattern of today's Peru became a reality. In the mid- to late 17th century many of these new haciendas or *chacras* were moderate in size and retained 20 Indian workers or less. The wine-producing vineyards in the Arequipa region are just one example of the successful chacras that emerged while silver production declined. Sheep and cattle *estancias* (ranches) formed also on the marginal lands of the Altiplano with labor often drawn from *forasteros* who had abandoned the failing reducciones to work as individuals in a new economic setting.

As the Spanish economy declined in the 17th century, native industries in Peru and especially Lima successfully responded to increased demand in the colony. In manufacturing, the production of textiles was paramount. But household goods, leather, and fine crafts also were produced in small artisan shops.[19] Lima's economy suffered significantly as a result of the highly destructive earthquake of 1687 and the decline of the fleet system that carried Peru's mineral wealth to Spain by way of Panama.

The ascendance of the Bourbons to the Spanish throne in the mid-18th century brought important changes to colonial Peru's economy. In the economic sphere, the reforms were designed to modernize the mercantilist structure of the Spanish empire thereby generating more revenues to strengthen Spanish administration and military defenses in the Americas. During the 1770s, in an effort to deregulate shipping and liberalize trade, the fleet system was abolished in favor of contracted vessels. Ships from the colonies could now trade with each other and enter any port in Spain, not just the mandated port of Seville. Additionally, the alcabala (sales tax) was tripled, further burdening indigenous traders who should not have been forced to pay this tax. The sales tax, imposed on top of tribute and repartimiento de mercancías obligations, was particularly onerous. This tax burden certainly contributed to the widespread discontent among the Andean peoples, which led to the uprisings of the late 18th century.

One of the most dramatic effects of the Bourbon economic reforms was the sharp increase in silver mining revenues during the 18th century. The great mines at Potosí once again flourished after 1740 and remained highly productive until the Independence era. There were many reasons for this resurgence: New mines were opened at Cerro de Pasco; Spanish capital was invested in Peru's mining sector on a more systematic basis; incentives for native mining investors were created by cutting the Crown's share of mining revenue from one fifth to one tenth; finally, improved mining technology and creation of guilds also contributed to increased production of silver. In the end, the vast treasures gathered by the conquistadores from the New World and later revenues generated by Peru's silver mines proved more damaging than beneficial to both Spain and its colony. Spain's other priorities and a lack of incentive to modernize its economy was in some measure encouraged by the wealth flowing from the New World. In Peru, the mita placed tremendous social and economic burdens upon the Andean peoples. Economic development outside of the mining sector was impeded in Peru as most internal investment was directed to the mining sector. Environmental degradation was also a highly negative consequence of Peru's mining economy. Mercury pollution from the patio process was particularly damaging. Still, even today the mining sector remains the dominant element of Peru's economy. It is easy to understand why the lives of Spaniards and Andeans alike were shaped by the rich ore from Peru's mountains.

As the quality of leadership in the Spanish state declined in the 17th century, its colonies in the Americas drew away from Spain. Smuggling was widespread, taxes and other forms of tribute were systematically evaded, and trade with Spain declined. The Enlightenment and emergence of the French Bourbons on the Spanish throne began a slow process of reform that would fundamentally alter Spain's relations with Peru and all of its other colonies. The Bourbon reforms sought to make the governance of the colonies more efficient, collect greater revenue, and strengthen their defenses against both internal rebellion and foreign interlopers. Nevertheless, as we have seen, the economic reforms such as the alcabala contributed to colonial unrest that would later create a climate of rebellion leading to the independence movement. Most of the substantive reforms were enacted during the reigns of Ferdinand VI (1746–1759) and Charles III (1759–1788). They included economic reforms that liberalized trade and business practices, creation of a colonial militia for purposes of defense, and greater control of the ecclesiastical orders. Administratively, the creation of two new viceroyalties in South America and the establishment of the intendant system were most important. The Bourbon reforms were often successfully implemented, but as with the case of the British colonists in North America, the reforms produced a backlash of resentment from colonists who had found previous colonial inefficiency and corruption often to their benefit. Let us now look at the Bourbon reforms more closely.

Rejecting orthodox mercantilism, the Bourbons deregulated trade with all ports of Spain to American trade, not just Seville. Regular ships could now carry this trade and the cumbersome *flota* (fleet system) was abolished. Overseas trading companies based upon the British model were introduced in the Americas and this infused private capital by means of the Caracas, Havana, and Barcelona venture companies. For defense purposes, colonial militias and a few army units were established in a number of areas, most notably in the viceroyalties of New Spain and Peru. Naval units were also present for coastal defense of Spanish possessions. The *fuero militar* (military special status) allowed for military status to be maintained in both colonies to assure a permanent military force as a basis for professionalism. Revenues for these reforms and improving and constructing new seaward defenses were raised in large part by the alcabala and had been increased substantially. The Viceroyalty of Nueva Granada was created in 1739 and established jurisdiction of much of present-day Ecuador, Colombia, and Venezuela. The Viceroyalty of Peru was reduced even further in size with the creation of the new Viceroyalty of Rio de la Plata in 1776. This viceroyalty administered part of present-day Bolivia and all of the geographic area that encompasses present-day Argentina. These measures consolidated Bourbon control of the colonies, but it was the intendancy system that was the key to their administrative reforms. Intendants were created as administrative subdivisions of the Viceroyalties by the Bourbons during the mid 18th century to reduce the influence of the creole administrators, lessen corruption, and reduce bureaucratic inefficiency. In New Spain,

12 new intendancies replaced 200 previous office-holders. Most of these new officials had been born in Spain with loyalties directly to the Spanish king. Bourbon reforms also led efforts to balance the power of the Church with those of Spain's more clearly delineated fiscal and political powers. The most contentious aspect of this effort was the clash with the Jesuit order in Peru and elsewhere. Ultimately the Jesuit order was expelled from Latin America in 1767, whereupon their missions and associated economic holdings fell into decline. Although the Jesuit order was reestablished in 1813 by the Papacy, Jesuits did not return to Peru until the mid-19th century.

The Bourbon reforms produced some immediate gains in revenue collection and administrative efficiency, and they reduced corruption. In the end, however, more efficient collection of taxes and tribute, and reduction of many loopholes in administrative practices produced significant animosity toward Spanish rule on the part of creoles. As we have discussed, the late 18th century was a period of great tumult in Peru. Significantly, the newly created colonial militia in the viceroyalty was incapable of suppressing the insurrection of Túpac Amaru II. Ultimately, even Spain's more professional armies were incapable of defeating the forces of independence that took their inspiration from the same movement that inspired the Bourbon reforms, the Enlightenment.

SOCIETY AND CULTURE IN COLONIAL PERU

The basic social unit of colonial Peru was the family. This was true among the Andean's ayllu as well the elite peninsular Spaniards newly arrived from Spain. Families were generally large, with multiple family members and close relatives living in the family household. Arranged marriages helped form alliances between elite families. These alliances had long-ranging effects on land ownership and other sources of power during the colonial era and beyond. Women played important roles in transmitting the values and ideals of Spanish culture to their children. This was true also of Indian women, who maintained the rituals of the domestic household and practiced weaving, which still remained of tremendous importance to the Indian communities. Despite the emphasis on family, very significant numbers of Peruvians born in the colonial era were illegitimate. The relatively small number of Spanish-born women in colonial Peru up to the mid-17th century assured the emergence of a large mestizo population. Thus the society of *castas* (castes) was well formed within the first century after the conquest.

From its earliest days the Spanish Crown decreed that there would be two social worlds in the Americas; the *república de indios* (Indian world) and the *república de españoles* (world of Spanish settlers). For religious, social, and economic reasons the crown sought to create two separate communities. But this idealistic notion was doomed from the start. Instead, the emergence of the mestizo and the introduction of African slavers in Peru created castas, the lower of whom suffer discrimination to the present day. At the heart of this discrimination was the concept of *limpieza de sangre* or purity of blood. All people of high rank, including those who held high positions in the viceroyalty, were expected have proof of this "pure blood" that was in part a goal of the Spanish Reconquista. This concept was being extended to the new world, with little chance of consistent enforcement except for physical appearance or phenotype. Mestizos faced bias on two counts. Early in the colonial period they were assumed to be illegitimate and also suspected of clinging to Indian religious beliefs that undermined their Catholic teachings. Mestizos truly lived in an isolated world. The *ladino,* a mestizo who learned the Spanish language with proficiency and had adopted Spanish customs, was often viewed with suspicion and disdain by the Indian peoples. Indeed, the ladino often exploited the Indian even as they were socially shunned by the upper levels of Peruvian society. Of course, the decline of the Indian population affected social relationships. For example, because of the low numbers of Indian laborers available to the mita, the forced relocation of Andean communities created thousands of forasteros. These people were compelled to create new social relationships in the Andean highlands or to drift into the ranks of ladinos if they chose to adopt the Spanish language or culture.

Andrien clearly explains the controversy over the impact of Spanish literacy and numeracy in the Andean region and throughout the empire. For some Indians living in an area without easily understood modes of communication, learning Spanish and numerical literacy allowed them to acquire a valuable "technology of the intellect." For others, adopting the language and culture of the conquerors was a form of cultural suicide. Still enormous contributions to understanding the Andean past were made by such individuals as Felipe Guaman Poma de Ayla, who authored a massive manuscript in both Spanish and Quechua that purported to tell the history of the Inca empire from the height of its power to its defeat by the Spaniards. Guaman Pomo set out to establish a basis for a new positive interpretation of Inca rule as a way to earn Madrid's respect for the Andean peoples. This was also the motive of another early colonial authority on Inca rule, the mestizo Garcilaso de la Vega, who was the son of a Spanish conquistador and a woman of Inca royalty. He tried to reconcile the violence and continuing tension between the Spanish and Andean world by arguing against the marginalization of Andean culture and suggesting that that enlightened cultural adaptation by both Spaniards and Andeans would be very beneficial.[20]

The task of teaching Spanish and numeracy to the Andeans fell to the clergy, as it did throughout Spanish America. As early as 1512, well before Peru was subjugated by Pizarro, the Spanish crown recognized the need to have the Castilian language be the cultural bond of the new Empire. But the volume and dialectical diversity of the Andean languages was an enormous burden to overcome. Even more directly, Spanish administrators felt the continued use of Andean native languages facilitated rebellion and cultural resistance. The Spanish colonial authorities were indeed correct in this notion, as proven by the numerous and widespread resistance movements that occurred throughout the colonial era. The main Andean languages, Quechua and Aymara, have endured to this present day in large part owing to the strength of Andean culture and a geography that has limited Andean cultural differentiation. Indeed, traditions such as backstrap weaving and the use of the *chaquitaclla* (digging stick) are in everyday use today despite the availability of supposedly superior technologies.

Andean weaving may be the most enduring of the traditional art forms that have transcended the conquest to remain vibrant in the modern era. Nilda Callañaupa, Director of the Center for Traditional Textiles in Cuzco, notes, "Here in Peru, weaving is an art that we live with every day, and for us it is more than an art, it is an historical part of the living culture." Callañaupa states unequivocally that Peruvian weaving is a deeply ritualistic activity that has carried many layers of meaning to the Andean people. In particular, these textiles honor Pachamama and the central Andean concept of connection to the natural world.[21] It is true that Peruvian weaving employs techniques that are unique in the world and as such are a treasure that must be preserved in order to continue more than a thousand years of ritual and tradition.

Representational or figurative painting, not a craft favored by the pre-Columbian Andean peoples, emerged in its finest form during the colonial period in the so-called Cuzco school. Largely done by indigenous and mestizo artists, the paintings of the Cuzco school often portrayed the Virgin Mary with perspective and decorative design drawn from Andean and not European influences. Thus, Andean artists were able to redirect even an art form new to them into a hybrid style of painting that could more accurately reflect their artistic worldview.

Hybridization of the newly imposed Spanish legal system could not be accommodated as easily by the Andeans. Indians were familiar with oral traditions and not sharply-nuanced written legal codes. The Andeans were at first confused and confounded by a system of order that was alien to them. However, as time went on, some were able to adapt to such legalities as the use of documentary evidence in the colonial courts. As we have seen, the Inca and their predecessors had a decidedly different concept of space, ordering much of their empire in accordance with *ceque* lines and their relationship to huacas. Further boundary lines were also established to adhere to community and perhaps even ayllu agricultural jurisdiction. The transition to a far different set of jurisdictional code was challenging and this struggle would continued well into the 20th century in Peru as large haciendas in the sierra continued to encroach upon the traditional lands of the Andeans. Of course, the main point of departure between the Andeans and the Spaniards was their conceptions of property. The Spanish introduced the concepts of private property and precisely delineated in boundaries to a region whose peoples had not known such concepts.

The Spanish religious campaign in Peru was really a continuation of the Reconquista that had been completed in the late 1400s against Islam. But the religious conversion of the Andeans to Catholicism never fully succeeded. Stern argues that the Andeans never fully accepted Christianity but rather embraced it selectively within the framework of their own indigenous beliefs.[22] Although this form of *mestizaje* occurred all over the Americas in different forms, it was facilitated in the remote Andes by the lack of sufficient priests to offer religious instruction and the sacraments and by the isolation of communities from Spanish mainstream culture. Five missionary orders took up the enormous task of religious conversion. These included initially the Franciscans, who first arrived in 1534, followed by the Jesuits, Dominicans, Augustinians, and the Mercedarians, all of whom had begun work in Peru by 1570. Nevertheless, in that year there were only nine Franciscan friars in the region of Jauja to serve the spiritual needs of more than 21,000 Indians.[23] Once again, the environment played a fundamental role in determining the evolution of society and culture in the Andes. The Andean peoples' spiritual world was all around them in the form of sacred places or huacas, which could be caves, rivers, or mountain tops. All of these were revered and remained as comforting reminders of a belief system that was more familiar to them than Christianity. Thus the particular form of Andean syncretism resisted a long and vigorous campaign of extirpation by Spanish clergy during the colonial period. Compounding the difficulty of the complete conversion of the Andeans to Christianity was the racial composition of the clergy. Overwhelmingly white, Spanish, and creole in origin, rarely could the clergy identify with the Andeans. Andeans and mestizos were barred from the clergy because of beliefs in their cultural inferiority or lack of legitimacy. Thus the shortage of priests assured the inability of the Peruvian church to administer to its scattered followers throughout the sierra. In modern times it has opened the way for Evangelical Christianity to make major inroads among the ranks of former Catholics.

The so-called barely concealed "idolatry" of Peru's Indians sparked anxiety on the part of Church leaders regarding "New Christians," or *conversos,* who migrated from Spain and Portugal after their union in 1580. Silverblatt notes, "the purported links between *Indios,* negroes and New Christians . . . heightened concerns about treachery." Spanish church leaders felt that clandestine Jews (New Christians) would incite these "simple minded" people to rebellion. The Inquisition, established in 1569, was used aggressively to extirpate the so-called sedition element of Judaism long after the Jews had been expelled from Spain in the late 15th century.[24] The "disease of the Indians," as one Spanish official termed Indian idolatry, was simply part of a far more pervasive lack of Catholic orthodoxy in colonial Peru. Silverblatt contends that the Inquisition's work may have been as much motivated by resentment of the New Christians' economic success as it was part of a process of "fear and blame." In any event, these early colonial religious practices were far more proscriptive than inclusive in regard to expanding Christian fellowship in Spanish Peru.

TOWARD INDEPENDENCE

By the early 1790s the French Revolution had set in motion events that would directly influence the course of events in Peru and the other Spanish colonies in the Americas. The Bourbon reforms, while successful to some degree, were never able to reverse the trend of greater de facto local control in Peru. With the rise of Napoleon and the eventual occupation of Spain by French armies after 1808, Spanish dominance in Peru all but disappeared. As the original seat of Spanish power in South America, Peru would be the focus of Spanish resistance to independence. But as we have seen, antipathy to Spain came from many directions during the last decades of Spanish rule. The Andeans who struggled so mightily to maintain their indigenous ways would face new challenges during and after the Independence wars, and their role in Peruvian society has remained poorly defined until the present day. Although Creoles and mestizos would have many of their own cultural and economic problems still left unresolved, much changed for them in Peru between 1810 and 1824. It is to the independence movement and Peru's early nationhood that we now turn.

NOTES

1. Noble David Cook, *Demographic Collapse: Indian Peru, 1520–1620* (Cambridge: Cambridge University Press, 1981), 165.

2. Ibid., 165–177.

3. Ibid., 198–206.

4. Kenneth J. Andrien, *Andean Worlds: Indigenous History, Culture and Consciousness Under Spanish Rule, 1532–1825* (Albuquerque: University of New Mexico Press, 2001). This scholarly and very readable study of colonial Peru is one of the very best works on this topic.

5. Ibid., 63–64.

6. Steve J. Stern, *Peru's Indian Peoples and the Challenge of the Spanish Conquest: Huamanga to 1640* (Madison: University of Wisconsin Press, 1982), xviii.

7. Andrien, *Andean Worlds,* 199–202.

8. Leon G. Campbell, "The Social Structure of the Túpac Amaru Army," *Hispanic American Historical Review* 61, no. 4 (1981): 691.

9. Andrien, *Andean Worlds,* 214.

10. Campbell, "Social Structure of the Túpac Amaru Army," 684.

11. Ibid., 691–692.

12. Andrien, *Andean Worlds,* 206–210.

13. Charles Gibson, *Spain in America* (New York: Harper and Row, 1966), 90.

14. James Lockart, *Spanish Peru, 1532–1560: A Colonial Society* (Madison: University of Wisconsin Press, 1968), 237–238.

15. Andrien, *Andean Worlds,* 49–50.

16. Peter F. Klarén, *Peru: Society and Nationhood in the Andes* (Oxford: Oxford University Press, 2000), 63–68.

17. Ibid. See also Karen Spalding, *Huarochiri: A Colonial Province Under Inca and Spanish Rule* (Stanford: Stanford University Press, 1984).

18. Andrien, *Andean Worlds,* 84–95.

19. For colonial shipbuilding see Lawrence Clayton, *Caulkers and Carpenters in the New World: Shipyards of Colonial Guayaquil* (Athens: Ohio University Press, 1980).

20. Andrien, *Andean Worlds,* 103–121.

21. Web site for the Center for Traditional Textiles of Cuzco. https://incas.org/SPchinchero.htm.

22. Steve J. Stern, "Paradigm of Conquest: History, Historiography and Politics," *Journal of Latin American Studies* 24 (1992): 20.

23. Andrien, *Andean Worlds,* 166.

24. Irene Silverblatt, "New Christians and New Fears in Seventeenth Century Peru," *Comparative Studies in Society and History* 42, no. 3 (2000), 532.

4

Independence to the War of the Pacific

INDEPENDENCE

The Viceroyalty of Peru was the last region of the Spanish Empire in the Americas to achieve independence. Coinciding with Napoleon's invasion of Spain in 1808, independence movements throughout Spanish America emerged as a result of the breakdown of Spanish authority in the New World. In Peru the struggle for independence was protracted. This was a reflection of the divided nature of the Viceroyalty of Peru between Lima and the interior provinces. It also reflected sharp divisions between ethnic groups who had very different ideas about the consequences of freedom from Spanish rule. The reluctance on the part of the Peru's elite to see independence as advantageous to them was partially responsible for this division but also at play was the failure of the Indians in Peru to identify with Independence after creoles and peninsulares alike united against them in the great rebellions of the late 18th century. There is little question that the Bourbon fiscal and administrative reforms enacted by Charles III resulted in great disenchantment to creoles, who saw their influence diminish after slowly but inexorably gaining influence in the colony during the early 18th century. Enlightenment thought, particularly that of John Locke and Adam Smith, also justified the proponents of independence in

Spanish America as it had in British North America in the late 18th century. Still, the pervasiveness of Enlightenment thought was not thoroughgoing. What emerged with independence after the final Battle of Ayacucho in December 1824 was a Peruvian nation that lacked a clear sense of social and political identity. This opaque national vision would confound leaders of diverse ethnic makeup throughout the first half century of independence and beyond. This process, of course, occurred with all emerging nations in the 19th century, but in the Peruvian case was at times more intense.

In some ways, Peru's independence movement seemed to have more of the characteristics of a civil war than those of a struggle for freedom from Spain. Creoles, mestizos, Indians, and blacks fought as both royalists and "patriots" in the independence conflict. In the sierra, armed guerrilla bands known as *montoneros* took advantage of the lawless time to harass *hacendados* who were far removed from the protection of a weakened state. *Limeños* were certainly isolated from most of the rest of Peru during the first decade of the independence wars in South America. But as Timothy E. Anna argues, the impoverished Indian population was still in no condition to unite against the relatively small numbers of loyalist creoles and peninsulares who ruled the viceroyalty from their Lima bastion. Anna does not link the Tupac Amaru II insurrection in the early 1780s directly to independence. Rather, he argues that the rebel leader claimed many times that he only wanted to reform the Spanish colonial system, not destroy it. Additionally, Spain took measures to strengthen and centralize its hold over the Viceroyalty of Peru in the three decades following the Tupac Amaru II rebellion. Old-line veteran soldiers replaced Colonial militias as the frontline of Spain's defense of its garrisons in remote areas of the viceroyalty. In effect, Spain changed the focus of the colony's defense from withstanding an attack by external forces to a caste rebellion from within. As Anna correctly argues, colonial authorities in Peru were far better prepared for an uprising by Indian and mestizo masses than Mexico, which suffered a terrible caste war after the rebellion of the Catholic priest and rebel Miguel Hidalgo in 1810. Compelling support for Anna's view is that indigenous forces did not bring about the Peruvian Independence. Freedom from Spain was realized by the armies of José San Martín, an Argentine, and Simón Bolivar, a general from Caracas.[1]

Not surprisingly, Cuzco and Upper Peru (Bolivia) were the centers of resistance to the Spanish. Rebels from the Rio de la Plata region joined with others based in La Paz to initiate the armed struggle for independence after the imprisonment of the Spanish king by Napoleon in 1808. These movements stretched as far as the city of Tacna on Peru's south coast. Still, they were characterized as unfocused in intent and shackled by poor leadership. When they were confronted by effectively led royalist forces they were soon dispersed.

The royalist cause in Peru also benefited enormously from the highly talented leadership of Viceroy José Fernando Abascal y Sousa (1806–1816). He introduced progressive reforms including the abolition of Indian tribute and strengthened royalist military forces. Nevertheless, rebellions continued to arise.[2]

A rebellion in Cuzco led by the curaca of Chincheros, Mateo Pumacahua, proved to be the stiffest challenge to Spanish leadership since the Tupac Amaru II revolt in the early 1780s. Other leaders of the rebellion were the brothers José and Vicente Angulo and Gabriel Béjar, all from Cuzco, and their actions were sparked by a disagreement between the regional audiencia and the local *cabildo* (city council), which was more representative of the creole interests. The cabildo members sought the full enactment of the provisions of Spain's new liberal constitution of Cádiz adopted in 1812. Although the rebellion was started by non-Indians for largely political reasons, it soon assumed the same caste war character as the Túpac Amaru II rebellion. Because of this, creoles and many mestizos refused to join its ranks or actively opposed it. When Pumacahua became the titular leader of the revolt with the intent of creating an independent Peru with its capital at Cuzco, royalist and creole opposition hardened further. The rebels succeeded in capturing Cuzco, Arequipa, and La Paz , but by March 1815 royalist forces contained the rebellion and were able to recapture Cuzco. Napoleon's defeat in Spain in 1814 freed Spanish troops to campaign in the colonies against rebel forces. At their strongest, the rebels may have numbered as many as 20,000. But they were poorly armed, having only 40 artillery pieces and fewer than 1,000 rifles in their defense of Cuzco.[3] Most of the rebels fought with traditional Indian weapons and were unable to successfully contest the well-armed and professional Spanish forces.[4]

THE LONG ROAD TO AYACUCHO

The deep social and political divisions in Peru during the independence wars were the legacy of Spanish colonial policy that called for *dos republicas* "two republics"—in other words, a Spanish world and an Indian world. These divisions could not be bridged to form a united front against the Spanish by internal forces for independence. Diverse Indian groups, especially in the Cuzco region, held on to their vague image of a restored Inca state or *Incari*. Liberal republicans voiced very little concern of the plight of the Indian and seemed to want to turn their back on the sierra and devote the bulk of their attention to Lima and the coast. This meant reaching out ideologically and commercially to the non-Andean world beyond Peru. It is revealing to note that there existed no intellectual currents among the independence thinkers who advocated any form of new state modeled upon aspects of the Inca Empire. Not until José Carlos Mariátegui in the 1930s posited his thoughtful amalgam of Marxist and Andean concepts as a formula for a more socially equitable Peruvian society, would Peruvians look to their impressive past for a guide to their future.

There were monarchists among the ranks of Peruvian independence fighters who believed strongly that the nation's Indians, blacks, and mestizos were not ready for democracy. Only Brazil among the Latin American nations would choose this path, but Peru's epic struggles with nation building in the 19th century led some to believe that monarchy would have been the proper course. Strong leaders or *caudillos,* who often ruled without democratic mandates, were the de facto answer to this problem of an undefined national vision.

After the suppression of the Pumacahua rebellion, Peru's insurgents would struggle for a decade before independence was finally won at the Battle of Ayacucho in December 1824. Ultimately, it took a revolutionary movement based in Lima to bring about the final struggle leading to Peru's independence. Interestingly, areas that had been heavily involved in insurrectionary politics in the past, such as Cuzco, Arequipa, Tacna, and most of the southern Andes, did not prove to be critical to the final phase of Peru's independence struggle.

If the patriot cause was to succeed, its leaders would have to control Lima and its port at Callao. But support for independence was never overwhelming in Lima. The upper classes reaped many benefits from the Spanish colonial system and economy. As always, they were afraid of caste war in the republican cause provoking a rising of the castes in the capital city. Significantly, Lima and the rest of Peru would eventually be liberated by outsiders. José de San Martín from the Rio de la Plata region in present-day Argentina and Simón Bolívar from present-day Venezuela fought their way to Peru, and the final phase of the independence for Peru and all of Latin America began.

San Martín, after a victorious campaign in Chile that concluded in 1818, landed 4,000 troops in Peru's southern town of Pisco in September 1820. Moving slowly while waiting for patriot volunteers to join his ranks, San Martín put military pressure on Lima and began sending probing operations into the Andes. His cautious strategy worked, as the Spanish viceroy was overthrown and the new viceroy, José de la Serna, evacuated Lima and began negotiating with San Martín for favorable terms of surrender. In an effort to gain support from the Peruvian black population, San Martín pledged to abolish slavery. Emancipation would actually not occur until the 1850s, but it did draw slaves and free blacks who joined with irregular guerrilla bands who then engaged royalist forces. Further weakening Spanish authority was a declining economy plagued by low silver production, which resulted from the disruption of mining activities by the independence movement. San Martín's campaign was aided in its initial stages by the fall of the northern city of Trujillo to patriot forces. This movement was led by the former royalist intendant, the Marquis de Torre Tagle, who abandoned the Spanish crown to support independence.

San Martín declared Peruvian independence on July 28, 1821, but his declaration was premature. He first tried to break the remaining potential for royalist resistance by ordering all Spaniards to be exiled. The Spanish population was now relatively small anyway as many had fled as the economic collapsed and taxes continued to increase in order to support the crown's defense of the colony. Despite his royalist tendencies, San Martín began to put Peru on the road to republican government during his early operations in Peru.

The effort to build a republican government in Peru under San Martín was established on a weak foundation. Peru's economy was in shambles. Silver production was practically nonexistent and agriculture was floundering. Most of the former royalists' land holdings were being contested by the patriot forces and would not be productive for years. There was also resentment against San Martín and his closest advisors for being outsiders. Adding to his difficulties was San Martín's declining health related to his tuberculosis. Like Bolívar, San Martín's exhausting military campaigns would take a terrible toll on his health. Eventually, San Martín's illness weakened him greatly. He was thus unable to lead the new nation with the vigor that characterized his campaign in Chile only a few years before. When the patriot squadron under the command of Admiral Thomas Cochrane abandoned the campaign and returned to Chile, San Martín's chances of consolidating his power in Peru largely disappeared.[5]

Unable to mount a campaign to finally defeat the royalist forces in Peru's interior, San Martín instead traveled to Guayaquil in present-day Ecuador in July 1822. His mission was to meet with Bolivar to plan the final defeat of Spain's forces in South America. The result of this meeting appears to be San Martín's decision to resign from his position of leadership in Peru in September 1822. Most likely his poor health, his eroding influence in Peru, and his lack of resolve to challenge Bolivar for power contributed to this decision. San Martín sailed for Argentina, disenchanted with the independence movement and early governance process. This feeling of dismay would also be shared by Bolivar during his last years as he struggled to find workable government systems in South America.

After San Martín's resignation, Peru was administered by its 56 members of congress. From the beginning of its nationhood, Peru's congressional leaders sought European assistance, in this case from Great Britain, to finance the fledgling country's needs. Britain extended Peru a $6 million loan. This loan did not bring the expected political stability, and eventually Bolivar was invited to become the military caudillo of Peru with powers to finally defeat the royalists.

Operating from a base in Peru's northern city of Trujillo, Bolivar began his campaign as Peru's new military dictator in September 1823. He defeated royalist forces at Junín in August 1824. He then returned to Lima to consolidate his power in the capital and left the final defeat of royalist forces at the Battle of Ayacucho to his able subordinate Antonio José de Sucre. With Sucre's victory at Ayacucho in early December 1824, Peru and all of Latin America was finally free from Spanish control for the first time in more than three centuries. The first decades of independence, however, would prove to be a hard road to travel for the Peruvian people. Issues of political legitimacy, economic independence and stability, the challenging diversity of Peru's peoples, and the formidable task of building viable institutions would all be daunting challenges during Peru's first half century of troubled republicanism.[6]

THE QUESTION OF NATIONAL IDENTITY

The unspoken question confronting Peruvian leaders at independence was similar to that which faced members of the United States Constitutional Convention in Philadelphia in 1787. What would the status of the indigenous peoples and blacks be under the new systems of republican government? Enlightenment principles informed the government charters of both the United States and Peru. Few people, however, openly questioned the viability of African slavery in both nations and certainly the large populations of indigenous peoples posed the very difficult problem of social and economic integration into mainstream society. In the end, Indian integration and harmonious racial relations have proven to be two of the most difficult tasks confronting the U.S. and Peru up to the present day. In effect, Peru's leaders after independence inherited from the colonial era what Klarén termed a "patriarchical, patrician and paternalistic order" that despite the provisions of Peru's republican constitution remained in effect for the first full century of independence.[7]

PERU'S FALTERING ECONOMY

Having gained its independence later than any other Spanish American former colony, Peru had a late start in creating a viable economy during its early decades of nationhood. The destruction and dislocation of the independence war in the mining and agricultural sectors was also severe. Also, agricultural and mine workers were drawn into the loyalist and patriot armies during the independence wars and were not immediately available as a labor source during the first years of independence. However, once the mines were restored after being destroyed by warfare and flooding, silver mining once again rose to prominence in the Peruvian economy. The most productive mining center was Cerro de Pasco in the central highland and silver exports by the late 1830s would account for nearly 90 percent of the value of exports from Peru. But as Klarén notes, while Peru engaged in more open trade with Britain, France and the United States, it would be inundated with cheap manufacturing goods, which severely undercut Peru's small manufacturing and artisan classes. The pastoral economy benefited from the growing importance of Andean fairs where wool from llamas, alpacas, and vicuña became a commodity sought by local merchants who traded in the international market. The most dynamic agricultural region in Peru was the Mantaro valley, an area not characterized by large haciendas, but rather smaller holdings and active peasantry that toiled in both their own small plots and in the mines of Cerro de Pasco on a seasonal basis. The traditional routes of trade from southern Peru to Chile for wines, grain, and other foodstuffs as well as sugar, cotton, and tobacco to Lima only became active again by the mid-1830s.[8]

Despite these bright spots, Peru's broad economic picture during its first decades was discouraging. Political instability produced by a lack of central authority and competing caudillos prevented any consistent revenue stream from developing. Additionally, debts owed from the independence wars needed to be paid. The answer to this problem was all to frequently foreign loans. British bondholders were the original holders of Peru's growing debt. This gave Britain an opportunity to become intimately involved in Peru's financial dealings for most of the remaining years of the 19th century. By the late 1840s, Peru's foreign debt was nearly $22 million. Indebtedness would plague the nation's economic and political relations with the leading economic powers of the world to the present day. It was nearly impossible for Peru to gain its economic footing as long as the national political picture remained so clouded with uncertainty as a result of *caudillismo*.

Caudillos or strongmen trace their origins in Latin American culture to the warrior knights of the Spanish Reconquista and to a degree from the curacas of Andean culture. In Peru during the first decades of independence, two caudillos, Andrés de Santa Cruz and Agustín Gamara, dominated the politics of the new republic. But these leaders really only provided a veneer of some continuity during a period when Peru experienced 24 different governments. Military and civilian factionalism for most of the first three decades after independence limited real progress in nation building. In an age of political self-aggrandizement, however, there still existed broader political movements. As was the case in much of the rest of Latin America, political outlooks were dominated by conservative and liberal factions. Conservatives tended to be based in Lima and in northern coastal Peru. They opposed free trade, supported a strong Catholic church, and wanted to maintain the castes system of the colonial era so as to retain the rigid social hierarchy of the pre-independence period. Liberals, hailing largely from southern Peru and Arequipa in particular, sought broad contacts with the outside world founded on a policy of free trade and immigration, primarily from Europe. They also sought a federalized or at least a weakened central government. Liberals were also wary of the power of the Church in Peruvian society. Weakened by their distance from Lima, their inability and/or unwillingness to enlist a popular base, and factionalism, Peru's liberals were not a decisive element in national politics early in the republic's history. With these two competing factions looking to impose their ideology upon the nation, Peru remained in a state of civil war for most of the period from independence until the mid 1840s. What makes this political strife confusing is that these caudillos were not consistent in their programs or viewpoints and often adopted positions from their opposing camps. Gamara usually championed the conservative's cause and Santa Cruz the liberal's. But opportunism and the ill-defined boundaries of these relatively new political ideologies encouraged them to be eclectic in their views.

Santa Cruz had grand ambitions. Having led Peru for a brief time after Bolivar departed, he served as President of Bolivia for a full decade (1829–1839). In the midst of his tenure Santa Cruz created the short-lived Peru-Bolivian Confederation (1836–1839). He sought to recreate the geographic unity of old Peru by uniting Peru and Bolivia under his supposed liberal but often autocratic rule. Called to intervene in Peru's internal war, he managed to create a confederation between Peru and Bolivia under his leadership. Santa Cruz had great difficulty thereafter keeping the confederation intact. He was staunchly opposed by Lima conservatives. Peruvians, both liberals and conservatives, disliked the idea of being ruled by a Bolivian. The confederation also aroused the fears of Chilean and Argentinean leaders who feared the economic and military potential of the confederation led by Santa Cruz. The combined population of Bolivia and Peru at this time was 4.1 million compared to only 1.1 million in Chile. Moreover, Chile and Bolivia were contesting control of valuable nitrate deposits in the Atacama Desert. This issue would have critically important implications for Peru, Chile, and Bolivia by the 1870s.

Chile and Argentina declared war on the Peru-Bolivia Confederation in 1836. After three years of intermittent conflict, Santa Cruz's army was defeated at the Battle of Yungay in 1839 and the confederation collapsed. Although the Chilean army and a dissident Peruvian force was smaller than the combined armies of Peru and Bolivia, the Chileans possessed a superior navy, which was decisive in these conflicts resulting from the creation of the confederation. Additionally, the Chilean army was a standing force, while the Peru-Bolivian Confederation fought primarily with ill-trained Indian conscripts. In the wake of these events, Peru suffered a protracted period of political instability where short-term rule by caudillos was the norm. Peru thus made little progress toward establishing the institutions of a stable democracy during these formative years after independence.

GUANO AND CAPTIVE LABOR SYSTEMS

Guano, or dried bird excrement rich in nitrogen and phosphates, is an excellent fertilizer that had been used very successfully by the Incas but less so by the Spanish colonists. Because of the exceedingly dry conditions of coastal

Peru and the rich marine resources of the Humboldt Current, conditions were perfect for huge deposits of guano to accumulate for hundreds of years on the Chincha islands off the coast of central Peru. In the early 19th century, the European and U.S. demand for organic fertilizer was intense. The market for Peruvian guano opened in the early 1840s and remained strong until the beginning of the War of the Pacific (1879–1883). These years constituted the Guano boom, and this commodity dominated the Peruvian economy like no product before or since. Sold at prices ranging from $25 to $50 a ton, guano proved to be a highly profitable resource. Although the government of Peru granted consignment contracts to British firms such as Arthur Gibbs and Sons, Lima was able to retain a significant share of the direct sales of the guano exports. Some estimates place the Peruvian share of the total sales at 60 percent, with annual sales in the 1860s averaging about $20 million per year. Still, as was often the case in the boom and bust commodity cycles of the Latin American nations, the guano boom produced little balanced economic growth while largely benefiting only the Lima elites. Paul Gootenberg and others have rightly characterized the guano age as a "lost opportunity" for Peru in that the riches provided by the seabirds did not lead to creation of an economic foundation for steady expansion and modernization of Peru's economy.[9] Still, as we shall see in the ensuing chapter, it did help stabilize Peru's political climate under Ramón Castilla and energized the nation's financial structures and real estate sector.

The principal source of laborers for Peru's guano fields were Chinese workers, or coolies. Between 80,000 and 100,000 of these Chinese "colonists" emigrated from China to Peru during the period from 1849 to 1874. They were essential to the expansion of Peru's coastal sugar and cotton plantation and the construction of the trans-Andean railroad lines engineered by the U.S. entrepreneur Henry Meiggs during the mid-19th century. Michael Gonzales argues effectively that Chinese workers on Peru's coastal sugar and cotton plantations offered an important transition labor source after African slavery was abolished in Peru in 1855. Further, he contends that hard-pressed Chinese labor allowed Peruvian planters to weather the wartime crisis of the 1870s and early 1880s and maintain their position as the dominant social class in Peru. Labor conditions on these plantations were never easy. Resistance and rebellion by the Chinese laborers was nearly a constant dilemma for the planters. Violence and opium were characteristically used to subdue resistance.[10]

But nothing could compare with the abject misery of the work in the guano beds. Under the tropical sun, Chinese laborers shoveled and bagged the stinking guano and loaded it into ship holds for transport to farm fields in Europe and the United States. An Englishmen, A. J. Duffield, aptly described these conditions during a visit to Peru in the mid-1870s: "No hell has ever been conceived by the Hebrew, the Irish, the Italian or even the Scotch mind for appeasing the anger or satisfying the vengeance of the awful gods that can be equaled in the fierceness of the heat, the horror of the stink, and the damnation of those compelled to labor there to a deposit of Peruvian guano when being shoveled into ships."[11] The Chinese coolie trade continued until the mid-1870s, when the pressure of humanitarian interests led to Peru negotiating the Tientsin Treaty with the Chinese government to end this inhuman form of contract labor. After African slavery had run its course by the middle of the 1850s, Chinese contract labor was seen as absolutely necessary to keep the economy of 19th-century Peru running.[12]

African slavery was primarily limited to Peru's coastal plantations throughout the colonial period and remained so until abolition in 1855. Unlike Brazil and the United States, a viable and assertive abolition movement never formed in Peru. Instead, coastal planters facing the flight of slaves from their plantations during the independence wars and the turbulent times following Peru's liberation from Spain were looking to Chinese bonded labor to fill the demand created by the slow demise of slavery. Peruvian slave owners held approximately 50,000 slaves at the time of independence, but as the plantation economy declined and haciendas were neglected or abandoned during the troubled period from independence to the 1850s, the slave population declined as well. Slaves simply ran away or were often drafted into the armies of the numerous caudillos struggling for power in troubled Peru. This differed sharply from the United States, where the slave economy was bolstered by the rising price of cotton in the mid-19th century. The U.S. Civil War and the resultant sharp increase in world cotton prices came too late for Peruvian cotton producers to bolster a dying institution. The immediate cause for the end of slavery in Peru was not a vibrant abolitionist movement. Rather it was the outbreak of yet another civil conflict in 1854 that prompted the abolition of the Indian Head Tax, which remained in place despite previous attempts to abolish it. Significantly, African slavery was outlawed soon thereafter. Strongman Ramón Castilla was seeking to be Peru's chief caudillo at this time. In an effort to recruit former slaves to his banner, Castilla referred to himself as Peru's "provisional president" and promised emancipation in return for support for his cause. His campaigning appears to have been successful as between 2,000 and 3,000 ex-slaves were reportedly recruited into his army. Formal manumission came with Castilla's decree of January 23, 1855. Still, the question of compensation and the future status of the former slaves remained to be resolved. Seeking to consolidate his support among the coastal hacendados, Castilla moved quickly on the question of compensation. He issued a decree in early March 1855 that ordered a generous indemnification of 300 pesos per slave regardless of gender or age, including slaves who had previously fled the plantations. In the end, 25,505 slaves were freed at a cost of 7,651,500 pesos.[13] Sadly, like the end of slavery everywhere in the Americas in the 19th century, there were no provisions for the freed slaves' transition into Peruvian society. No attempt was made to facilitate the acquisition of land or employment beyond the plantations that most ex-slaves had fled. As everywhere else in the Americas, former bondsmen, both Chinese and Afro Peruvian, were left to forge new lives with only their wits and strong backs to contend with a society that continued to regard them with disdain and distrust. For some of these unfortunate ex-slaves, the Catholic Church at least provided some solace.

THE CATHOLIC CHURCH IN EARLY REPUBLICAN PERU

The Catholic Church in Peru was organized into 10 dioceses at the time of independence; Lima, Cuzco, and Arequipa were the most important dioceses at this time. Two categories of priests resided in Peru, the secular clergy, or those who lived in society and administered to the spiritual news of the nation's Catholics, and those in the religious orders, who resided in monasteries or missions and followed a much more strict regimen. The Jesuits, however, were expelled from all of Latin America in 1767, and the loss of their influence in the missions and in education in Peru was substantial. Jeffrey Klaiber characterizes the Church during the first decades of independence as a corporate body that although distinct from Peruvian society was still reflective of its dominant trends. In this sense, the church, as it was in many areas of Latin America, was caught up in the ideological struggles between liberalism and conservatism. These years were difficult times for the Church in Peru, as much of its property was lost as a result of the independence wars, and membership in the religious orders dropped significantly. For example, as of 1790 there were 711 priests in Lima, but by 1857 the number had dropped sharply to 155.[14]

With the end of the Spanish royal patronage, Peruvian patriots sought to create a national church with minimal interference from Rome in the appointment of the leadership of the 10 dioceses. The Vatican vigorously opposed this and many of the dioceses were leaderless for long periods of time in the early 19th century. Yet another serious blow to the church was the abolition of tithes by the Castilla government in May 1859. Tithes were one of the most important sources of wealth for a church that already had lost significant sources of its fixed wealth. It is likely that Peru's liberals were not motivated by the desire to destroy the church, but rather to control it. But their efforts left the church badly weakened during a time when strong institutions were badly needed to build foundations for a nation that was badly floundering. Peru's church and state difficulties were not unique. Differing views over the role of the church in society plagued nearly every Latin American nation at various times, particularly Mexico. Certainly Peru would not experience anything like the widespread violence of the Cristero Rebellion in Mexico (1926–1929). Yet it would be well into the 1960s until the church and the government were of the same mind regarding public policy on major issues of reform.

THE NATIONALIST CAUDILLO: RAMÓN CASTILLA

Peru's early leaders after Simón Bolívar lacked the vision or the ability to create the conditions for a viable nation-building process. Aided by the guano boom in the mid-19th century, Ramón Castilla, a caudillo from Tarapacá in southern Peru, was different. Castilla is credited today with making substantial contributions to the creation of Peru's republican state as the nation made slow progress to distance itself from the chaos of its early years. His concern for establishing at least a modicum of constitutional government earned him the sobriquet "soldier of the law." As indicated earlier, Castilla's most notable acts were the abolition of slavery and the head tax, which occurred while he struggled to build a power base during the mid-1850s. No matter what his motives were, these enormously important reforms helped reshape Peruvian society from this point forward. Castilla also sought to attract immigrants from Europe, especially Irish and Germans who were fleeing both hunger and social unrest. Like most future efforts to draw immigrants from Europe to Peru, Castilla's efforts met with relatively little success. Castilla also negotiated the guano contracts with British and French firms that would create the basis for the immensely profitable guano trade.

Castilla's attempt to establish a corporate legal basis for the modern Peruvian state was embodied in the constitution of 1856. This document validated the abolition of slavery as well as the religious and military *fueros.* In addition, the conditions for creating a national budget were outlined. In an attempt to reduce caudillismo, the presidential term was reduced from six years to four.

Interestingly, the caudillo Castilla's government established at least the legal, if not the practical basis for civilian control of the military. Congress was given the power to approve promotions to the senior leadership of the armed forces. More importantly, the constitution mandated that the armed forces must submit to civilian control. At the same time, a *Guardia Nacional* or national militia force was created. These efforts did not end caudillismo, of course, and Peru's national police have almost always been underfunded. Nevertheless, these constitutional measures indicated that at least Castilla was looking to create the framework for a modern nation at a time when government revenues from guano gave elements of the Peruvian population some reason for embracing a nationalist vision.

How did these reforms affect Peru's impoverished indigenous population? Not at all. Jacobsen concludes that they "did nothing to improve the situation of the Indians in terms of their social treatment and recognition of their rights by local power holders." A contemporary reformer, Juan Bustamante, bitterly criticized "these local power holders (hacendados), claiming, 'The persons opposed to the regeneration of the Indian and frustrating every well intentioned effort . . . enrich themselves by abusing the ignorance, humiliation and abandonment of the Indian.' "[15] Clearly, notions of nationalism and modernization might be stirring among liberal elites in Lima, but in the highland regions of Peru, local elite economic and political interests were developing their particular response to modernization and liberal capitalism. Peru's rugged geography and precarious climatic conditions limited the expansion of agriculture, especially in the highlands. But it also afforded hacendados the breathing room to delay the impact of world capitalism. They were thus able to chart their own course in response to changing economic conditions. As Jacobsen argues quite effectively, in the Azángaro province in the southern Peruvian Altiplano, the high altitude environment with its killing frost, long dry season, and exhausted soils can only support a limited population. Still, a vibrant pastoralist economy involving alpaca, sheep, and cattle sustained the region. At times of high prices for wool, the area's products became an important component in Peru's links to the world economy. With a population's diet based on tubers, they supplemented their food products with hunting and fishing from Lake Titicaca.[16] Other areas in highland Peru fraught by harsh environmental conditions presented a similar story. As the 19th century unfolded, it was becoming increasingly clear to astute observers of the Peruvian economy that guano provided a very uncertain future for Peru's economic well-being. The demands of the changing world economy and national rivalries in the Andean region would shake Peru to its very foundations throughout the course of the next three decades.

ABORTIVE NATION BUILDING

Peru's process of nation building during the guano age came to an abrupt end with the collapse of the guano-based economy and the terribly destructive War of the Pacific (1879–1883) with Chile. As Klarén has noted, by the 1860s a guano-based plutocracy, which included merchants, lawyers, coastal planters, and bankers, began to exercise substantial influence in national affairs. Increasing levels of economic power allowed civilians to challenge the traditional control of national affairs by military caudillos. This era saw the emergence of Peru's first civilian political party known as the Civilistas. The founder of the Civilistas, Manuel Pardo, was elected Peru's first civilian president in 1872. But civilian democracy would never fully mature during this era or at any point during the first part of the 20th century.

Peru began moving away from the guano-dominated economy when a consortium of Peruvian businessman wrested control of the lucrative guano concession from British concessionaire Anthony Gibbs 1862. This group's economic interest soon diversified into banking, railroads, mining, and agriculture. Arising out of these activities was a powerful oligarchy that dominated political and social affairs until the 1960s. This group nevertheless remained heavily tied to the land.

The leaders of this oligarchy also yearned to push the military caudillos aside and claim political leadership of the nation. Their brand of liberalism differed substantially from that which emerged from the Enlightenment and the French Revolution. Indeed, anti-clericalism was relatively moderate in Peru, especially compared with its profound importance among Mexico's liberals, for example. Primarily centered in Arequipa in southern Peru, the liberals of Peru wanted to dismantle the autocratic Lima-centered protectionist structures that were rooted in the colonial past.

Advocating free trade as the primary means of building a modern nation, liberals were limited until the late guano era by their inability to build a political base beyond southern Peru. Many were successful, however, in advancing their economic agenda, which included acquisition of increasingly valuable land previously held by Indian communities in the sierra.

Events in southern Peru did not exactly mirror those of the rest of the nation because of the region's substantial distance from Lima. But they did reflect general economic and social trends that were changing the face of Peru's leadership during the three decades prior to the War of the Pacific. Klarén argues that foreign debt consolidation in the 1850s enabled a "guano-era plutocracy" to emerge. Composed of planters from the coastal sugar and cotton plantations, wool and cattle producers from the sierra, merchants and professionals from Lima, and commercially connected military men, the plutocracy was never large. Many church lands were opened to private ownership during this era and the newly emerging elite gained control of much of this property. And, as we have seen in southern Peru, this new liberal capitalist sector progressively encroached upon Indian lands, solidifying its base in the countryside throughout the early 20th century. The oligarchy functioned primarily through family ties and other close-knit social networks. One member of this exclusive group would years later characterize the oligarchy's role in Peruvian society as a type of "Democratic Caesarism" with pronounced elitist and paternalistic characteristics.[17] Most of these elites had little faith in the worth of Peru's Indians and mestizo masses as agents of change and progress for Peru.

The civilian leader who first attempted to put the liberal's nation-building vision into reality was Manuel Pardo (1872–1876). A well-educated liberal who made a fortune in guano and banking, Pardo was the founder of the Civilista party, which would dominate Peruvian politics until the first decades of the 20th century. Pardo's vision for Peru rested with the modernization of the country's internal infrastructure through railroad construction. Looking perhaps to the U.S. and Argentine models, Pardo felt that agricultural revenues, like those from Peru's guano industry, should be substantially diverted to railroad building. He argued that "material progress" and the "population's well-being" would languish without opening up Peru's rugged interior for economic development.[18]

When Pardo assumed office in 1872, an ambitious railroad building program had already begun under the direction of a colorful and somewhat shady U.S. engineer, Henry Meiggs. After business failures in New York and California, Meiggs achieved renown for constructing a rail line in Chile from Santiago to Valparaíso and another from Chile's capital to the south. Hired by Peru to construct the central railroad from Lima to the mining town of La Oroya, Meiggs completed the difficult task with well-paid and decently treated Chilean, Peruvian, and Chinese laborers. Rising at times to heights over 15,000 feet in altitude, the central railroad is one of South America's most impressive engineering marvels, opening the way to the rich mineral deposits at La Oroya for export.

Heavy borrowing to pay for railroad construction and a banking crisis during Pardo's first two years in office quickly placed the Civilista president in political jeopardy. Worsening his political standing was his stance on Peru's military. Quite understandably, Pardo wanted to reduce the size of the armed forces and make it less intrusive in Peruvian politics. Pardo maintained that Peru's national security must be based on negotiated treaties with Peru's neighbors rather than a large permanent armed forces establishment. At a time when social Darwinist thinking was prompting world powers such as Germany and even emerging militaries like Japan to enact national conscription, Pardo's views had little appeal among conservatives and the military in Peru. His idea to create a National Guard (*Guardia Civil*) to assume police function for Peru's internal affairs also met with suspicion by military men. Peru's men in uniform pointed to the recent naval war with Spain in the mid-1860s as evidence that the nation was still vulnerable to threats from non-hemispheric foes. During the mid-1860s Spanish naval forces seized the guano-rich Chincha island and bombarded Chilean and Peruvian port fortifications before being driven off by fire from shore installations.

This brief conflict ended inconclusively but it added strength to the arguments of both diplomats and militarists during the ensuing decade. Never had the Andean nations been more unified than during the brief naval war with Spain. On the other hand, Spain, now a power clearly in decline, had come dangerously close to depriving Peru of its principal source of national income with a relatively small naval force.

In the midst of the growing economic crisis at the beginning of his presidency, Pardo was facing an uphill struggle to modernize and professionalize an armed forces establishment that lacked a professional ethos, a consistent training regime, and permanent training academies. Most of all, the army was still atomized by caudillismo. As Peru plunged into a deep economic crisis in 1873, the armed forces found themselves very poorly prepared for an impending war with Chile over the rich nitrate deposits in the southern Atacama desert. The economic crisis was a response to the worldwide depression of 1873 but it had deep roots in a growing national debt, the transfer of the guano contract to a French firm headed by Augusto Dreyfuss, and a sharp decline in guano revenues at the beginning of the 1870s. As might have been expected, the guano fields were nearing exhaustion, and domestic and foreign speculators were turning their attention to the rich nitrate fields that lay in the coastal desert territories of Peru, Bolivia, and Chile.

Discovered in the mid-19th century in the Atacama Desert, nitrates were the main components of fertilizer and explosives. As guano stores declined and the world's population expanded dramatically in the late 19th century, nitrates became a valued commodity until the invention of the Haber-Bosch process for producing synthetic nitrates in the World War I era. Seeking to safeguard this valuable natural resource, President Pardo nationalized the nitrate industry in 1875. This action alienated Chilean and European mining interests that had been granted earlier contracts to exploit the nitrate fields in Tarapacá. Except during the brief period in the mid 1860s when Chile and Peru had diplomatic ties to confront the threat from Spain, the two Pacific nations always viewed one another with suspicion. Once Bolivia entered the diplomatic picture these suspicions soon turned into open warfare.

In an effort to confront a possible military threat from Chile, Pardo signed a secret mutual defensive alliance with Bolivia in February 1873 but failed to get Argentina enlisted in this alliance. As William Sater and others have noted, the War of the Pacific was thus not just rooted in the economic issues relating to the nitrate industry but was also was a result of in longstanding geopolitical issues among the Pacific nations, which originated well back into the Spanish Colonial era. President Pardo has been consistently criticized for reducing the size of Peru's army and leaving the nation vulnerable before the War of the Pacific. Still, Pardo left office as scheduled in 1876 and was replaced by the military man General Mariano Ignacio Prado. Uncharacteristically, the military president did not take steps to prepare for possible war with Chile. The army had not been mobilized on the southern borders as would be expected, and Peru's fleet was generally not seaworthy. At the same time, Bolivia was also ill-prepared for the conflict, in the aftermath of the Bolivian government's decision to place a tax on the nitrates extracted by a jointly owned British and Chilean mining firm in province of Antofagasta. The small tax of 10 centavos per ton was in seeming violation of an earlier treaty between Bolivia and Chile. The refusal of the Antofagasta mining company to pay the Bolivian tax resulted in the seizure of the company and the arrest of his manager. Chile responded by conducting joint naval and infantry operations again the port city of Antofagasta in mid-February 1879. Bolivia responded by declaring war on Chile. While Peru pondered its course of action, Chile declared war on both Bolivia and Peru on April 6, 1879. The most important military conflict on the west coast of South America had then begun.

THE WAR OF THE PACIFIC: THE SEA CAMPAIGNS

The War of the Pacific, which pitted Chile against Peru and Bolivia, shaped the geopolitics and economic destiny of these three nations for the ensuing century. The war involved both naval and land campaigns that combined modern weaponry with tactics largely rooted in the Napoleonic era. In a fundamental sense, the naval battles determined the course of the war because the coastlines of both Bolivia and Peru were poorly defended once their own sea powers were destroyed early in the war. Contemporary wars such as the U.S. Civil War and the Franco-Prussian War are not good points of reference for the War of the Pacific because of the significant differences in scale. But it is useful to note that the technologies employed in these wars such as the railroad, telegraphy, breach-loading rifles, machine guns, ironclad steam-driven vessels, underwater rams, and mines, all played important roles in the War of the Pacific.[19]

Chile's advantages in this conflict were clear from the outset. Due to its independence from Spain, Chile enjoyed much more political stability than had Peru or Bolivia. Although not a true democracy, legitimate presidential succession and constitutional order were commonplace in Chile. The relative populations of the war nation's mattered little because Chile's population was not as deeply divided by caste and class as was that of Peru or Bolivia. Additionally, Chile enjoyed closer relations with Britain because of partnership in the nitrate trade. This relationship with one of the leading financial and military powers was critical. As we have seen, Peru's rugged geography precluded the effective communications and transport that were critical to their war effort. Bolivia was in even worse shape than Peru with regard to its infrastructure. The littoral of Bolivia, Peru, and Chile in the contested areas were far from their main urban centers. However, Chile was able to establish a profoundly important presence in Peru in the decade before the war due to foreign investment and migrations of large numbers of Chilean workers into the Peruvian provinces of Tarapacá Tacna, Arica, and the Bolivian province of Antofagasta.

None of the armies of the combatants were ready for war in 1879. Chile's military had had battle experience in the suppression of the Mapuche Indian peoples, but these battles were fluid cavalry-dominated affairs that had little relevance to the fixed formation infantry tactics of the time. Still, issues of discipline, leadership, logistics, and supply were better understood in the

Chilean army than that of her two foes. Chilean armaments were also more modern. Adding to Peru's woes was the demobilization of nearly 8,000 soldiers in the 1870s after the resolution of the conflict with Spain. Although Peru possessed relatively modern Krupp artillery pieces, they were generally outgunned by the Chileans during the first stages of the war in the desert. Peruvian soldiers were armed with a variety of small arms that offered the army little uniformity for training and resupply. Rifles manufactured by Comblain, Chassepot, Remington, and Peabody were distributed throughout the ranks. Peru's cavalry carried 22 caliber carbines, which lacked the firepower to engage the better-armed Chilean cavalry and infantry units.[20]

Bolivia was in no better position to prosecute the war, as its armed forces were in disarray due to economic instability and chronic caudillismo, which undercut any semblance of military professionalism. Still, undermanned and poorly armed Bolivian units fought bravely. At the Battle of Campo de Alianza, for example, the Bolivia Colorados and the Amarillos took heavy casualties in both offensive and defensive operations.[21]

The balance of naval forces at the beginning of the war held the key to victory. Peru's navy included three monitors (*Huáscar, Manco Cápac,* and *Atahualpa*), all with two main guns. The British-built *Huáscar* was Peru's primary fighting vessel and carried three artillery pieces, but its turret range was limited. The two remaining ironclads were American built but were not really seagoing vessels. They were underpowered with very shallow drafts and thus were used as floating batteries for coastal defense off Callao. Augmenting the three ironclads was the armored frigate *Independencia,* a corvette, and a gunboat.

Chilean naval forces were led by the central battery ironclads *Almirante Cochrane* and *Blanco Encalada,* which were built in Hull, England, in 1874 with the up-to-date technology. The engines of these two vessels generated far more horsepower (13 knots) than Peru's two capital ships and thus had a decided advantage at sea. They each carried nine cannons. Four corvettes, two gunboats, and two aging sloops comprised the remainder of the fleet as the war commenced. Chile thus enjoyed a significant advantage in firepower and with the modernity of its vessels. As the war progressed, Chile augmented its fleet by purchasing 11 torpedo boats, giving the nation an enormous naval advantage over its opponents. Even before the war began, Peru recognized the disparity in naval power. Thus, Peru made furious diplomatic efforts in Argentina, France, Turkey, and the United States in order to acquire more naval firepower, to no avail.[22] The first naval battle of the War of the Pacific would largely determine the course of the conflict thereafter. As Bolivia lacked a blue water fleet, the war at sea was a straight up match between Peru and Chile.

In mid-April 1879 Chilean naval forces blockaded the Peruvian port of Iquique. This was the first step in the Chilean navy's plan to blockade all major Peruvian and Bolivian ports as the key to naval strategy. Still, as William Sater has argued, the relative inactivity of the blockade allowed the Peruvians at least four weeks to refit their naval vessels and move troops into the war zone while the Chilean commander Admiral Williams Rebolledo dallied offshore at Iquique. Finally, Peruvian and Chilean naval forces were joined in battle at Iquique on May 21, 1879. There the *Huáscar,* captained by Miguel Grau, rammed and sank the Chilean corvette *Esmeralda,* commanded by Arturo Pratt, who died in a failed boarding attempt of the *Huáscar.* Peruvian forces suffered a huge setback however when the frigate *Independencia* was destroyed on a reef. Peru's naval forces were then reduced to only one remaining capital ship, the *Huáscar.*

Even with the disadvantage in naval power, Grau led the *Huáscar* against Chilean shipping and shore installations in an audacious few months of splendid seamanship. The Peruvian naval hero captured a number of important vessels, including the transport *Rimac,* which was soon pressed into service supplying Peru's troops in the battle zones. The inaction of the Chilean naval commander Williams Robelledo allowed Captain Grau nearly a free hand during those critical months. Eventually Williams Robelledo resigned. Grau's brilliant high seas operations would come to an end in October 1879 at Angamos, which lay to the north of the former Bolivian port city of Antofgasta, when Chile's fleet commanders became far more aggressive.

At the naval battle of Angamos, Peru's fate in the War of the Pacific was virtually decided. After refitting most of its capital ships to make them battle ready, the Chilean fleet was deployed in two groups to the west and north of point Angamos. Grau's retreat north to home waters was thus blocked. Badly in need of repairs, the *Huascar* could not outrun its foes to the south. When Grau engaged the Chilean monitor *Chochrane,* he was soon outmaneuvered. After taking several hits from a *Cochrane* broadside, Grau was killed by a shell from the Chilean vessel. The *Huascar*'s companion vessel, *Union,* escaped the battle of Angamos, but Peru lost its main capital ship when the *Huascar* was disabled and captured after Grau's death. Peruvian naval forces continued to resist using vessels with spar torpedoes and small booby-trapped vessels, but without their brilliant naval commander Grau, and with only one seagoing ship remaining in its fleet, Peru could not defend itself again Chilean attacks along its vast and exposed southern coastline. Fittingly, Grau became one of the central icons of Peruvian patriotism. Over the years the Peruvian navy has named its main capital ship after this hero of the War of the Pacific. Chile would quickly take advantage of Peru's vulnerability to press the war against both Bolivia and Peru.

THE WAR IN THE DESERT

As armies still discover today, defeating an enemy's regular forces and occupying the enemy's territory is often easier than defeating lingering guerrilla resistances. Such was the case in Chile's advance again Peru's defenses on their way to capturing Lima. Sater notes that the land battles during the war were particularly brutal. Often the number killed exceeded that of the wounded, as often Chilean soldiers followed a no prisoners policy. Slashing a wounded enemy's throat was a common practice of rampaging Chilean soldiers during the battles in the desert. The tenacious Peruvian resistance during the subsequent Chilean occupation of Peru can be explained in some measure by the conduct of Chilean troops during the early stages of the war. In fact, the land campaigns of the War of the Pacific can be divided into two phases: conventional war by Chile against the coastal cities of the allies during the period from 1879 to 1881, and the ensuing guerrilla operations led by the Peruvian military leader Colonel Andrés Cáceres that extended until 1883.

The first phase of the coastal desert war began with Chile's invasion of Peru's province of Tarapacá. With no naval capability, Peruvian troops in their south-ernmost province, Tarapacá did not pose a serious threat to supply line com-munications necessary for amphibious landings at the port of Pisagua. Chilean soldiers went ashore during early November 1879 and overcame heavy Peru-vian and Bolivian resistance. Once Tarapacá was taken, Chile financed the war effort from the significant revenues gained from the newly captured nitrate op-erations. Peru, of course, was deprived of its principal revenue for not only the war but for the daily operations of its government. Peru's units fought bravely, defeating Chilean forces at the battle of Tarapacá in late November 1879. Nev-ertheless, isolated from their supply lines, Peruvian defenders could not hold the strategically important town. More importantly, some of Peru's best officers and regular soldiers were lost during these early campaigns. This influenced the course of the war in the provinces of Tacna and Arica to the north.

The battles for the provinces of Tacna and Arica were bitterly fought in some of the worst terrain in the world. Disease and lack of medical equipment and personnel significantly increased the death toll. Battles were contested in desert with constantly inadequate water supplies. Chile's soldiers fought the allies in key battles at Tacna and Arica. Often no quarter was given by the Chileans when they overran allied positions. This encouraged Peruvian and Bolivia soldiers to often fight to the death to avoid capture. Peruvian army colonel Francisco Bolognesi, who led the defense of the city of Arica atop El Morro Mountain, exemplified the bravery of many of the Peruvian defenders. Outnumbered by Chilean forces 3 to 1, Bolognesi died in hand-to-hand com-bat with Chilean infantry units amid the defenses atop El Morro. Bolognesi's sons Enrique and Augusto died later defending Lima against Chilean assault. Some Bolivian and Peruvian units suffered 80 percent casualties in the con-flicts in Tacna and Arica. Yet these losses often occurred as units fought out of sequence with other allied personnel. Clearly, the allied command structure was weakened at the mid-grade officer level by casualties in Tarapacá and the early phases of the Tacna campaign. The lack of leadership deprived Peru of the critical direction it needed to defend Lima from ensuing attack.

THE BATTLE FOR LIMA

By June 1880, Peru was in a desperate position. Its nitrate resources were lost with the fall of Tarapacá. Tacna and Arica were in Chilean hands. Its regular army with valuable experienced officers was barely intact. Nearly Peru's entire navy was either at the bottom of the sea or in Chilean hands. Chile's terms were presented in negotiations during 1880, but Peru refused to concede.

Any possible truce negotiations were stymied anyway by the departure of President Mariano Ignacio Prado from Peru to Europe in mid-December 1879. Claiming he was leaving Peru to acquire badly needed arms, Prado's departure paved the way for a coup d'état by his political rival Nicolás de Piérola, who seized power less than a week after Prado's departure.

Piérola could have turned to European diplomatic intervention at this point to possibly end the war. France, Italy, and Britain offered a settlement that would have ceded the province of Tarapacá to Chile with Tacna and Arica likely to revert back to Peru. Bolivia, however, would still remain a landlocked nation. Peru and Bolivia hoped for a strong diplomatic intervention by the United States to thwart Chilean military advances. But the Arica peace conference that convened in October 1880 came to nothing. In reality, Bolivia was no longer Peru's military ally now that its army had disintegrated in the Arica campaign. Now Chile's complete superiority in naval forces allowed it to undertake the difficult task of an amphibious assault on Peru's capital through Lima's port city of Callao. Before the invasion of Lima was launched, Chile sent Naval Captain Patricio Lynch to northern Peru to lead a Sherman-like incursion against military and economic targets in the area from Paita south to Quilca. In early September 1880, Lynch sought to divert troops from the defense of Lima, train new recruits in battle conditions, and raise war revenues through taxes on the local population.[23] Like Sherman, Lynch left a path of devastation and fury in the wake of his campaign.

Lima was taken in a series of pitched battles in the Lima environs at Chorrillos and Miraflores. Chilean soldiers occupied Lima on January 22, 1881, and much looting followed. But like modern war has shown us many times, the capture of Lima would only mark the transition to a different and brutal form of Peruvian resistance. The Chilean occupiers now faced a protracted guerrilla war in the sierra led by one of the most able commanders of the desert campaign, Colonel Andrés Cáceres.

MONTONERO RESISTANCE AND THE TREATY OF ANCÓN

Chile's task after occupying Lima was to establish a puppet government that would sign a treaty ending the war. This proved to be an extremely difficult process because few Peruvian figures of prominence wanted to be associated with defeat and the loss of Peruvian territory. Most parties, including U.S.,

British, and French diplomats, agreed that Peru would likely have to cede the nitrate-rich province of Tarapacá to Chile. The real issue was the fate of the other Peruvian provinces of Tacna and Arica. With its army destroyed, Bolivia had effectively withdrawn from the war after the battle of Tacna, and thus the loss of the Bolivian province of Antofagasta to Chile was a certainty. When acting President Nicolás Piérola could not generate support for his own resistance movement to Chile, he left Peru in late 1881. Various military leaders would claim the Peruvian presidency over the course of the next two years. But these individuals did not have any political legitimacy until the guerrilla war in the mountains ended and until the way was opened for a military leader who could command the respect of the alienated serranos. That leader was the Quechua-speaking hacendado and veteran of the desert campaign, Colonel Andrés Cáceres. This caudillo rallied the Indian fighters, known as the *montoneros,* to join him in a war without mercy against the Chilean occupiers.

As Sater correctly concludes, the principal problem for the Chilean army in the sierra campaign was a lack of manpower to conduct an irregular war in the extremely rugged and vast expanses of the sierra. Of his 15,000 man army in Peru, Chilean Commander Patricio Lynch was able to spare only 4,000 for duty in the sierra. The rest were used for garrisoning Lima and Callao. This left practically no effective Chilean forces in Peru's northern and southern provinces. Complicating Lynch's situation was a Peruvian military force in the Arequipa region commanded by Admiral Montero. These regular forces were, however, not as active or as threatening to Chile's dominance as Cáceres's montoneros. [24]

In classic guerrilla fashion, the montoneros used the sierra terrain to ambush Chilean columns by isolating stragglers or rear guards, blocking mountain passes and immobilizing small contingents of Chilean troops. In addition, they would lead the occupiers on long chases until their provisions and their strength gave out. Peru's irregular forces had few firearms but instead did battle using traditional tactics such as employing *rejoneros* (spearmen) and *honderos* (slingmen). The montoneros' primary ally was the terrain. *Soroche* or altitude sickness took a heavy toll. Characterized by severe headache, nausea, and weakness, soroche could kill or weaken a lowlander for days at time. Communicable diseases such smallpox, yellow fever, and typhus took their toll as well, as did hypothermia and frostbite. The Peruvian serranos knew their mountains intimately, and, of course, the Chileans did not. In order to enforce order in an extremely hostile land the Chileans used draconian measures. Entire towns suspected of harboring the resistance were torched. Local serranos were interrogated and shot on the slightest pretext. As in the desert campaigns, few prisoners were ever taken. If not burned, many sierra towns were looted. Rape of serrano women by Chilean soldiers was distressingly common. These actions engendered a violent reaction by the montoneros, who routinely mutilated the corpses of Chilean soldiers after armed engagements.

The turning point in the sierra campaign did not come until July 10, 1883, with Cáceres's defeat at Huamacucho. His forces weakened by the desertion of 600 soldiers, Cáceres nevertheless fought a pitched battle against superior Chilean forces. Both sides were fortified by artillery but the telling feature of the battle was a shortage of ammunition by Cáceres forces that cut short an assault against Chilean positions. Peruvian forces were then dispersed by Chilean cavalry and the battle was over.[25] Although Cáceres was able to escape and go on to dominate Peruvian politics for the next decade, Peruvian resistance to the Chilean occupation was effectively over in central and northern Peru. With the capture of Arequipa in the south in late October 1883, effective Peruvian resistance came to an end.

The Treaty of Ancón brought the disastrous War of the Pacific to an end on October 20, 1883. Signed by an agent of General Miguel Iglesias, who had become an instrument of Chilean policy in Peru, the treaty validated Chilean dominance on the west coast of South America. Bolivia's hopes that Chile would return at least a corridor to the sea through its lost province of Antofagasta were predictably denied. The impoverished Andean nation remains landlocked to the present day. Peru agreed to permanently cede the nitrate-rich province of Tarapacá. A decision on the future status of the provinces of Tacna and Arica was to be delayed 10 years until a plebiscite could be held to determine whether they would revert back to Peru or remain in the hands of the Chileans. Not surprisingly, the plebiscite was not held in 1893. In fact, it would not be until 1929, with the assistance of U.S. arbitration, that the Tacna and Arica controversy was finally resolved. At the time, Arica became the permanent possession of Chile and Tacna reverted to Peru. The terrible War of the Pacific significantly delayed Peru's development as a nation, embittered the Andean nations against one another, and fueled old class and ethnic hatreds that would linger far into the next century. In many important ways, the Indians of the sierra resisted the Chilean conquest as bravely as the regular army that fought in the desert campaign. Whether they were fighting for the larger concept of the nation or merely in defense of their homes and villages mattered little to the Chilean soldiers. They often held the serranos in very low regard until they had to cope with them in battle. Out of the ashes of that conflict would emerge a caudillo who could unite the country under his forceful rule. Given Peru's nineteenth century experience, it is not surprising that the military hero of the montonero war, General Andés Cáceres, would be chosen by the people to lead the shattered nation in its rebuilding process.

RECONSTRUCTING THE NATION

Some of the more thoughtful Peruvians who dared to risk deep self-examination after the War of the Pacific concluded that the lack of an integrated national awareness was at the root of Peru's defeat. Some of these thinkers will be examined later, but for now it is important to note that the marginal role of the Indian in national life, the nation's still backward infrastructure, and its poorly integrated economy all were critical elements in Peru's defeat. The heavy dependence on nitrate revenues left Peru nearly helpless economically after the province of Tarapacá was captured by Chile. Had Peru been able to manufacture even relatively small amounts of firearms and ammunition, such defeats as Arica may have been reversed. Further, the Peruvian army simply did not have not the trained officers necessary to carry on the long war after the desert campaign. Robust service academies to train officers were badly needed before 1879, but their creation would only come after the war was lost. Peru's military heroes Grau and Bolognesi would become icons in Peru's military pantheon that would not be marked by successful military commanders until the war with Ecuador in 1941. General Andés Cáceres, perhaps the keenest military mind of all of Peru's soldiers, had his reputation sullied by his embrace of caudillismo in the aftermath of the War of the Pacific.

Significant changes were wrought in Peru's social fabric as a result of the war. In the central sierra and to a lesser extent in southern Peru, regional oligarchies did not survive the destruction of the war. With their properties ruined and little chance to gain credit to rebuild, Lima-based investors and later international capital assumed control. Within little more than a generation, the sierra was plugged into the world economy as never before.[26] Peru's oligarchy, however defined, was forced to make major adjustments in the years after the War of the Pacific to maintain its dominance in the country's national life. This would require some very agile economic adjustments as Peru's single-product economy (guano or nitrates) was very much a reality of the past. In October 1883 Peru was a shattered nation. All elements of society from wealthy hacendados to the poorest serrano peasants suffered severe financial losses. Klarén notes that Peru's revenues fell from 35 million soles in 1879 to a dismal 1 million soles at the end of the war in 1883. Most of Peru's banking institutions did not survive the conflict. The north coast sugar estates suffered from the double calamities of the Lynch column's destructive forays and the loss of manpower as Chinese contract laborers escaped. In 1878, Peru derived 26% of its national revenue from nitrates. With the loss of Tarapacá, this revenue was completely gone.[27]

Following the retreat of the Chilean forces, Cáceres rebelled against president Miguel Iglesias and with the support of his montoneros was able to occupy Lima and unseat Iglesias and drive him into exile. Cáceres took office as the elected president of Peru in early June 1885. He could only achieve the presidency, however, by turning away from his Indian allies to gain the support of Peru's still powerful landholding classes. The hacendados wanted guarantees that reforms would not be enacted that resulted in the liberalization of the land laws in favor of the Indians. Moreover, in a desperate effort to raise critically needed revenue, Cáceres reinstated the Indian head tax, which echoed the oppressive tactics of Spanish rule during the colonial period. Thus, Peru's Indian peoples lost the opportunity in the wake of the highly destructive War of the Pacific to establish their genuine right to have their economic welfare considered as the nation was rebuilding.

Cáceres certainly gave Peru a period of badly needed stability as in his role as Peru's chief caudillo during the period of Second Militarism, which lasted from 1885 until 1895. Ruling through political surrogates after 1890, Cáceres sought to expand his government's revenue base by imposing new taxes on alcohol, tobacco, and other consumer items. Peru's commercial and agricultural institutions began to rebuild, and as it's the economy grew, so did the confidence of investors. Administrative reforms were undertaken in the army and the navy, but they did not prove to be substantive, as both institutions were rooted in Napoleonic era strategy and tactics. This would not change until foreign military missions from France and the United States offered alternative viewpoints for Peru's armed forces after the Cáceres years.[28]

Cáceres was again elected president in July 1894 with expansive executive powers. But he was becoming increasingly unpopular. The Civilistas who yearned for a civilian president with direct ties to the landed classes wanted badly to occupy the Pizarro Palace. Not having a strong enough political figure of their own, the Civilistas turned to the exile Nicolás de Piérola as their revolutionary standard-bearer. Organizing support throughout Peru, Piérola launched a movement know as the Revolution of 1895, which plunged Peru into civil war.

Known as the democratic caudillo, Piérola was able to unite the diverse opposing forces arrayed against Cáceres and depose him in March 1895. With his inauguration as president in September 1895, after an uncontested victory in the presidential election the previous July, Piérola laid the groundwork for the Aristocratic Republic (1895–1919). The dominance of the caudillos in Peruvian politics would go into abeyance but would certainly not disappear from Peruvian politics.

CONCLUSION

As the former center of Spanish colonial power in South America, Peru was a latecomer to the ranks of republican nations in the region. In the aftermath of Bolívar's efforts to free Peru from Spanish colonialism, the new nation was fraught with fractious caudillismo and resultant civil strife that delayed the process of nation building until the mid-19th century. The highly profitable guano trade connected Peru to the world market system, and its profits provided an illusion of prosperity that masked an economy that was poorly integrated, lacking in sufficient capitalization, and slow to modernize.

Ramón Castilla, the most politically astute of Peru's early caudillos was able to begin Peru's formal nation building process by eliminating the Indian head tax, abolishing slavery with compensation, and overseeing the drafting of the constitution of 1856.

Only the era of the Sendero Luminoso insurgency in the late 20th century surpasses the age of the War of the Pacific in its destructiveness for the Peruvian people, economy, and national spirit. Although Peru made rapid and important strides toward recovery in the decade after the War of the Pacific concluded, there was also a great deal of soul searching during that time among all sectors of Peruvian society. But ongoing issues such as the status of Tacna and Arica, the modernization of the military, and the development of the concept of national defense as an economic and social reality would all be issues of supreme importance in the ensuing decades.

NOTES

1. Timothy E. Anna, *The Fall of the Royal Government in Peru* (Lincoln: University of Nebraska Press, 1980), 29–30.

2. Leon G. Campbell, *The Military and Society in Colonial Peru, 1750–1810* (Philadelphia: American Philosophical Society, 1978), 223.

3. Charles Walker, *Smoldering Ashes: Cuzco and the Creation of Republican Peru, 1780–1840* (Durham: Duke University Press, 1999), 100.

4. John Fisher, "The Royalist Regime in the Viceroyalty of Peru, 1820–1824," *Journal of Latin American Studies* 32, no. 1 (2000), 59–62.

5. Peter F. Klarén, *Peru: Society and Nationhood in the Andes* (Oxford: Oxford University Press, 2000), 130–131.

6. Ibid., 131–133.

7. Ibid., 134.

8. Ibid., 142–143.

9. For a valuable analysis of Peru's guano-based economy see Paul Gootenberg, *Between Silver and Guano: Commercial Policy and the State in Postindependence Peru* (Princeton: Princeton University Press, 1989).

10. For the conditions of bonded servitude for Chinese plantation workers in Peru see Michael Gonzales, *Plantation Agriculture and Social Control in Northern Peru, 1875–1933* (Austin: University of Texas Press, 1985).

11. Watt Stewart, *Bondage in Peru: A History of the Chinese Coolie in Peru, 1849–1874* (Westport, CT: Greenwood Press, 1951), 97. Stewart's work remains the standard study of Chinese coolie labor in Peru after more than a half century.

12. Ibid.

13. Jorge Basadre, *Historia de la república del Perú, 1822–1933* (Lima: Editorial Universitaria, 1983) vol. 3, 313.

14. Jeffrey Klaiber, *The Catholic Church in Peru, 1821–1985: A Social History* (Washington, DC: Catholic University of America Press, 1992), 55.

15. Nils Jacobsen, *Mirages of Transition: The Peruvian Altiplano, 1780–1930* (Berkeley: University of California Press, 1993), 146.

16. Ibid., 20.

17. Klarén, *Peru,* 213–214.

18. Ibid., 172.

19. William F. Sater, *Andean Tragedy: Fighting the War of the Pacific, 1879–1884* (Lincoln: University of Nebraska Press, 2007), 23–24. This work is the best recent scholarship on the War of the Pacific and its military aspects.

20. Basadre, *Historia,* vol. 6, 105

21. Sater, *Andean Tragedy,* 238–239.

22. Basadre, vol. 6, 54–55.

23. Sater, *Andean Tragedy,* 259–262.

24. Ibid., 325.

25. Ibid., 336–337.

26. Jacobsen, *Mirages of Transition,* 178.

27. Klarén, *Peru,* 191–192.

28. Basadre, *Historia,* vol. 7, 116–127.

Valle Sagrado: The Urubamba Valley shown above was considered the most important lands of the Inca and was known as the "Sacred Valley." Courtesy of Jorge Ortiz-Sotelo.

Club Union: Hotel Maury and the Club Union were established in the mid-19th century facing Lima's main square. The Club was the center of Lima's conservative social elites. The welcoming sign "to our American Friends" reflected the strong pro-U.S. foreign policy of the Augusto B. Leguía administration (1919–1930). Courtesy of Jorge Ortiz-Sotelo.

An open regional market in Tarapoto in the Department of San Martín. These markets are a vital component of rural Peru's interchange of agricultural products and other goods. They have blossomed after road networks have been rebuilt since the systematic destruction of the Shining Path War. Courtesy of Jorge Ortiz-Sotelo.

A monument to the humble street peddlers of Peru in Juliaca, Department of Puno. Throughout Peru and Latin America, peddlers such as these have formed what is called the "informal" economy that goes untaxed and unregulated but provides incomes for large sectors of the work force. Courtesy of Jorge Ortiz-Sotelo.

Three generations of Peruvian highland women preparing cloth for dyeing in the village of Chinchero. Courtesy of Erin C. Masterson.

5

Aristocrats to Populists in Peruvian National Affairs, 1895–1930

Peru continued to recover from the ravages of the War of the Pacific during Piérola's second presidency and beyond. These years also witnessed the consolidation of power of an oligarchy that had aggressively diversified its economic holdings into all sectors of the Peruvian economy. Nevertheless, the economic and political hegemony of this powerful elite did not go unchallenged. Peru's working classes and middle sectors began to mobilize during the first decades of the new century. Innovative political thinkers also challenged the old order in ways that were quite appealing to the emerging classes. Finally, the armed forces, so badly battered after their defeat by Chile, began to slowly rebuild and modernize.

After World War I, the military would become the principal arbiter of Peruvian political affairs and often the primary political player. The legacy of caudillismo would linger even as the armed forces sought desperately to professionalize and eradicate personalism from their ranks. These events evolved against the backdrop of increasing dominance of foreign capital in the Peruvian economy. This was made possible by the economic cooperation of the Peruvian elites with the dictator President Augusto Leguía (1919–1930). During this *Oncenio* (11-year rule), Leguía forged very strong alliances with U.S. capitalists in most areas of Peru's economy.

PHILOSOPHERS OF PROGRESS

Following the disastrous defeat in the War of the Pacific, a creative and influential school of Peruvian intellectuals known as the Generation of 1900 began a searching examination of themes relating to Peru's national character in hopes of understanding the tragedy that had befell the nation. These Peruvian thinkers were somewhat comparable to the Spanish Generation of '98, especially the influential Miguel de Unumuno.

Though not of the same intellectual prominence as Unamuno, Manuel González Prada subjected all members of Peruvian society to a biting iconoclastic critique that was unsparing in its sweep. Badly disillusioned by Peru's military defeat by Chile, González Prada sought answers away from Peru in Europe for most of the 1890s. González Prada was particularly inspired by the positivism of Auguste Comte, and he began to espouse the importance of scientific reasoning, technocratic education, and European (white) immigration. González Prada bitterly attacked the Hispanic traditions and the subjugation and isolation of Peru's Indians. He called for Peru's young leaders to replace the older corrupt generation, whose members should be in their "tombs" rather than in positions of power. However, he soon despaired of Peru's elitist political leaders ever being capable of passing meaningful reforms that could mitigate the suffering of the nation's indigenous masses. By the early 1900s González Prada was espousing anarchist views and advocating revolutionary solutions to resolve problems of poverty and misery. González Prado's ideas would influence the thinking of many other revolutionists, including the early anti-imperialist Víctor Raul Haya de la Torre.

Grounded in a much more conservative form of positivism were three intellectuals from Peru's elite. Philosopher Javier Prado, legal scholar Vicente Villarán, and social philosopher Mariano Cornejo all argued that Peru must move forward and away from the traditions of its Spanish past. Like the followers of Comte in Brazil, they had great faith in the power of education and technology to modernize Peru. But in their minds, this could only be accomplished by a select elite of highly educated scholar/technocrats and not by the masses. Regarding the Indian population, this group saw ethnic assimilation through education as the only solution for the "Indian problem." Few Peruvian thinkers had yet arrived at an acceptance of what would be called *indegenismo* (Indianess) or the acceptance of indigenous culture as viable path for Peru's social affairs. This would await the powerful and creative thinking of Mariátegui and others in the 1920s. Víctor Andrés Belaúnde, a prominent educator, philosopher, journalist, and diplomat in Peru during the mid-20th century, would amalgamate the ideas of these positivist pioneers with French idealist and Catholic philosophy to arrive at the concept of *Perunidad* (Peruvianess). This theory called for an integrated national consciousness that could be achieved through social and cultural conciliation and not through revolution or class conflict.

TOWARD A NEW MILITARY TRADITION

Of all the problems facing the Piérola administration in 1895, none was more pressing than the need to rebuild Peru's badly damaged armed forces. First and foremost a caudillo, Andrés Cáceres, Peru's leader after the War of the Pacific, did not really address the institutional weaknesses that lay at the foundation of Peru's military defeat by Chile. Seeking a more professional army that he could better control, Piérola looked to Europe to recast the military in a new professional framework. Peru's past military defeats and the continuing military expansion of Chile under the aegis of a Prussian military mission contracted in 1885 convinced Piérola of the need to develop a small but battle-ready army subordinate to civilian presidential control. As a counter to the Prussian model, Piérola looked to its European rival, France, for military inspiration. Despite the latter's defeat in the Franco-Prussian War of 1871, Peru's president was impressed with the French army's progress in preparing border fortifications and sustaining discipline in civil military affairs. What was not fully understood by Piérola or any of his presidential successors until the 1960s was the French army's expertise in colonial affairs. The French army's civilizing mission would be inculcated into the Peruvian army's sense of mission with great intellectual impact during the seven decades following the arrival of the military mission in 1896.

This small French army mission was headed by Colonel (later General) Paul Clément, and arrived in September 1896. All of its officers boasted experience in the French colonies. Major institutional change was initiated very quickly. The Peruvian military academy, the Escuela Militar del Chorrillos, was established to train and educate new officers for the army. Previous attempts to establish a military institution had been fraught with inconsistencies in funding, curriculum, and the divisive influence of caudillismo. The first class at Chorrillos graduated in 1898. Very soon a national conscription law was passed and a new military justice code modeled on that of France was enacted. Most important in the professionalization of the army, modern norms for determining promotions, tactical organization, fiscal policy, and administration were also enacted. For the first time, Peru's soldiers now had a mission that was guided by traditions applicable to both standard military doctrine and what would later be called civic action, or the developmental doctrine. These development initiatives were being implemented in North Africa and Indo-China by the French army at the very time of the first French military mission to Peru. Thus the Peruvian army benefitted from this evolving perspective of nation building in the poorest of lands.

While teams of French trainers were working in Peru, the French army was consolidating its administration in Algeria and Indochina, and French soldiers were dying by the millions in the trenches of the Western Front. Awed by the French army's courage, Peru's soldiers were prepared to listen to nearly all aspects of their mentors' professional principles except one. Yet, the concept of the "great mute," as the apolitical French army was known, was never accepted in Peru's military barracks. This fact would have enormous implications for Peru's pubic affairs in the 20th century.[1]

Little more than a decade after the arrival of the French mission, the Lima army garrison, under the command of Colonel Oscar R. Benavides, overthrew elected president Guillermo Billinghurst in February 1914. When Billinghurst reduced the army's budget, armed Lima's workers, and initiated a broad-based social and political challenge to Peru's ruling oligarchy, he was arrested by the army and exiled. Benavides himself had an aristocratic pedigree. He would become one of the foremost military caudillos of the 20th century. Although the officer corps may have been studying how to deal with the nation's poor, its leadership was not prepared to allow the workers to mobilize and potentially pose a major threat to the stability of the established order. Not yet feeling comfortable as the chief political leader of the nation, Benavides handed over power to a civilian successor in 1915 and returned to the barracks. At that time, World War I was increasingly affecting economic trends in the Peruvian economy, a development that would be profoundly important for Peru's future.

EXPORT-LED ECONOMY

During the first three decades of the 20th century, Peru's economy was dominated by exported commodities, especially cotton, minerals, and petroleum. The sugar industry, a mainstay of the economy in the 19th century, had not yet recovered from the devastating war with Chile. The rate of growth in the export sector of the Peruvian economy was dynamic, averaging 7 percent per year during this period. The mining and petroleum sectors especially catered to the demands of a modernizing world economy that heavily emphasized construction materials and petrochemicals. In the mining industry, copper assumed leading importance and maintained its place throughout most of the 20th century. In the early 1900s, domestic producers enjoyed a relatively robust role in the cotton and petroleum sectors. This changed as foreign capital, most particularly large U.S-owned industry, overwhelmed the native producers and captured large sectors of these formative industries.

The cotton industry, a crop originally produced with African slave and Chinese coolie labor in the 19th century, was forced to adopted new labor systems after the War of the Pacific. Sharecropping, known in Peru as *yanconaje*, was adopted on the large coastal haciendas. With the financial means to reclaim marginal land, wealthy cotton growers cultivated substantial new lands by expanding irrigation and clearing new acreage. Smaller farmers, particularly Japanese immigrants, were also able to enter into cotton production as prices remained favorable until the Great Depression. Control of the marketing of cotton by British firms did not substantially reduce profits from the cotton sector in Peru. Nevertheless, with the exception of the Banco Italiano, Peruvian financial firms were reluctant to capitalize the native sector. This was unfortunate, since cotton, along with copper and petroleum, offered great economic possibilities for independent Peruvian producers. Peruvian cotton producers demonstrated energy and skill in adapting to the challenges of the demanding agricultural setting. A Pisco, *hacendado* Fermin Tanguis, developed a hybrid and disease-resistant strain of cotton after World War I that would soon be adopted by Peruvian growers. Innovations such as this assured that the cotton sector in Peru would be more domestically oriented and diversified in ownership than any other major sector of the Peruvian economy. But while profits were substantial, especially between 1916 and 1925, they were not sufficient enough to be reinvested in other prominent sectors of the Peruvian economy. Given the amount of economic pressure generated by foreign investors in the burgeoning mining and petroleum sectors, this further reduced Peru's control over its key resources.[2]

Peru's mining industry had been the foundation of its economy since the conquest. But the country's as-yet inadequate infrastructure and the damage wrought by the War of the Pacific posed heavy obstacles to the future development of gold, silver, iron, lead, zinc, and vanadium deposits. Thorp and Bertram note that because of the high costs of production the defining characteristic of the Peruvian mining sector in the period from 1901 to 1930 was denationalization. For example, the U.S.-owned Cerro de Pasco Mining Company and the Anaconda Company came to dominate the copper industry by the beginning of the Depression. The growth rate of copper value from 1890 to 1930 increased spectacularly. Two U.S-owned companies benefited most from this copper boom. This is significant because copper accounted for nearly half of the value of Peru's metal production in 1930.

Significantly, the U.S penetration of the mining industry was not aimed at exploration and development of new mines. Rather, highly capitalized corporations, such as Cerro de Pasco, focused their attention on the purchase of many undercapitalized Peruvian mining ventures that had little chance of long-term success without some form of subsidies from the Peruvian government. This type of aid was certainly not forthcoming from Peru's political leadership during this era. Peru's weak state was unwilling or unable to regulate the business practices of these huge corporations. The most blatant example of corporate misdeeds during this era was the Cerro de Pasco's decision to build a massive smelter in the La Oroya district in 1922 without installing pollution filters. As a result, within a decade toxic wastes from the smelter had degraded surrounding pastureland and killed livestock to the extent that more than a half million acres were rendered unproductive. Local landholders were forced to abandon thousands of hectares of previously productive land. Cerro de Pasco then bought much of the devalued land, installed the necessary filters, and soon became the dominant cattle producing operation on newly restored pasture land.

Peru's petroleum deposits were originally exploited in the northwest coast region where access was relatively easy. The Negritos oil field close to the hacienda La Brea y Parinas was joined by the Lobitos and Zorritos fields in the same general region. From the beginning of reasonably large-scale petroleum production, foreign interests were heavily involved. Initial exploration and development by the Michael Grace firm and a London-based company were eventually supplanted in power and profits by the International Petroleum Company, a Canadian-based subsidiary of Standard Oil of New Jersey that gained control of the highly productive Negritos field. When a petroleum law, highly favorable to foreign interests, was passed in 1922 by the Leguía administration, petroleum production soared.

Oil led all Peruvian exports by value in 1924, and by 1929 it accounted for nearly a third of all export earnings.[3] Because of the very low royalty tax on petroleum that had been negotiated by the Leguía government, in addition to very favorable labor costs and a near monopoly on the local market, I.P.C. was able to sustain an astounding profit margin of 70 percent well into the 20th century. Perhaps no other aspect of Peru's export-led economy reflect the depth to which foreign interests came to dominate the nation's economy than I.P.C.'s role in oil production. It is not surprising that it would be the first foreign corporation nationalized by the Velasco regime when it claimed power in October 1968.

Other sectors of the Peruvian economy, such as sugar, wool, and rubber, lagged behind the previously mentioned commodities in export earnings. Still, these were labor-intensive industries that witnessed significant changes in production strategies in the decades before the Depression. North coast sugar estates in Peru sustained serious damage by the forays of Captain Patricio Lynch during the War of the Pacific. By 1900 one of the most productive areas for sugar production in Peru, the Chicama Valley in the department of La Libertad, saw the consolidation of sugar production to three main producers, all with recent immigrant origins. The Larco family, Italian immigrants who settled in Peru in the 1860s; the Gildemeisters, German immigrants who arrived in the 1880s; and the Grace Corporation, based in New York and founded by William R. Grace, who originally immigrated to Peru from Ireland in the 1850s. All three enterprises were well capitalized and expanded by purchasing smaller and less competitive haciendas in the Chicama Valley. Similar but less pronounced patterns of concentration of sugar holding occurred in coastal areas to the Cañete valley south of Lima.

One of the most acute problems in the sugar sector was a lack of labor. After the abolition of African slavery and the ending of Chinese contract labor in the 1870s, the planters tried to make do with seasonal Indian labor from the sierra. This rarely proved satisfactory and in the late 1890s, planters turned to contracted Japanese immigrant labor to meet their needs. This proved to be a failure, as harsh working conditions quickly drove the Japanese workers off the plantations and into the coastal cities, where they sought new forms of work. By the first decades of the 20th century, Peruvian sugar planters were mechanizing their production as much as possible in the face of continuing labor shortages. Still, the sugar industry did very well through World War I as world prices of the commodity remained high. Significantly, sugar production remained largely in Peruvian hands throughout the first three decades of the 20th century, unlike most of Peru's main commodity exports. The 1920s, however, witnessed a decline in sugar prices that prevented this particular agricultural sector from contributing to surplus income for the Peruvian state, as it had done during the previous three decades.

Rubber and wool production occupied the lower rungs on the ladder of Peruvian exports during this era. Rubber experienced a boom in the remote regions of the selva in the years before and during World War I. The labor supply was provided by local Indians and small numbers of Japanese migrant laborers who had drifted in from Bolivia and harvested the rubber from isolated groves of rubber trees. The Peruvian Amazon Company was the primary business operation in the selva region along the Putumayo River. This company's treatment of its Indian laborers was so harsh that it drew vocal international protests. The *seringeros* (rubber workers) often made as much as four times what a sugar worker would earn on the coast. But the laborer's life was terribly lonely and subject to an array of hardships, most especially illness from tropical diseases. Rubber production peaked in Peru and the Western Hemisphere as a whole in 1912. Rubber plantations in the Far East were better organized and financed and eclipsed rubber producers in Peru, Brazil, and Bolivia by World War I. The economy of Iquitos, Peru's Amazon River town, was closely tied to the rubber boom. The collapse of the industry after World War I had a devastating effect on the city's economy and population, which had dropped to only 15,000 by the beginning of the 1920s. The rubber industry never really influenced the mainstream economy of Peru, since the export of this commodity was directed through the Amazon basin by way of Iquitos. Those relatively few local businesses in the city lost everything in a saga that was repeated among the *seringeros* in Bolivia and Brazil after World War I.

Wool, of course, was a primary commodity of the Peruvian sierra for well over a thousand years. The coarser wool of the llama warmly clothed the commoners of the Inca Empire. The finer fleece of the alpaca and highly prized wool of the rare vicuña was reserved for the finer fabrics worn by the elites. In Peru after 1900, wool declined as a valued commodity for external trade to only about 10 percent of the value of exports in the years before the Depression. Wool exports were roughly divided equally by volume between sheep wool and alpaca wool during this period. Most wool from sheep was produced on the increasingly larger haciendas in the central and southern sierra. Most of the alpaca production occurred on indigenous lands in the southern sierra. Cattle were also raised in the central sierra by the hacendados, thus reducing the amount of pasture land available for wool production. From a regional perspective, the southern sierra suffered a long decline in wool exports throughout the 1920s. These hardships continued during the 1930s as major changes in land ownership occurred in the south of Peru. Arequipa was the center of the southern wool trade and the city's economic fortunes reflected the long downturn in the wool economy during this era. Landholding relationships between the often absent hacienda owners and Indian herdsmen were characteristic of this era. Community solidarity and Andean traditions were thus put to a very severe test among the indigenous population. Jacobsen notes that the fluctuation of wool prizes, population pressure, and an increasingly powerful Hispanicized class of landowners forced thousands of Indian herdsman from their lands. Their fate would be to become colonos on the haciendas of the moneyed and powerful.[4]

In examining the Peruvian export sector during the first three decades of the 20th century, it is important to understand that strident economic nationalism, while proclaimed by the Peruvian left in the 1920s, did not become government policy until the late 1960s. In sum, economic nationalism, at least in some limited form, might have allowed the Peruvian mining sector to further develop local technical skills and reduce the dependence on foreign firms to extract Peru's uniquely diverse mineral resources. It is not difficult to imagine that if Peruvian producers developed new strains of disease-resistant cotton, then others in the mining industry could have perfected and installed better smelters with financial support from the government. But this was not the mindset of the political or financial leadership of Peru before 1930.

IMMIGRATION AND LABOR

During the first decades of the 20th century Peru was still unable to attract large numbers of immigrants in the manner of Brazil and Argentina. Brazil, and Argentina to a lesser extent, became settler destinations because of their substantial amounts of arable land. Peru had neither the available agricultural land nor the economic opportunities of the two larger countries. Yet, it still became the destination for a substantial number of Japanese and Italians, and smaller numbers of Spaniards and Eastern Europeans. Let us first turn to the experience of the *Nikkei* (Japanese immigrants), which began in Peru in April 1899.

Like earlier Japanese immigrants to Hawaii, those 790 Nikkei who arrived in Peru in 1899 aboard the *Sakura-maru* were males destined to labor in the sugarcane fields of the north coast. They were required to work 10 to 12 hour days in the fields or the sugar mill for approximately $12.00 per month. Rarely, however, were the hours so limited or the wages that high. Most of the Nikkei were from Southern Japan and nearly all had the intention of returning to their homeland after earning enough savings to ease their family's poverty and provide for better lives for themselves. This re-migration rarely occurred for Japanese in Peru as the return rate for these immigrants was less than 15 percent. From the outset, the Japanese sugar workers' circumstances on the sugar haciendas were miserable. Sickness, especially malaria, took a heavy toll. Relations with the management of the haciendas were often hostile. Conditions on the Cayaltí and San Nicolás were particularly bad. Japanese sugar workers struck in protest over the failure to pay wages and the poor working conditions. Soldiers from nearby garrisons were sometimes called in to suppress the very militant sugar workers. Many of the original Nikkei petitioned their government's officials in Peru to arrange for their return to Japan. But a lack of ships and no money for the return fare stranded all but a few of these first immigrants in Peru. Many of these Nikkei protested by fleeing the plantations and going to the urban center of Lima and its environs.

Despite continuing harsh conditions on the sugar haciendas, Japanese colonization companies and the government in Tokyo paid little heed to the plight of the immigrants. So the flow of the Nikkei from Japan's southern provinces continued well into the early 1930s. But by this time the core of the Japanese community was situated in metropolitan Lima, where eventually 85 percent of the Japanese in Peru would come to reside. Still, some hard-working Japanese tried their fortunes in agriculture, where the odds were very long against success. Still, Japanese cotton producers did quite well in the Chancay, Rimac, and Pachacamac river valleys after the early 1920s. Using intensive agricultural techniques, clearing and improving marginal non-irrigated land with long hours of hard work, these Peruvian Nikkei did not achieve spectacular economic success, but they made a solid economic place for themselves in a country where they were not generally accepted or admired.

The Japanese immigrant community in Peru was very close knit. Centered primarily in Lima, they organized themselves by prefectural associations known as *Kenjinkai* (home districts in Japan), by occupation as well as commercial, agricultural, and industrial activity. The Japanese in Peru often created their own lending agencies that were restricted to their own communities. This created access to credit that they would otherwise not have had.

Japanese language schools and an active press served the Nikkei community after 1920.

During the 1920s the Nikkei population grew to more than 20,000 under the supportive leadership of Leguía, who had been instrumental in bringing the first Japanese to Peru in 1899. Helping to keep the Japanese informed was a Japanese press, best represented by the *Rima Nippo* (*Lima Japanese News*). The circulation of this paper was substantial, reaching about one in four of the Japanese residents in Peru. Originally, Japanese newspapers were published exclusively in Japanese, but as time went on and the second-generation Japanese (*Nisei*) struggled with their native language, bilingual editions in Japanese and Spanish were published. By the end of the 1920s the Japanese were the dominant group in commercial enterprises in the Lima metropolitan area.[5]

As previously noted, because of the Italians' early settlement patterns and the relative ethnic homogeneity of the Italian immigrants, the Italian community was well established in Peru by the beginning of the 20th century. Most of the Italians in Peru had origins in the Ligurian region in Italy's northwest. These immigrants were reasonably well educated, unlike those from southern Italy who were migrating in much larger numbers to Argentina and Brazil. They had come individually and not as part of the subsidized groups who were brought to Argentina and Brazil to toil on the docks of Buenos Aires, as agricultural laborers on the Pampas or as coffee pickers in southern Brazil. The Italian community in Peru achieved its population peak in 1906 at 13,000. Thereafter, with the Italian economy improving and Fascist propaganda discouraging emigration, the Italian community declined significantly in population but certainly not in influence. Italians were vital participants in textiles, insurance, and manufacturing. But it was in banking where they most dominated the economy, controlling half of Peru's banking activities including the formidable Banco Italiano. More than 100 of Peru's manufacturing establishments were Italian owned. Peru's Italians were well integrated into Peruvian society by the late 1920s, unlike their counterparts in Argentina and Brazil. The *descamisados* (shirtless ones) had no counterparts in Peru, as few Italians remained within the ranks of the laboring classes as the Great Depression approached. What must be understood about Peru's Italian community was that it was very small compared to those in Argentina, Brazil, and the United States, where their numbers were well over one million. Therefore, the Italian emigrant profile in Peru was nearly invisible. However, despite the small size of the Italian community in Peru, they still had a great deal of economic power, which allowed them to influence Peru's government of the 1930s, especially the pro-Fascist regime of Augusto Benavides (1933–1939). In no way were Peruvian Italians subjected to the virulent prejudice manifested in the United States or to the prejudice the Japanese would be subjected to in Peru.[6]

LABOR, THE INDIAN, AND THE ALIANZA POPULAR REVLOUCIONARIA AMERICANA

Like most other Latin American nations, Peru's laborers began to organize with some effectiveness during the last decade of the 19th century. Because the nation's economy was so diverse and important sectors such as mining and plantation agriculture were so distant from urban centers, large national unions such as the American Federation of Labor in the United States did not arise in Peru. Estimates place the size of the laboring classes at approximately 120,000 by the turn of the 20th century, with the largest concentrations in mining, sugar, cotton, wool, rubber, petroleum, and transportation. As might be expected, the best organized laborers were in the Lima-Callao metropolitan area. Strikes began to become commonplace among dockworkers and factory and railroad workers in Lima as the last century came to a close. These work stoppages were usually in response to the standard issues of pay, working hours, and labor conditions. Peru's Congress did pass an important law in 1911 creating workman's compensation for work-related accidents. In fact, significant numbers of mutual aid societies were providing their own low-cost insurance for their members in the years before World War I. Nevertheless, militant agricultural workers often faced a grim fate. A strike in the Chicama Valley by sugar refinery workers in 1912 resulted in the deaths of 500 workers. Local police and army units were often brought in to quickly quell strikes on cotton and sugar plantations.

Anarcho-syndicalism, a powerful ideology that became very appealing to workers in Spain and Argentina, also found significant followers in Peru. One of the most prominent of these anarchists was Manuel González Prada, who had by then despaired of a ever reaching a peaceful solution to Peru's divided society. Anarchist ideas may have flourished as a result of the arrival of immigrants from Italy and Spain, where anarchist ideas were widely promoted. Radical periodicals such as *La Parias* founded by González Prada in 1904 found avid readers among the laborers in Lima, Trujillo in northern Peru, and Arequipa in the south. González Prada proclaimed, "[Strikes] awaken the conscience of the worker, make him understand his value as a human being, as a social factor, as an element of production, they link the destiny of workers of every country by teaching them they are the largest and strongest element in this absurd and egotistical society."[7] The newspaper *La Protesta* (*Protest*) was founded in 1911, furthering the anarcho-syndicalist line. That year witnessed the first general strike in Lima. Led by textile workers, the strike was quite successful and marked the high point of labor organizing in Peru before World War I. In essence, the election of Guillermo Billinghurst in 1912 also served as evidence of how powerful labor had become. His election is generally considered to be the first example of a popularly elected president in Peru's modern history. Presaging a strategy adopted by Juan Perón in Argentina after World War II, Billinghurst tried to use the support of the laboring classes to balance growing opposition to his policies by the oligarchy and the army. It was a dangerous game, and he lost. Once Billinghurst tried to arm a workers' militia, the army acted under the leadership of Colonel Oscar R. Benavides, commander of the Lima garrison. They overthrew the Billinghurst government in early February 1914 and the short-lived worker's republic came to an end.[8]

As might be expected, the World War I years brought an upsurge in prices for much of the commodities in Peru's export-oriented economy. Mining and wool exports experienced substantial gains, as did copper after 1917. Most of all, the war allowed the United States, particularly economic giants like W. R. Grace and the I.P.C. to extend their control of key sectors of the Peruvian economy. With the opening of the Panama Canal in 1913 and the decline of British and German economic interests as a result of the war, the configuration of foreign economic interests in Peru began to change dramatically.[9] This had significant implications for Peruvian labor as they now confronted powerful economic forces such as Cerro de Pasco, W. R. Grace, and I.P.C., which could not be as easily coerced through collective action as native companies had been during previous decades. The dominance of U.S. capital would become even more pronounced during the Oncenio, or 11-year dictatorship of Augusto Leguía (1919–1930). This period in Peruvian history was launched just as organized labor showed its strength with the Lima general strike of May 1919. Led by many anarcho-syndicalists leaders, the strike drew substantial support from the working class but was a failure in terms of gaining concessions from management. Tellingly, the violence and looting that accompanied the strike was directed at shops owned by Chinese and Japanese merchants. These groups would be targeted again over the course of the next three decades, in times of political and economic uncertainty.

In northern Peru, especially in the Chicama and Santa Catalina valley near Trujillo, the consolidation of medium- and small-scale sugar operations into big sugar, as represented by the W. R. Grace Corporation estates and those lands gathered together by the Gildemeister and British Sugar Companies, gave rise to a large and militant rural working class, many of whom continued to be activists from World War I through the Velasco reforms in the mid-1970s. These sugar workers provided an important political base for the emergence of Peru's first and foremost populist political party of the 20th Century, the *Alianza Popular Revloucionaria Americana* (American Popular Revolutionary Alliance, or APRA). In its initial phase APRA was primarily an expression of the many grievances expressed since the first decades of the 20th century by the wage laborers and displaced small capitalists associated with the north coast sugar industry. However, as Peter Klarén noted in his study of the early

ARPA, the party leadership was always trying to balance the support of the radical sugar workers and other labor elements with that of the emerging middle class, who also resented foreign capital but feared the consequences of radical politics.[10]

The labor organization and strife of the World War I era created a venue for one of Peru's most prominent political leaders to emerge. Víctor Raúl Haya de la Torre emerged as a student organizer during these years. He soon expanded his activities to labor organizing and agitation. By the mid-1920s he was one of Peru's most well known voices of anti-imperialism. Born on February 22, 1895, in Trujillo to a family with aristocratic origins but of relatively modest means, Haya (as he came to be known) had an interest in politics from an early age; he is said to have spurned childhood toys for self-made models of make-believe nations he would then administer. Haya was raised near the ancient ruins of Chan Chan, which he frequently visited. He often claimed that he had a physical resemblance to the people of Chimú and often insisted that he was spiritually linked to the ancient pre-Columbian civilization of Peru's past. Much of his complex philosophy was shaped during his early 20s through his association with the Trujillo Bohemians, a group of artists, poets, and journalist that included the renowned poet César Vallejo and the journalist Antenor Orrego. The prevailing mood of this group was disdain for the ruling classes of Trujillo and a profound distrust for foreign capitalism.[11]

When Haya moved to Lima in 1919, he quickly seized upon the momentum of the university reform movement that was then sweeping Latin America, and he placed himself at the center of university and working-class politics. As president of the student federation at the venerable University of San Marcos, Haya established intimate contacts between student activists and militant workers. The ranks of the working class were growing rapidly during the 1920s in Lima as economic prosperity drew more than 60,000 migrants from the sierra to the urban center. Haya took a major role in the establishment of an institutional link between students and workers with the creation of the González Prada popular universities. These universities staffed by college students in Lima were an attempt to unite the working classes and the young intellectual community. In January 1921, for example, nearly 1,000 Lima workers graduated from a popular university program staffed by students. These classes were held in theaters and other venues and provided important educational opportunities for the city's poor. These popular universities had the potential for creating one of the most powerful multi-class alliances Peru had yet witnessed. But a permanent union was not to be.

Haya was criticized by his opponents as a demagogue or an opportunistic charlatan. His opponents at San Marcos University deeply resented his efforts that politicized the university and undermined the learning community for traditional students. But to the APRA leader, the popular universities were a phenomenon that saw the "great divide between intellectuals and workers bridged in rituals that had some of the qualities of baptism into a new life."[12]

Haya's activist politics culminated in May 1923 when he organized a large demonstration of workers and students in Lima that opposed Leguía's campaign to dedicate Peru to the Sacred Heart of Jesus. This campaign was the dictator's attempt to reduce religious freedom and build an open alliance with the Catholic Church. Haya united many anti-Leguía groups together in opposition, including Free Masons, workers, students, and the far left. The rally was a success and Leguía backed down. But Haya had overplayed his hand and was soon exiled from Peru along with many of his key political supporters, including Luis Heysen, Manuel Seoane, and leaders of his workers vanguard. Haya would remain abroad for the next eight years in North America and Europe, drawing on the heady doctrines of Trotskyism in Soviet Russia, Nazism in Germany, and *Indigenismo* from one its founders in revolutionary Mexico, José Vasconselos. Haya would later confirm that these travels were the most formative period of his life, when much of his later ideas began to crystallize.[13]

Haya's overseas travels brought him in 1923 to Mexico, where he was influenced by José Vasconselos, the country's minister of education and a vocal proponent of the glorification of Mexico's indigenous past. It was not long before Haya felt comfortable enough in the highly nationalist and evolutionary atmosphere of Mexico to announce the formation of a political alliance with hemispheric ambitions. This alliance was an off-shoot of the APRA in Peru. This political group represented a synthesis of anti-imperialist, indigenous, and populist ideals. Haya chose, for example, to refer to Latin America as Indo-America in deference to both its Indian origins and the large numbers of native peoples who were seen to be exploited by foreign capitalism and the elites in their own countries.

APRA would never have any real appeal outside Peru, but the image of a pan-American alliance of like-minded reformers was a device that Haya exploited for most of his long political career. It must be said that for all of its ups and downs in the nearly nine decades of its existence, APRA is the only political party that has sustained itself as a meaningful political entity. The election of Alan García to the presidency in 2006 as the candidate of the APRA serves as evidence of this.

While Haya was in exile throughout the 1920s, an alternative and influential voice from the left emerged. José Carlos Mariátegui (1894–1930) is viewed today as one of Latin America's most modern and innovative Marxist thinkers. He was born in Moquegua in southern Peru in 1894. He lived an early life of poverty and thus lacked extensive formal education. Still, he read widely. Remarkably, although Mariátegui was slowed all his life by debilitating illness, he nevertheless produced an important body of work that belies his short life span. His intellectual awakening apparently had rather practical beginnings as a copyboy for one of Lima's most important newspapers, *La Prensa.* This led to a career in journalism and as an essayist. While working at *El Tiempo* during the last years of World War I, Mariátegui commented on daily political events in Lima with acerbic wit. He also found time to write poetry. It was his penchant for biting political commentary on Peru's powerful institutions that would be his initial undoing. In June 1918, in the first issue of the newspaper *Nuestra Epoca,* the journalist attacked the social make up and the moral character of the Peruvian army. The newspaper closed its doors after the publication of only two issues. Within a year, Mariátegui had so alienated the newly installed Leguía regime that the radical journalist was given the choice of the Lima penitentiary or exile to Europe with a modest government stipend. This exile would last from October 1919 until March 1923.[14]

Very much like Haya de la Torre, Mariátegui's European travels shaped his later thinking dramatically. He spent most of his time in Italy where he met and married his wife Ana Chiappe His travels also took him to France, Germany, Austria, Switzerland, and Czechoslovakia. During his time in Europe, Mariátegui became aware of the growing militancy of the European working class, made contact with the nascent communist party cells, became familiar with the workings of the Third International, and came to understand better the Bolshevik Revolution and Mussolini's Fascism. Unlike Haya, Mariátegui found nothing to admire about Mussolini's ideas or methods. But like the APRA leader, he was much impressed with the energy and discipline of these dynamic European political movements.

Despite a worsening of his health that led to the amputation of his one functioning leg, Mariátegui produced his most vital work during the four years before his premature death in 1930. With the publication of the highly influential journal *Amauta* (*Teacher*) in 1926, the Peruvian left finally found its most articulate journalistic voice. The editor of *Amauta* sought works from abroad, to include essays by the Mexican painter Diego Rivera, the Spanish philosopher Miguel de Unamuno, and his French contemporary Henri Barbusse, but mainly the journal focused on literary criticism and socialist commentary. Indeed, *Amauta* is seen by many Peruvian intellectuals as one of the most important mediums for the exchange of ideas on national issues ever published. With Haya still in exile, Mariátegui's influence with the left grew significantly. Mariátegui took his influence further by openly challenging APRA's view of a gradualist approach to socialism in Peru, which would have allowed for a multi-class party that would make room for the incipient bourgeoisie in Haya's ascent to power. Breaking with APRA completely in 1928, Mariátegui helped found the Peruvian Socialist Party in 1929. This would become the Communist Party of Peru after his death in 1930.

Among his many significant works, Mariátegui's *Seven Interpretive Essays on Peruvian Reality* remains his most seminal. Published in 1928, these collected essays are directed to three major themes. Foremost was *Indigenismo,* or Indian identity, a theme that was being addressed by increasing numbers of scholars and activists at that time. However, Mariátegui brought the discussion of indigenismo to a much higher level than ever before. He claimed that land ownership patterns were of central importance to the political system of nations. As alternative to the continued exploitation of feudalism of Peru's Indians, Mariátegui argued for its replacement with an Andean variety of socialism, to be constructed on the ancient ayllu system still functioning among the serrano population. He argued powerfully for a faith in the indigenous past as a way of formulating a system that would end feudalism and the continued exploitation of Peru's native peoples.

Revisionist Marxism was the second primary concern of Mariátegui. He noted that the working class in Peru was 80 percent Indian and thus socialism must be built upon an Indian base. Using the Inca Empire as the point of reference, Mariátegui viewed the ancient social structure of the ayllu as the essence of the community or the "nucleus" of the Inca Empire. He argued, "The Inca unified and created the empire, but they did not create the nucleus. The legal state undoubtedly reproduced the natural pre-existing state. There were should be praised . . . as the expression and consequence of thousands of years and myriad elements."[15] This highly original political thinker thus saw the Indian community with its age-old and proven system of land use and labor reciprocity as the basis for a socialist model for Peru. The ayllu had in fact endured, through the onslaught of the conquest, disease, *gamonalismo* (bossism), and modern foreign capitalism. To Mariátegui the ayllu's endurance was sufficient evidence of the innate strength and integrity of the Incan system.

For Mariátegui the vehicle for the liberation of the Indian from poverty was two fold: (1) the end of feudalism in Peru and (2) the reform of the educational system. Mariátegui believed that education should be removed from politics and be made far more widely available in the sierra. He believed that there must at least be primary education and technical training for the masses and that for those who had the aptitude, university education should be free and accessible. Teachers at all levels should be paid a living wage, and university reform was badly needed to revitalize clearly outdated curricula. What was not clear within the writings of Mariátegui were his ideas on what education could do for Peru's indigenous peoples. Would it lead to the abandonment of their traditional values as they developed a more modernist outlook, or would western-oriented learning reinforce their wariness of modern culture? Prophets of revolution, like the leaders of Sendero Luminoso, addressed these issues head on in the 1970s.

Haya de la Torre and Mariátegui ended their cooperative relationship in 1928 as a result over their differing approaches to change in Peruvian society. Haya accused Mariátegui of falling victim to "tropical illusions and absurd sentimentalism."[16] In essence they fundamentally disagreed on the nature of class-based change in Peruvian society. This was certainly not a battle of wills by the powerful forces of the left in Peru. By most accounts, the Haya and Mariátegui followings were very small. Still, Mariátegui and six other associates decided in September 1928 to form the Socialist Party of Peru. Mariátegui wrote the program for Peru's first socialist party. The party then established affiliations with other Latin American socialist parties. A sharp debate then ensued as to whether Peru's socialist party should, in fact, reject affiliation with any element in Peru other than workers and campesinos. In fact, great pressure was exerted to have Peru's socialist party to become a more monolithic communist party, more favorable to Moscow. Mariátegui did not live to see this debate through, dying April 16, 1930 at the young age of 35. Within five weeks, on May 20, 1930, the Communist Party of Peru was formally created. For the next half century, the Communist Party of Peru was unsettled and ideologically divided. By 1980, one faction that came to be known as the Shining Path (Sendero Luminoso) would create the greatest threat to the nation by the Left in Peru's history.

It would be far from accurate to think of Haya or Mariátegui as the best reference points for understanding indigenismo in Peru. Recent work by Jaymie Heilman and Marisol de la Cadena highlight how significant grassroots indigenous movements in the sierra were during the 1920s. One of the largest and most radical peasant movements of the 20th century in Peru was the Tawantinsuyu movement. This campesino alliance arose in most of the central and southern sierra departments in protest to land tenure issues, labor demands of the Lima government, and the many grievances the Indians had with local hacendados and government officials. In many ways, the Tawantinsuyu movement reflected the rich history of peasant alliances in colonial and republican Peru. It also presaged peasant land invasions in the three decades after World War II.

The Tawantinsuyu movement was actually founded in Lima in mid-June 1920. Indian men with some education began the alliance with the intention to "unify our race and make them aware of their political, economic and social rights."[17] The founding members of the movement articulated a set of principles that they hoped would provide the framework for the movement's growth throughout Peru. Among these principles were cooperation with workers; protection against exploitation by gamonales, government officials, and priests; and most importantly, the unification of the suppressed indigenous peoples. The Tawantinsuyu movement elected delegates to national congresses that were held into the mid-1920s before they were suppressed by the Leguía administration.

An important theme in the Tawantinsuyu movement was the reawaking of campesinos' links with the Inca past. A flurry of archeological discoveries during the first decades of the 20th century helped confirm the wonders of Peru's pre-Colombian past for all Peruvians. The most important of these, at least for international significance, was Machu Picchu. Small-scale rebellions with professed links to the Inca empire such as the Rumi Maki rebellion from 1915 to 1916 actually strengthened the ideal of an indigenous framework for the remaking of 20th-century Peru.[18]

Heilman argues effectively that while Mariátegui became best known for advocating an all-encompassing socialism involving urban workers, campesinos, and indigenous principles, the Tawantinsuyu movement was actually working to bring these ideas into effect. Cooperation between this campensino movement and anarcho-syndicalists in Peru was quite close. Indeed, the campesinos frequently referred to themselves as "workers of the indigenous race."[19] Another critical centerpiece of the movement was its commitment to education and literacy for the Indian masses. Without literacy, the Indian could not exercise political power, as the ability to read had long been a requirement to vote. In this vision, the Tawantinsuyu movement mirrored exactly what Mariátegui saw as one of the key components for giving power to the Indians in Peru.

One issue more than any other brought the Tawantinsuyu movement in direct conflict with the Leguía government. This was *Conscripción Vial.* This measure was a government draft of Indian labor to construct and repair roads for a period of up to two weeks per year. The labor draft was imposed upon nearly all adult males. It was terribly disruptive of family and ayllu labor requirements, a financial hardship, and reminiscent of the forced labor of the colonial past. Peasants in Ayacucho complained that the draft labor was being abused by local hacendados, who were conspiring to have private roads to the holdings built by the *Conscripción Vial* laborers. The most effective forms of protest to this draft labor system (noncompliance and flight from labor recruiting gangs) remained the same as it had been during the colonial era for the mita. The level of resistance was so widespread in the sierra that road building projects were all but crippled in many areas. In a broad sense, abuse and corruption by local authorities tended to galvanize the movement throughout most of the early 1920s. In the end, however, Leguía responded by sending the *Guardia Civil* (National Police) to crush the Tawantinsuyu movement, but the foundations of later peasant activism were laid.

CONSERVATIVE VOICES: LEGUÍA AND THE UNITED STATES

The most prominent conservative voice challenging the view of Mariátegui and Haya was Víctor Andrés Belaúnde (1883–1966). Patriarch of one of Peru's most prominent families, Belaúnde was born in Arequipa and educated in law, political science, and literature at Arequipa's main university and the University of San Marcos. Very early in his public career he was engaged in the diplomatic service in Spain, Argentina, Bolivia, Colombia, and Germany, where he became a specialist in boundary controversies. Although exiled for most of Leguía's rule, Belaúnde continued a prolific writing and teaching career, which serves as his lasting contribution to Peruvian thought. Belaúnde's works reflect his Catholic upbringing and the middle-class values that were stronger in Arequipa than anywhere else in Peru. Belaúnde argued that Peru's social problems were not as much an issue of class as Maríategui contended but rather an issue of race and culture. In Belaúnde's mind, a deep-seated Catholic faith and middle-class reformist values held the key to the future of Peru's masses. The acceptance of the mestizo as the legitimate heritage of indigenous and Hispanic culture was one of the key components of Belaúnde's views. Like Mariátegui, Belaúnde stressed education as the key element of progress for the Indian peoples, but he did not favor a fundamental change in existing land tenure systems, thinking those reforms to be too disruptive to Peruvian agricultural stability.

José de la Riva Aguero also represented Peru's conservatives with a carefully constructed vision of Peruvian history in his *La historia en el Perú*, originally his doctoral dissertation, completed in 1910. Riva Aguero spent most of the Oncenio in exile after opposing the Leguía regimes policies. His *La historia en el Perú* was an analysis of the best-written histories of the country by natives. Beginning with the writings of Garcilaso de la Vega, this work established an important literary and historical structure for Peruvian scholars as the 20th century began to unfold. Riva Aguero envisioned Peruvian society as a "mysterious community of the ages" whose soul had fallen into lethargy and sleep. According to Riva Aguero, only an informed elite could awaken Peru from this lethargy, and Peru had not been fortunate in the quality of its leadership. This is apparently why he felt comfortable with fascism in the 1930s when his more liberal views before 1919 made him an enemy of Leguía. Fred Bronner insists that the relatively human Italian fascism of the 1920s was seemingly leading to a more unified and prosperous Italy.[20] It might also be said that Riva Aguero felt more affinity for the corporate nature of *Hispanidad* than the volatile populism that was emerging in Peru in the 1930s and after. Despite a lack of clarity in the implications of his work by supporters and critics alike, Riva Aguero became one of Peru's most important men of letters.

Surpassing all previous intellectuals in his acceptance by the Peruvian people was the historian Jorge Basadre. Revered in Peru as much or more than Daniel Cossio Villegas in Mexico or George Bancroft in the United States, Basadre examined the complex aspects of Peruvian society with more precision than anyone else to date. Born in Tacna, Basadre was educated in leading educational institutions in Lima. He spent his professional life seeking to characterize what he termed the *país profundo* (authentic country) of Peru. His multivolume history, *Historia de la republica del Perú* (1822–1933), is the foundation upon which all histories of the Peruvian nation are based. Basadre was a nationalist and a historicist who sought to balance the rejection of Peru's Hispanic past by virulent social critics such a González Prada. Instead, Basadre saw Peruvian history in organic terms wherein the Spanish conquest was "the alluvium that was added to the fertile soil cultivated by the Incas." The seeds planted in the republican era were only beginning to take root and flower as the nation began to mature in the 20th century. Thus he rejected those who despised the early republic period and explained that Peru, as a result of its geography and diverse cultures, was a necessarily divided but still self-perpetuating society that was shaped in the "abyss" of historical events such as the conquest and the disastrous War of the Pacific. Above all, Basadre was a nationalist who was recognized by Peruvians of all classes as a patriot who strove to define a notion of the Peruvian nation that was very elusive.[21]

THE UNITED STATES AND THE ONCENIO

Peruvian intellectuals and political leaders from Mariátegui to Basadre to Haya de la Torre were alienated by Leguía's unabashed cooperation with the United States' capitalism and its ancillary military cooperation with Washington. Haya de la Torre, in particular, built the APRA program largely on the basis on anti-imperialism. This opposition mattered little to Leguía who embraced United States business and military assistance more aggressively than any other country in South America. As indicated earlier, the "big three" corporations in Peru were W. R. Grace, which dominated shipping, sugar, and textile production; Cerro de Pasco, which successfully exploited a large part of the mining sector; and the I.P.C., a Canadian subsidiary of Standard Oil, which dominated the petroleum sector. Lawrence Clayton argues that Leguía sought to Americanize Peru by appointing United States citizens to important posts in the Peruvian government. At the same time, U.S. companies were granted lucrative long-term contracts that assured low or nearly nonexisting taxes while enjoying nearly complete autonomy in their zones of production. The dominance of these companies in the Peruvian economy would be nearly complete until they were all nationalized by the military government in the 1960s. Leguía's rationale for this action was based on the "business model" made famous by the Coolidge and Hoover Administrations in the United Sates during the 1920s. The economic power and ruthlessness of these economic giants is perhaps best demonstrated by Cerro de Pasco's operations in the central sierra.[22]

Extracting copper, silver, zinc, lead, and bismuth from its mines in La Oroya, Cerro employed 13,000 laborers and managers during its very profitable operations in the 1920s. The company constructed railroad lines and a massive smelter to support its mining activities. Originally constructed without filters, the smelter emitted a highly toxic residue of arsenic, lead, zinc, and sulfur. Soon the pasture and farm lands within range of the smelter were poisoned by the emissions. Both local hacendados and Indian communities alike protested the Cerro's lack of concern for the environment and their lands. Even protests by Lima newspapers and court action by the Indian communities proved to be of no avail. Finally, over 400,000 acres of the degraded land was purchased by Cerro at significantly reduced prices and a less than effective filter was installed in 1925. The mining company thus became the largest landholder in Peru. Soon Cerro diversified into cattle and grain production on their newly purchased lands, and the company was therefore able to become self-sufficient in food production for its work force. That work force, composed mainly of Indian laborers from the surrounding communities, was highly volatile, engaging in numerous protests and strikes in the ensuing decades. Attempts to organize these mine workers were marked by intense competition between APRA, the Peruvian Communist Party, and other elements of the radical left. The most lasting legacy left by Cerro was the disregard for Peru's fragile environment, which is still evident in some of the operations of Peru's extractive industries today.[23]

Leguía was also enamored of the growing strength and prestige of the United States Navy, and thought that a U.S. naval presence in Peru would encourage further business ventures. The dictator was also wary of the potential strength of the Peruvian army, particularly allies of the former military president, General Oscar Benavides, and Captain Luis M. Sánchez Cerro. Leguía was compelled to suppress a number of coup attempts against his government in the early 1920s. Accordingly, he expanded the Guardia Civil to a manpower level nearly equal to that of the army. The Guardia was trained by a highly professional Spanish police mission. Seeking to further neutralize the army, Leguía established a separate naval ministry, which was independent of the Ministry of War in 1919. He dramatically increased naval spending, especially on capital purchases such as new submarines from the Connecticut-based Electric Boat Company. A new naval base was also established on San Lorenzo Island in Callao Harbor.

A U.S. Navy training mission contracted by Leguía arrived in Peru in September 1920. Led by Captains Frank Freyer, Charles Gordon Davey, and Lewis D. Causey, this mission reshaped the Peruvian navy along the lines of its U.S. counterpart. A Peruvian naval aviation service was also established in the 1920s under the leadership of Lieutenant Commander Harold Grow. Grow soon became a close friend of Leguía and was instrumental in the establishment of domestic air service in Peru and long-distance air passenger service between Lima and the United States. Leguía heavily politicized the armed services with his favoritism toward the navy and the Guardia Civil. The navy would be almost constantly at odds with the army in the coming decades over issues of national policy and arms purchases. In the end, divisions within the armed forces, national trauma over the eventual settlement of the Tacna Arica controversy, and the economic blow of the Great Depression delivered the final shocks to the Oncenio that would end along with the Leguía dictatorship in August 1930.

It will be recalled that with the Treaty of Ancon ending the War of the Pacific, the future status of Peru's former southern provinces of Tacna and Arica were to be determined by a plebiscite held within 10 years of the signing of the Treaty. Predictably the plebiscite was never held. Peru then claimed the terms of the treaty regarding the two disputed provinces were null and void. As a result, for much of the early years of the 20th century, diplomatic relations between Peru and Chile were broken. During the 1920s the United States actively sought to resolve the dispute. The high priority placed upon this arbitration was reflected in the appointment of General John J. (Black Jack) Pershing as the principal arbiter in 1925. Eventually the dispute was resolved diplomatically with the direct participation of U.S. President Herbert Hoover with the division of the two disputed territories. Peru was awarded the northernmost province of Tacna, and Chile was awarded Arica. Chile agreed to pay Peru a $6 million indemnity and awarded Peru legal rights of transit with the use of rail and port facilities in Arica. Bolivia, the third participant in the war, was excluded from the negotiations and was left completely empty handed, with no access to the sea to this day.[24]

The final loss of Arica brought painful reminders to Peruvian nationalists and Leguía's enemies in the army of the disastrous War of the Pacific. The U.S. role in negotiating the settlement and the Peruvian president's intimate relations with U.S. capital alienated a broad array of students, workers, middle-class businessmen, and, of course, the army. The Oncenio was indeed tottering upon a fragile foundation, and when the Great Depression ravaged the Peruvian economy, the Leguía regime could not withstand its impact.

THE COLLAPSE OF THE ONCENIO

Built on a fragile base of foreign loans and investments, Leguía's regime was further undermined by massive corruption and waste. When the shock waves from the Wall Street collapse reached Peru in early 1930, the government was compelled to reduce spending by at least 50 percent. Soon the country's banks were facing insolvency. When commodity export prices, particularly copper, wool and cotton, fell as much as 70 percent, a crushing level of unemployment, especially in the mining industry, ensured massive opposition to the continuation of the Oncenio.

The instrument of Leguía demise was Lieutenant Colonel Luis M. Sánchez Cerro, an extremely ambitious and politically oriented army officer. Sánchez Cerro, a dark-skinned *cholo*, had been involved in a plot to unseat Leguía in Cuzco in 1923 and thus was exiled on military missions abroad for most of the remainder of the decade. Upon his return to Peru, Leguía made the inexplicable mistake of promoting Sanchez Cerro to lieutenant colonel and giving him command of a garrison in Arequipa. Aided by widespread organized opposition to the dictator among Arequipa civilian political leaders, Sánchez Cerro "pronounced" against the government on the afternoon of August 24, 1930. By the next day, three of five of Peru's military districts had renounced the Leguía government and the dictator stepped down. Through excellent planning Sánchez Cerro was able to outmaneuver General Manuel Ponce, commander of the Lima garrison, and consolidate power as head of an all-military provisional government. Leguía's attempt to escape Peru aboard the navy's flagship, *Almirante Grau*, was thwarted, and he was imprisoned. The former dictator, given little medical attention, died in February 1932 after a painful illness. As Peru confronted the Great Depression, political forces were at work that would dramatically change the face of Peruvian politics and society. Populism as a manifestation of working-class discontent would characterize Peruvian politics throughout the decade. Confronted by a military that was itself conflicted by deep schisms, the nation would experience serious violence during the first years of the 1930s.[25]

CONCLUSION

Peru did make steady progress in national reconstruction during the first three decades of the 20th century. Still, the Peruvian government, especially that during the Leguía dictatorship, made a commitment to export-led growth that sacrificed Peru's economic autonomy in critical sectors such as the extractive industries and textiles. The highly pro-U.S. policies of the Oncenio would fuel deeply anti-imperialist strains in Peru's politics until Velasco's military government. The Peruvian army, deviating from the dictums of its French tutors, intervened twice (1914 and 1930) to overthrow the civilian government. The pattern was thus set for an interventionist mindset for decades to come.

All but forgotten during these years were Peru's campensinos. The Tawantinsuyu movement demonstrated that Peru's Indians were fully aware of their needs and could act as advocates for themselves. This was particularly true in their understanding of the value of literacy and basic education. In this, the Indians were in tune with Mariátegui, their foremost advocate at the national level. But meaningful reforms would remain in abeyance as Peru confronted the very troubled times of the 1930s and World War II.

NOTES

1. Daniel M. Masterson, *Militarism and Politics in Latin America: Peru from Sánchez Cerro to Sendero Luminoso* (Westport, CT: Greenwood Press, 1991), 26–27.

2. Rosemary Thorp and Geoff Bertram, *Peru 1890–1977: Growth and Policy in an Open Economy* (New York: Columbia University Press, 1978), 51–62.

3. Ibid., 95–98.

4. Nils Jacobsen, *Mirages of Transition: The Peruvian Altiplano, 1780–1930* (Berkeley: University of California Press, 1993), 285.

5. Daniel M. Masterson with Sayaka Funada Classen, *The Japanese in Latin America* (Urbana: University of Illinois Press, 2004), 34–42, 63–73.

6. Orazio A. Ciccarelli, "Fascist Propaganda and the Italian Community in Peru during the Benavides Regime, 1933–1939," *Journal of Latin American Studies*, 20, no. 2 (1988), 369–373.

7. Peter Blanchard, *The Origins of the Peruvian Labor Movement, 1883–1919* (Pittsburgh: University of Pittsburgh Press, 1982), 54. Blanchard is the standard treatment of the early labor movement in Peru.

8. Peter F. Klarén, *Peru: Society and Nationhood in the Andes* (Oxford: Oxford University Press, 2000), 219–224.

9. Ibid., 226–227.

10. Peter F. Klarén, *Modernization, Dislocation and Aprismo: The Origins of Peru's Aprista Party, 1870–1932* (Austin: University of Texas Press, 1973), 152–153.

11. Fredrick B. Pike, *The Politics of the Miraculous in Peru: Haya de la Torre and the Spiritualist Tradition* (Lincoln: University of Nebraska Press, 1986), 24–31.

12. James Billington as quoted in Pike, *Politics of the Miraculous* , 44.

13. Haya de la Torre interview with the author, July 13, 1974, Lima, Peru. This interview occurred at the *Casa del Pueblo,* the APRA headquarters. Of all the prominent leaders Haya met during his travels he spoke most highly of Albert Einstein. Haya attempted to integrate components of quantum physics into his concept of "Historical-Space-Time."

14. José Carlos Mariátegui, *Seven Interpretive Essays on Peruvian Reality* (Introduction by Jorge Basadre) (Austin: University of Texas Press, 1971), xii, xvi.

15. Ibid., 75–76.

16. In a July 14, 1974 interview with the author Haya de la Torre, he elaborated on his relations with many Peruvian national figures including Mariategui.

17. Jaymie Heilman, "By Other Means: Politics in Ayacucho Before Peru's Shining Path War, 1879–1980," PhD dissertation, University of Wisconsin, 2006, 105.

18. Ibid., 108.

19. Ibid., 112–113

20. Fred Bronner, "José Luis Riva Aguero (1885–1944), Peruvian Historian," *Hispanic American Historical Review* 36, no. 4, (1956), 490–502.

21. Mark Thurner, "Jorge Basadre's 'Peruvian History of Peru,' or the Poetic Aporia of Historicism," *Hispanic American Historical Review* 82, no. 2 (2008), 247–283.

22. Lawrence Clayton, *Peru and the United States: The Condor and the Eagle,* (Athens: University of Georgia Press, 1999), 104–130.

23. The best study of the Peruvian mining industry is Elizabeth Dore, *The Peruvian Mining Industry: Growth, Stagnation and Crisis* (Boulder, CO: Westview Press, 1988).

24. Clayton, *Peru and the United States,* 137–141.

25. Masterson, *Militarism and Politics in Latin America,* 39–55.

6

Populism and Dictatorship in Depression and War, 1930–1948

Driven by tumultuous world events, Peru's social and political cultures were very unsettled during the two decades after 1930. APRA emerged as a potent political force after Haya de la Torre returned to Peru in 1930. Andean peasant unrest continued in the face of continued pressure by the gamonoles to divest Indian communities of their land.

Labor emerged as a potent force in the 1930s and APRA worked hard to capture its support. The armed forces continued to witness its professional progress impeded by the caudillismo of Colonel Luis M. Sánchez Cerro (1930–1933) and General Oscar Benavides (1933–1939). Junior officers and enlisted personnel remained unhappy with the pay and the professional standards of their respective institutions. They were targets of subversion by APRA and right-wing proto-fascist elements that became quite active during the 1930s. World War II did not bring the terrible suffering of European and Asian nations to Peru. Its Japanese population, however, was particularly mistreated. The nation remained mainly in a non-combatant status against the Axis, but Peru did cooperate closely with the United States in protecting the approaches to the Panama Canal. Vital resources such as sugar, cotton, copper, iron ore, and other strategic metals were supplied to the Allies at bargain prices. Still, the war years were not without military operations. Peru fought a brief border war with Ecuador in July 1941. The repercussions of that conflict divided these two nations until the end of the 20th century.

SÁNCHEZ CERRO AND APRA

Steve Stein's important study of populism in Peru reveals some important legacies of the Oncenio, which shaped the politics of the 1930s. The encroachment of hacendados on the Indian community's lands in the sierra and the coast accelerated as world prices for sugar, cotton, and wool advanced. Through legal and illegal means, and often by brute force, the Indian communities lost their ancestral lands and often their only recourse was to seek wage labor in the mines or in Lima. The capital's working and middle-class sectors expanded dramatically during the Leguía years. The government's many public works projects provided construction jobs. The three-fold increase in the government budget allowed for a nearly 500 percent growth in public sector jobs. Accountants, lawyers, engineers, and technicians found work. Nearly all of these were centered in Lima. With good times, labor union membership lagged. Anarchists through their newspaper *La Protesta* were the most active union organizers during the 1920s. The *Federación Obrera Regional Peruana* (Regional Federation of Peruvian Workers; FORP) was one of the first important unions in Peru. By 1929, *Confederación General de Trabajadores del Perú* (General Confederation of Peruvian Workers; CGTP) had substantial support. The Depression and Leguía's outlawing of unions in 1929 weakened the labor union movement just as it was beginning. By 1930, what Stein calls the "massification" of Lima was well underway. Elite politics was about to change fundamentally. Even though the electorate would not expand to include the non-Spanish-speaking indigenous population until the 1970s, new working- and middle-class voters largely determined Peru's political leaders. These changes were not always peaceful and the 1930s proved to be one of Peru's most violent until the Sendero Luminoso years. The migrants who abandoned their traditional homes in the highlands for Lima were now confronted during the Depression with 25 percent unemployment in Lima and many longed for home. A song called *Provinciano* ("The Provincial One") conveyed their feelings of being drawn to Lima by false dreams of better life. Instead, what they found was loneliness, disappointment and a tormented nostalgia for their country home.[1]

After the fall of Leguía, Sánchez Cerro governed Peru as the *jefe* (chief) of a military junta from September 1930 to early 1931. Born in the northern city of Piura in August 1889 to a family of very modest means, Sánchez Cerro's career demonstrates that the army was an agent of social mobility. He enlisted in the army as a private in 1910. Soon, however, he entered the military academy at Chorillos. He was afforded this opportunity because of his intelligence and his high scores on the academy's entrance exam. This is the same manner used by General Juan Velasco Alvarado to gain entrance to the army's officer corps, which would have normally been barred to him. In the parlance of the U.S. military, they were "mustangs" who struggled throughout their careers for recognition by more "establishment" officers. In this period of great instability in civil-military relations, Sánchez Cerro became an accomplished conspirator. This talent opened political avenues for him, but it would also lead to his demise.

Soon after overthrowing Leguía he shrewdly prepared for popular elections by arresting many of Leguía's government officials, distributing food to the poor, and decreeing civil marriage and divorce. These measures were designed to enlist the support of the urban poor. But his abolition of Conscripción Vial was immensely popular in the sierra well. Now many male campesinos were freed from public labor obligations imposed during the Oncenio. Sánchez Cerro's appeal to the poor was also enhanced by his own dark-skinned cholo appearance. He professed to be a man of the people, but in reality he was quite conservative in the manner of old guard civilistas of the late 19th century. In preparing for the coming elections, however, Sánchez Cerro overplayed his hand. He purged officers from the army who were not loyal and took swift measures to counter the *Guardia Republicana* that Leguía established as a virtual praetorian guard. in 1919. Some senior army officers, particularly Major Gustavo Jiménez, resented the "upstart Lieutenant Colonel" who usurped the chain of army command to achieve power. APRA, beginning a long history of collaborating with the armed forces to further its political aims, backed Jiménez, and Sánchez Cerro, now facing formidable opposition in the army and civilian sector, stepped down from the presidency and went into a brief political exile.

A civilian junta that ruled Peru during the Sánchez Cerro interregnum enacted an immensely significant electoral law in May 1931. Property qualifications for voting were abolished and the secret ballot was established. Now literate males 21 years or older could vote. This law increased the electorate by nearly 60 percent and essentially began the era of mass politics in Peru. Importantly, the indigenous peoples could not vote as Spanish literacy was a requirement. Also, women continued to be barred from voting until early 1950s.

With the expanded electorate, the 1931 election campaign became one of the most contentious ever held in Peru. Supporters of Sánchez Cerro, especially Antonio Miró-Quesada, owner of the powerful conservative newspaper *El Comercio*, formed the *Union Revolucionaria* (Revolutionary Union) party as the political vehicle for his election. *El Comercio* launched a steady series of attacks on Haya de la Torre and the Apristas that clearly hurt their campaign in Lima. Thus, the political lines were drawn between the populist forces aligned with APRA and those supporting Sánchez Cerro. The decisive elements in this election, however, were Lima's poor and the limited numbers of literate campesinos who could vote in the sierra. The election also badly divided the army with many senior officers opposed to Sánchez Cerro because of his ambitious opportunism, and others, especially in the Navy who were wary of Haya de la Torre's strong public antipathy for the United States and "imperialist" ventures in Peru. Both Sánchez Cerro and Haya de la Torre returned from their respective exiles in July 1931. The APRA chief immediately began making adjustments to the party's political platform so as to expand its appeal to a broader political base. Registered in Peru as the *Partido Aprista Peruano* (PAP; Peruvian Aprista Party), the APRA jettisoned its international standing to appeal more directly to Peruvian voters. From this point on, this party would be known to Peruvians as APRA and its members as *Apristas*. Most importantly, Haya de la Torre made a direct appeal to the middle class, small- and medium-size farmers and small businessmen in northern Peru who had suffered by the expansion of the Grace Corporation's holdings in the Trujillo region. This would be the core of APRA support. Ultimately, the party grandly hoped to create a broad alliance of the disaffected middle sectors, urban working classes and the Indian peasantry in the sierra.[2]

For many reasons, this alliance was never achieved, and APRA remained primarily a regionally based party for the next half century. Unable to vote because of literacy restrictions, most of Peru's campesinos were non-factors in the 1931 elections. Still, it appears that those that did vote, with the exception of those in the north, tended to support Sánchez Cerro. Haya de la Torre's rhetoric, which drew on much of Mariátegui's thinking, appeared to many to be unconvincing. APRA's greatest strength, its highly disciplined and rigid party structure with Haya de la Torre as its maximum leader, was also its most significant liability with regard to the armed forces. The army feared APRA's capability to mount an armed challenge to the military. APRA was recruiting sugar and textile workers, mechanics, and laborers of all kinds into its militant ranks. On a much smaller scale, this party forces calls to mind the fascist models in Germany and Italy during the 1930s. Just as the Wehrmacht feared the *Sturmabteilung* (Assault Division) for its militant potential in Germany, Peru's army feared the APRA as it was being mobilized in 1931.

When election day arrived October 11, 1931, Sánchez Cerro's relief efforts for Lima's poor and his abolition of Conscripción Vial in the sierra seemed to be the decisive factors in leading him to an electoral victory over Haya de la Torre by a vote of 152,148 to 106,088. Almost immediately, APRA leaders began seeking an alliance with dissident army and Guardia Civil personnel to overthrow the newly installed Sánchez Cerro regime. The response by the government was a declaration of martial law and the arrest of Haya de la Torre on May 6, 1932. Almost immediately, lower deck sailors of Peru's two main warships, the *Almirante Grau* and *Colonel Bolgnesi* mutinied in protest. This rising was quickly put down, but a massive civil-military rebellion was soon activated in Trujillo on July 7, 1932.

The O'Donovan army garrison in Trujillo was to be the epicenter of a nationwide revolt that envisioned Trujillo falling to Aprista-led civil military rebels once they gained the arms and ammunition from the garrison. When the fighting began in Trujillo, this would be the signal for other risings throughout Peru. The plan misfired when the army garrison was attacked prematurely and a coordinated national effort was lost. Aprista rebels did seize the city of Trujillo, but they were soon isolated by overwhelming government forces who surrounded the city. Most of the rebels remained in Trujillo to confront government forces. Some Apristas sought to start a guerrilla campaign in the mountains, but that hope never materialized. Of great historical importance was the decision of some rebel leaders to execute 35 army and Guardia Civil personnel held in the Trujillo jail. Five of the corpses were mutilated. When government troops discovered the atrocity, they took terrible vengeance on rebel prisoners. The prisoners were removed to the nearby ruins of the ancient city of Chan Chan. There between 1,000 and 6,000 rebels were executed by firing squads. Exact figures will likely never be available. The Trujillo uprising, the jail killings, and the government's retribution opened a wound in Peruvian civil-military relations that would not fully healed for most of the 20th century. In a letter from his prison cell Haya de la Torre expressed his troubled feelings to an associate. "The civilized person who falls into the hands of a horde of savages, defends himself, but does not become a savage himself. . . . we must avoid becoming barbarians ourselves which would be to forget the civilizing mission of the party."[3]

For most armed forces officers, Apristas now became demons bent upon the destruction of the military and the nation. But ironically, for other ambitious or discontented military men, APRA was now even more appealing as the only disciplined and militant political force in Peru. APRA was their only hope for leveraging important change within both the military and the society. Almost always the handmaiden of APRA—military interaction was violence and disorder. Sánchez Cerro would be the author of much of this violence, and he would be consumed by it.

With the suppression of the Trujillo revolt, Sánchez Cerro was forced to deal immediately with the depression-ridden economy that was bottoming out in 1933. Peru defaulted on its foreign debt in 1932, as most South American countries would do in the 1930s. With plunging commodity prices, Peru had no choice in the matter, but it did allow the government leeway to play a waiting game to allow prices for copper and other metals to recover. Moreover, demand for Peruvian cotton remained relatively stable keeping some export income flowing in. Because Peru's export sector was so dominated by foreign firms, these corporations absorbed a good deal of the losses from the decline in export earnings after 1929. Peru was thus able to recover more quickly from the Depression than most Latin American countries. The government's internal problems were overshadowed in September 1932 when armed hostilities began between Peruvian and Colombian forces in the border town of Leticia, a former Peruvian territory. This territory was ceded to Colombia by the Solomón-Lozano Treaty of 1922. About 200 armed Peruvians seized Leticia on September 1, 1932. On October 21, the Colombian town of Tarapacá on the Putumayo River was also taken. It is not certain whether Sánchez Cerro instigated these hostilities, but he certainly tried to benefit from them by making the small Leticia operations a national crusade. As Colombian forces mobilized 1,000 infantry and six river craft to retake their lost towns, Sánchez Cerro ordered the entire army mobilized, the draft fully activated, and, most importantly, he named General Oscar R. Benavides as chief of a military defense board charged with prosecuting the military campaign. Benavides was the most prestigious officer in the armed forces. As will be recalled, he was provisional military president in 1914, and he had confronted Colombian forces successfully in 1911. Unlike Sánchez Cerro, he boasted "impeccable" social credentials; he hailed from one of Peru's elite families; and he was well connected to Lima's economic and political centers of power.

APRA–associated violence reached a climax in April 1933 when a 17-year-old party member shot and killed Sánchez Cerro at Lima's San Beatrice race track while he was reviewing troops training for the Leticia conflict. This was the second attempt on Sánchez Cerro's life by Apristas, and it further solidified the party's radical nature. In a 1974 interview with the author, Haya de la Torre denied APRA's involvement in the assassination. Rather he claimed that "Benavides was the intellectual author of the death of Sánchez Cerro."[4] Suspicions were raised regarding Benavides involvement largely because he was made provisional president of Peru for the remainder of Sánchez Cerro's term by the nation's Congress. Interestingly, the Congress violated the newly adopted constitution, approved that same month, which barred active duty military officers from holding the presidency. Sánchez Cerro's death brought to an end one of the most violent periods in Peruvian history up to that time. But the legacy of this violence would color Peruvian domestic affairs for many decades to come.

THE BENAVIDES ERA, 1933–1939

It is a telling statement on Peru's weak civilian political culture that the Peruvian congress would call upon a military caudillo legally barred from assuming office to quiet the nation's turmoil. Still, Benavides was the logical choice. Easily the most respected military man in the nation, he had the capacity to heal the divisions with the armed forces that Sánchez Cerro had incurred by his ambitious ways. Benavides also had the trust of Peru's wealthy and powerful as he was born into their ranks. He also had diplomatic experience, having served as ambassador to the United Kingdom before being named president. He would use this skill to quickly resolve the Leticia dispute through diplomacy rather than armed conflict. Benavides also tried to be a political conciliator by announcing a policy of "peace and concord" regarding the hard-edged politics that he confronted during his first months in office.

Toward this end, a general political amnesty was declared, and most Apristas, including Haya de la Torre, were released from prison. Martial law was also ended. Nevertheless, Benavides was wary of APRA's political power and the party remained illegal. This prompted the party to continue plotting to overthrow the government. Violence continued. In May 1935 Antonio Miró-Quesada, the owner of *El Comercio,* and his wife were assassinated by an Aprista.

The 1936 elections were considered critically important for Peru's future by all political factions. Right-wing fascist groups were gaining adherents as the threat from the left increased. Peru's small Communist Party was really a non-factor in national politics, but APRA, with its proven record of radicalism and violence was steadfastly opposed by the fascist Union Revolucionaria. The Union Revolucionaria boasted a party army of about 6,000 militants and was headed by Luis Flores. The Miró-Quesada family, along with other traditional conservatives, were beginning a long feud with APRA, which was responsible for the death of the Miró-Quesada's patriarch and matriarch. *El Comercio* was the influential voice of these traditional conservatives. Pedro Beltrán, a wealthy cotton planter, and the intellectual José de Riva Aguero were also prominent in the opposition to APRA. As noted earlier, Riva Aguero became the most literate and influential advocates of fascism in Peru during the 1930s. Detesting Bolshevism and Aprismo as anti-Catholic and anti-Peruvian, he admired Mussolini's brand of Fascism and his concord with the Catholic Church. The army and navy officer corps held on to their vendetta against APRA, but this did not stop some disgruntled officers from maintaining contacts with the party.[5]

Benavides and the National Election Jury took measures to prevent a likely APRA victory in the 1936 elections. First APRA was barred from participating in early September. Then when it appeared an APRA-backed candidate would win, Benavides had the congress cancel the elections in November. He then named an all-military cabinet and convinced the congress to extend his presidential powers until December 1939. By this time, the caudillo was able to exercise dictatorial power because of favorable economic conditions and reforms within the armed forces that broadened his support.

The new administration benefitted from the slow but steady recovery of the Peruvian economy from the worst years of the Depression. The Benavides administration had little choice regarding the pace of recovery since foreign investment in Peru virtually halted after the government defaulted on its loan obligations. A similar situation in many other Latin American countries prompted them to resort to import substitution and the subsidization of native industries in order to become more economically independent. Such was not the case in Peru because commodity prices for its key exports recovered relatively quickly. As previously indicated, cotton led the recovery. A minimum of 100,000 laborers worked in the cotton fields of northern Peru in the 1930s offering steady if not well-paid work in troubled economic times. As Thorp and Bertram note, cotton remained a "small and medium cultivator's crop."[6] Because of the moderate scale of crops, immigrants, particularly Japanese immigrants, were able to enter cotton agriculture and prosper even during the Depression.[7] Cotton production from the mid-1930s to Pearl Harbor continued to expand in Peru both in total number of acres in cultivation and productivity. Better fertilizers, better agriculture techniques (especially among Japanese farmers), and more readily available credit from the Banco Agricola (Agrarian Bank) were important factors. Labor organizers also targeted the cotton fields in their efforts to build a rural organized labor base. The 1930s witnessed the beginnings of Peru's fish meal industry. By the end of the decade four canneries were in operation, and World War II gave a further boost to an industry that would be one of the world's largest by the 1960s.

World prices for metals varied considerably during the 1930s. Copper prices remained depressed as construction lagged world wide during the 1930s. But most of Peru's copper production was in foreign hands, and multinational companies absorbed the losses. As one would expect, prices for all of Peru's commodity exports recovered dramatically during World War II. As we shall see, however, price arrangements for these commodities were such that Peru did not benefit to nearly the degree that her South American neighbors did. Moreover, environmental degradation in the mining zones, particularly near the Cerro de Pasco operations in La Oroya, was becoming an immense problem.

National income rose 61 percent between 1935 and 1939 reflecting rising world prices for Peru's cotton and mineral exports. This added revenue was used by Benavides to begin ambitious public works and housing projects along with a social welfare program. Thousands of miles of roads were built and repaired. More than 110,000 acres of new land was brought under cultivation through new irrigation networks. Mirroring New Deal legislation in the United States, a social security system was created. A council for Indigenous Affairs was established to help adjudicate the myriad land claims Indian communities were asking the government to review as they were pressed ever harder by the gamonoles to surrender their land rights.

Florencia Mallon's landmark study, *The Defense of Community in Peru's Central Highlands*, offers strong evidence of the erosion of traditional community values and land use patterns in central Peru, especially after World War I. Miners and peasants in the Cerro de Pasco region were forced to deal with mining accidents, environmental degradation, and the cutback of the labor force with the onset of the Depression. Capitalism modified peasant lifestyles by privatization of communal lands. Mallon employs the term *commodification* to describe how land and labor systems that were shared communal experiences for hundreds of years became simple commodities to be quickly bought and sold. The Depression actually gave rise to an agrarian middle class that altered class relationships on the highlands significantly. Commercial agriculture began to emerge in the 1930s and became an important aspect of the income of select "farmers" in the Yanamarca Valley. Growing Bermuda onions for an expanding market in Lima, a new class of commercial farmers emerged that significantly altered communal relationships in the central highlands of Peru. The growth of capitalism in the Yanamarca and Mantaro Valleys of central Peru, according to Mallon, came at the expense of subsistence agriculture as increasingly more land was converted to commercial use. As is always the case, some peasants adjusted to these changes and others did not. Those that did not became part of a rural labor force that had little resemblance to the reciprocal labor relations of the traditional community. Change did not necessarily mean progress for these communities in central Peru. It is likely that these same changes were occurring in other parts of Peru, but they are especially well documented by Mallon's study of central Peru. What emerges from this study is the elaboration of an economic process that certainly benefited a new class of middle-class agrarian capitalists, but left many others in a new form of dependent poverty.[8]

Benavides's programs rarely touched Peru's serranos, but he could not ignore the armed forces. A new naval hospital and 18 new army barracks were constructed throughout Peru. Training teams from Spain, for the national police, and from Germany and Italy for the army and the nation's fledgling air force were also contracted in 1937. The German and Italian teams replaced the long-established French and U.S. training missions and led to charges that Benavides had established close ties with Europe's fascist powers. On the other hand, the shrewd Benavides may have been attempting to diversify Peru's sources of arms and supplies in the event that the United States refused to sell Peru military equipment. Indeed, this would happen a number of times in the course of the next four decades. Importantly, the government eliminated the possibility of future conflict with Colombia by settling the Leticia dispute diplomatically soon after Benavides assumed the presidency in 1933.

Although Benavides encouraged friendly relations with Germany and Italy, he adopted a strongly anti-Japanese policy throughout his administration.

Reflecting anti-Japanese sentiment throughout Latin American after the invasion of Manchuria in 1931, Benavides was playing the anti-immigrant card that is so popular with politicians then and now.

Anti-Japanese riots occurred during the Sánchez Cerro regime. Working and lower middle-class Peruvians were angered by self-sufficient Japanese immigrants farmers and small business owners who seemed to be weathering the rigors of the Depression. In October 1937 the Benavides government renounced a 1924 treaty of friendship, commerce, and navigation that was negotiated by the pro-Japanese Leguía government. Japan held a highly favorable trade balance with Peru, and this angered the country's nationalists. The Japanese were the largest immigrant group in Peru by the late 1930s, and they had created a stable, hard-working, and relatively prosperous community mainly in the Lima metropolitan area. The 1936 Immigration Act effectively ended further Japanese settlement in Peru. Peru's immigrant legislation mirrored that of the United States and Canada in 1908. Brazil, the home of nearly 200,000 Japanese by 1941, limited Japanese immigration in the early 1930s.

In characterizing the Benavides regime it is now possible to refer to it in the terms of later military regimes in Latin America. *Dictablanda* or soft dictatorship is a good characterization. Although he ruled mainly by decree and maintained emergency laws throughout most of his rule, he allowed some political space for his opponents. He knew, for example, that the imprisonment of Haya de la Torre prompted high levels of violence by his Aprista supporters. He thus released Haya de la Torre from prison early in his administration. Despite numerous plots against his government, Haya de la Torre was allowed to remain at large in living an underground existence that was not overly secretive. During these years in the catacombs, Haya adopted the nom de guerre Pachacútec (Inca royalty). Clearly, Benavides did not want Haya de la Torre to be a martyr. Still, Haya's enemies were many, and Haya de la Torre escaped a number of assassination attempts during these underground years.

By early 1939 Benavides appeared ready to step down from the presidency, but his successor was an open question given Peru's volatile political climate. In yet another case of civil-military intrigue, APRA tried to seize power in February 1939 by means of a military coup head by an army senior officer, General Antonio Rodríguez Ramírez. Benavides, the Minister of Government and Police, and a former army chief of staff was suborned. Apparently thinking he could rule Peru with APRA's support, Rodríguez gained widespread support with the armed forces officer corps. Poor timing of the rebellion led to immediate confusion among the conspirators. Then General Rodríguez was shot dead by a pro-government officer in the National Palace. This effectively ended the last armed challenge to the Benavides regime before the 1939 elections.

Given its radical history during its first decade of political activism, APRA had no chance of legally participating in the 1939 elections. Benavides settled on an established member of Peru's aristocracy, Manuel Prado y Ugarteche, as his favored candidate. Manuel Prado's brother Jorge was Benavides's candidate in the 1936 election. The brothers were from one of the oldest and wealthiest families in Peru. Their father, President Mariano Ignacio Prado (1876–1879) had extensive holdings in banking and insurance. The elder Prado's reputation had been diminished, however, by his decision to leave Peru during the first months of the War of the Pacific, ostensibly to seek funds for the war in Europe. Thus the Prado family's patriotism was in question in the minds of many Peruvian nationalists. It appears that APRA reached a tacit agreement before the election to support Prado in return for the possibility of future legalization of the party during Prado's presidency. Moreover, APRA leaders, despite its radical activism, were clearly moderating their strong anti-imperialist rhetoric and praising the Good Neighbor policy as they sought Washington's support for their party. This was the first of many significant shifts in APRA's ideology that would occur over the course of the next three decades. These revisionist initiatives caused major party schisms and frequently alienated the party's younger and more radical membership.

Promising to cut taxes on the middle classes, Prado won an easy victory in the 1939 elections over the lackluster José Quesada Larrea, the candidate of the extreme right. Prado emerged from the election with 55 percent of the vote. Very likely Prado won many middle-sector votes that would have likely gone to APRA because of his tax pledge. Moreover, despite Prado's refusal to legalize APRA, his politically moderate views and opposition to the radical right in Peru seemed to make him the better choice. Washington was pleased with his victory since he quickly drew away from Benavides's close ties with Germany and Italy. Prado promoted himself as a conservative modernizer. His most significant challenges, however, would not be domestic issues but rather a border war with Ecuador and Peru's policies regarding World War II.

WORLD WAR II AND PERU

As war loomed in Europe in 1938, the Eighth International Conference of American States was held in Lima. The resolution produced at that conference stated that if the peace of the hemisphere was threatened, any member group could call for a consultation to address the danger. U.S. policy before Pearl Harbor was, of course, to remain neutral but to provide England with as much assistance as possible within the scope of the neutrality laws. Above all, Washington sought to protect the Panama Canal and keep Axis elements within Latin American neutralized. Toward that end, Peru was considered of major importance because of its proximity to the approaches to the canal and its relatively significant numbers of Japanese, German, and Italian aliens.

World War II redefined Peruvian national affairs in many ways. Never a real beneficiary of the Good Neighbor Policy during the 1930s, Peru became one of Washington's best allies. Peru broke relations with the Axis in January 1942 in accordance with the wishes of the United States. Lima did not declare war on the Axis until three years later on a timetable that reflected U.S. wishes as well. Economic and military cooperation between Peru and the United States was extensive throughout the war, although the United States clearly got the better end of the exchange. The war did not touch Peruvian soil or significantly trouble her sea approaches. Still some Peruvian Jews were murdered in the Holocaust, and hundreds of Japanese, Germans, and Italians were arrested and deported to the United States as "dangerous" enemy aliens. In the end, Peru's strategic exports of cotton, metals, sugar, and oil were of major importance to the Allied cause.

No Latin American nation cooperated more closely with the United States on the enemy alien issue than Peru. The nation's Japanese population was an unpopular minority almost from the arrival from *Nikkei* immigrants in 1899. Most of Peru's Japanese settled in the Lima-Callao metropolitan area, where they were more visible than in Brazil, for example, where most settled in relatively remote areas of São Paulo state. The majority of the Japanese in Lima were engaged in small-scale commerce where they had daily contact with Limeños. Very few became spectacularly wealthy, but most *Nikkei* did well enough during the depression years to arouse the enmity of the city's struggling middle and working class. The Japanese rarely mixed socially with native Peruvians. This provoked allegations that they could not or would not assimilate and were thus threats to the nation. Making matters worse, of course, was the rampant militarism of the Tokyo government after the invasion of Manchuria in 1931. With the invasion of China proper in 1937, anti-Japanese sentiment heightened even more. The Peruvian government essentially refused to admit Japanese immigrants after 1936. The Japanese community in Peru also showed an uncharacteristic insensitivity to nativists' animosity. In 1938, for example, the Central Japanese Association of Lima donated funds it had raised among its members to fund two Japanese war planes for the campaign in China. This was done with the full knowledge that serious anti-Japanese disturbances occurred during the early years of the Sánchez Cerro regime. Not surprisingly the worst anti-Japanese riots ever to occur in the Americas erupted in Lima in late May 1940.

A hostile press and consistent false rumors of a Japanese "invasion" of Peru sparked the riots on May 13 and 14, 1940. APRA seems to have been linked to the anti-Japanese campaign. While the city's police largely stood by and did nothing, 600 Japanese businesses were looted or totally destroyed. Ten

Japanese lost their lives and hundreds were injured in the rioting. Since many Japanese lived in the same building as their business, they lost everything. The only refuge for many Japanese who were made homeless by the riots were the Japanese schools in Lima. Total property damage in the rioting was estimated by the Japanese embassy in Lima at $7 million. Interestingly, the extremely hostile anti-Japanese attitude in Peru apparently discouraged the Tokyo government undertaking an sabotage campaign in Peru after Pearl Harbor. The feat of mob action in retribution against Peru's *Nikkei* was seen as highly likely. Thus, after Pearl Harbor the soon-to-be-expelled Japanese ambassador implored the many Japanese-Peruvian associations in Peru to remain calm, obey Peru's laws, and prepare for a protracted period of sacrifice.[9] This is exactly what Peru's 25,000 Japanese Peruvians did. Still, many lost theirs jobs, businesses, families, homes, and even their nationalities. They joined other millions of displaced persons during the Pacific war who became "pawns in a triangle of hate."[10]

Soon after Pearl Harbor and at the instigation of the U.S. State Department, Immigration and Naturalization Service, and the Federal Bureau of Investigation, the Prado government drew up a black list of Japanese business and community leaders who were viewed as possible enemy aliens. Peruvian military intelligence and the F.B.I, which had assumed responsibility for counterespionage in Latin America, did not have substantial evidence of Japanese espionage activity in Peru. Tokyo, through its embassy in Peru, actually instructed Peru's *Nikkei* to maintain a low profile to avoid repeats of the May 1940 riots. Still, the safety of the Panama Canal was a concern, and the same kind of imagined subversion that prompted the internment of the U.S. Japanese prompted many Peruvians to push for Peruvian Japanese to leave the country. A domestic internment program involving most Japanese Peruvians was considered but rejected as too costly. Peru's *Nikkei* were also considered as possible barter for U.S. citizens caught behind enemy lines in Asia.

In the final analysis, a lack of wartime ships limited the deportation program. Over the three-year period after April 1942, a total of 1,800 *Nikkei* were arrested and deported to the camps in the North American southwest. The majority were eventually sent to war-torn Japan; only a handful returned to Peru.[11]

Peru's small Italian and German populations were also subjected to black listing and deportation but not in the same numbers as the large Japanese community. Both these communities were well established before World War II and enjoyed good relations with the Benavides administration. Peru's Italian population actually declined during the inter-war years to only 7,618. Still, its members were prominent in banking (Banco Italiano), utilities, manufacturing, and commercial enterprises. Their small numbers, similar cultural traditions (particularly Catholicism) and significant critical press support from Miró Quesada's *El Comericio* newspaper helped their cause. Moreover, as Orazio Ciccarreli convincingly argues, Peru was not critical to Mussolini's interests after the War with Ethiopia.[12] Fascist parties in Latin America were primarily oriented toward the Nazi model. Most staunch right-wing political figures such as Benavides and Riva Aguero felt far more comfortable with Italian fascism than the very hard-line Nazi beliefs. Accordingly, during the Second World War, the Italians were never a real target of the counterespionage campaign of the Peruvian or U.S. government. John Emmerson, Third Secretary of the U.S. Embassy in Lima, summed it up best when he concluded that "the Italians hardly mattered."[13]

The small German community in Peru has yet to be researched in depth. It can be said, however, that the German government and the *Abwher* (Intelligence Service) had limited objectives in Peru. Despite numbering only 2,122, the German community was concentrated in the exclusive Lima suburb of Miraflores and was thus quite accessible to Allied surveillance. Germans in Lima usually socialized with Peru's elite and had little contact with "street people" as was the case with the Japanese. There were no overt anti-German or anti-Italian demonstrations in Lima before or during the war. Yet, the Allied-Peruvian government dragnet still found, arrested, and deported a few Italians and Germans on the F.B.I. black list. These arrests attest to President Prado's desire to cooperate closely with the United States in its hemispheric security campaign. One of the last shipload of deportees from Peru in late March 1944 reflects well the ratio of deportees throughout the war. Bound for the "family internment camp" at Crystal City, Texas, the immigrants numbered 7 Italians, 165 Germans, and 368 Japanese. Of the German group only 42 were females and the number of children was very small. This was strange since the group was being sent to a "family camp." The youngest of the German group was 4 months, and the oldest 65 years. Most German men apparently chose to leave their wives and children in Peru while apparently planning to reunite with them in Germany after the war.[14]

In the economic sphere, the Prado government also signaled its emphatic support of the Allies by agreeing to commodity price controls to further the war effort. As a result, Peru's foreign exchange reserves grew at a smaller rate than any other major Latin American country during the war. The nation's reserves grew only 55 percent while those of Brazil, Colombia, and Mexico expanded at rates 10 times that of Peru.[15] Unfortunately, Peru's manufacturing sector grew only minimally during the war. Native investors remained tied to the traditional sectors of mining and agriculture, despite the commodity controls, which limited profits in such sectors. High taxes on exports actually reduced the number of acres in cotton. Major U.S. corporations such as I.P.C., Cerro de Pasco, and W. R. Grace solidified their dominant role in Peru's economy during the World War II–boom years. One of the most encouraging developments in the economy was the continuing emergence of the fishing sector. Spurred by the cutoff of fish exports from Japan and Scandinavia, Peruvian fishing interest began supplying U.S. buyers canned fish, fish livers, and smoked and salted fish. Thus, Peru's fishing industry, so vital to its economic viability in the 1960s and beyond, was established.[16]

The Prado administration seemed unable to devise "a coherent development strategy" during the economically beneficial war years. Instead, because of the cutoff of most alternative markets throughout the world, Peru became excessively dependent on U.S. economic assistance and investment. On the other hand, because Peru adhered to such restrictive commodity prices in the spirit of the war effort, the Prado government had very limited options.

Before December 1941, the United States and Britain worked to eliminate Axis elements in Peru. Once the Italian air mission that had trained pilots since the mid-1930s left Peru in March 1940, Peruvian pilots traveled to the United States and Britain to train. A U.S. naval aviation advisor team headed by a marine colonel arrived in Peru only five months later. In addition, Captain William Quigley, USN, was named to the critical command post of Inspector General of the Navy. Within months Quigley became the Navy's Chief of Staff. Clearly the bond between the navies of Peru and the United States were never stronger than during World War II.[17] The Peruvian navy performed its mission of coastal defense quite well during the war. Its primary responsibility was to protect shipping and ports, particularly the facilities at Talara. Additionally, it aided the U.S. navy in protecting the approaches to the Panama Canal. Before these operations began, however, the navy and nearly the full force of the Peruvian armed forces were committed to conducting a border war with Ecuador which commenced in July 1941.

BORDER WAR WITH ECUADOR

Of the many border disputes in modern Latin American history, the conflict between Peru and Ecuador may well be the most complex. Resolved only during the last years of the 20th century, the dispute had its origins in the imprecise boundary decisions made by Spanish colonial authorities. The common border also ran through some of the most remote mountain and jungle regions in South America. Since independence, Peru and Ecuador disagreed over the exact location of their common boundary.

In the 1880s the two nations negotiated the García-Herrera Treaty that proposed a settlement. The Peruvian Congress, however, failed to ratify the treaty. During the opening years of the 20th century, small detachments of Peruvian and Ecuadorian soldiers periodically skirmished along the Napo and Angosteros rivers northwest of Iquitos. Further attempts by the King of Spain to arbitrate the dispute during the 1930s failed. Peru's tactical defeat by

Colombia in the 1933 Leticia dispute convinced Peru's general staff during the Benavides era that a modernization of the armed forces was mandatory. Benavides met these demands with arms purchases and contracting of military mission from Italy, Germany, and the United States. The army alone grew from 8,000 men in 1933 to 25,000 in early 1941. Ecuador's army, by contrast, numbered only 4,000 on the beginning of hostilities. With significant foresight Peru acquired 24 Czech-made light tanks and 26 Italian Caproni bombers during the late 1930s. Roads, bridges, and airfields were also improved along key border areas with Ecuador.[18]

As tensions mounted on the borders with Ecuador, Peru's military planners correctly surmised the United States would not allow an extended military conflict in an area that would imperil the defense of the Panama Canal. Prepared to immediately take the offensive if hostilities began, armed forces leaders convinced President Prado that they were not prepared to accept a negotiated settlement until after military operations were complete. General Eloy Ureta commanded Peru's forces in the north, and it was his intention to occupy large areas of Ecuadoran territory and hold it until international diplomacy ended the conflict. Peruvian military leaders knew that with Germany's Wehrmacht driving on three fronts into Russia and the Japanese advancing into southeast Asia, that Washington and other Latin American nations would want a settlement for hostilities on the approaches to the Panama Canal resolved as quickly as possible. They were completely correct in that assumption.[19]

Major hostilities began on July 5, 1941, along the border areas of the Zarumilla-Marañón rivers. In one of the most sophisticated military operations in Peruvian military history, joint operations including a naval blockade of the Jambeli channel, motorized infantry, tanks, and even small paratroop units, Peruvian forces launched a small blitzkrieg against Ecuadorian forces. Other areas of conflict were Ecuador's Pacific coastal region near the towns of Puerto Bolivar, Santa Rosa, and Machala, and in the eastern selva region near Corrientes, Curaray, and Tarqui. By the time these military operations were halted in mid-August, the Ecuadorian army had all but disintegrated. It is possible that Peruvian forces could have captured Guayaquil had the conflict not been terminated by a cease-fire on October 2, 1941. In this short but devastating war, Ecuador suffered a defeat at least equal to Peru in the war of the Pacific. Peruvian troops remained in captured Ecuadorian territory until a settlement of the dispute was hammered out at the Third Meeting of Foreign Ministers of the American States at Rio de Janeiro in January 1942. Faced with a hard line by Peru with its troops occupying expanses Ecuadorian territory, the foreign ministers from the United States, Argentina, Chile, and Brazil convinced Ecuador to sign the Rio Protocol. The agreement confirmed Peru's control of the provinces of Tumbes, Jaén, and Maynas. El Oro province was evacuated by the Peruvian army. Ecuador retained access to the Putumayo river but more importantly lost its access to the Amazon. Ecuador eventually rejected the Rio Protocol in 1960 stating it was signed under duress and the boundary line was inaccurate in the Cordillera del Condor region. And as we shall see, hostilities again erupted between these two nations in 1981 and 1995. But for the Peruvian military, the Ecuador campaign was one of profoundly satisfying professional experiences.

Military commanders in the conflict including Ureta and Lieutenant Colonel Manuel A. Odría emerged as very prominent national figures after the border war. President Prado took great pains to grant liberal numbers of military citations to veterans of Peru's Northern Army Group. APRA, although still technically illegal, praised the military campaign and even visited Ureta military headquarters to wish him well. APRA followed a strict policy of refraining from civil-military intrigue during the Ecuador War and most of World War II. The party adopted a pro-U.S. policy and purported to be the most prominent anti-Axis element in Peru. Particularly aggressive in attacking Peru's Japanese population was Haya de la Torre, claiming repeatedly that his party members could be effective counterespionage forces if used properly by the United States.

Peru was the recipient of significant Lend Lease equipment during World War II with a stated value of $18 million. However, it is not clear how much of this was delivered before the war's end. Most of the equipment went to Peru's fledgling air force including 30 P-36 fighters, 13 A-33 bombers and PT-19 trainers.[20] The United States built an air base at Talara during the early war years to help patrol the approaches to the Panama Canal and protect the oil fields administered by I.P.C. This base, called El Pato, was turned over to Peru at the end of the war. It became one of the Peruvian air force's main installations in the post-war years. The navy and the army did not fare as well in this largess. Prado's preference for the air force was likely a reflection of his close friendship with air force chief Fernando Melgar, who may have been Prado's most important compadre in the armed forces. This favoritism sullied Prado's relations with junior officers who wanted their technological capabilities upgraded when the times were most opportune.

The centerpiece of U.S. economic development assistance was an Export-Import Bank loan for the planning and construction of a large industrial complex near the northern city of Chimbote. Unfortunately, the domestic financing for this steel complex was not forthcoming. Not until 1956 was financing obtained for a steelmaking and hydroelectric facility at Chimbote that is known today as Siderúrgica del Perú. The slow development of the Chimbote facility bears out Thorp and Bertram's conclusion that important opportunities for basic industrial development were allowed to slip away during the war years and after. An important figure for promoting good Peruvian–U.S. relations during the war years was Nelson Rockefeller. With funds largely contributed by the Rockefeller Institute, health programs were established in the largely neglected Amazon basin near Loreto and Chimbote. Agricultural training programs were also begun near Tingo Maria. Subsequently, hospitals were built and health workers trained through initiatives begun by Rockefeller. The son of the oil magnate, Nelson Rockefeller assumed a very prominent role in Latin American affairs during the war. His interest in Peru remained active well into the 1960s.[21]

The labor sector in Peru during the war years remained relatively docile as APRA leader and the Communist Party of Peru understood the implications of seeming to undermine the campaign against fascism. In rural Peru, *Yanaconaje* was still being used throughout the sierra. With origins deep in Peru's past, Yanaconaje was a system wherein an owner advances land and water rights for a specified period in exchange for about a quarter of the tenants gross production. In many cases the colonos already have some land of their own. They in turn employ landless peasants (*aparceros*) to work their rented holdings. Usually, these aparceros are paid by the colonos with a portion of the crop that remains after payment to the primary landlord.

In the very large and corporate-owned coastal sugar and cotton estates, three different kinds of labor arrangements prevailed. First there were permanent resident wage laborers who worked full-time, received housing, food, and general benefits. Seasonal migrant workers were employed at a higher cash wage rate than permanent workers but did not receive benefits. A third type of agricultural workers were daily wage workers who would often pick up odd jobs only when they were available. These lower level laborers were usually recent migrants from the sierra, who were just beginning their transition from communal to commercial agriculture.[22]

Peru's mining industry did not really benefit from World War II. The United States fixed metal prices and pressured Latin American producers to do the same. European metal markets were also cut off by the war. Dore notes that prices for Peruvian copper production remained stagnate from 1940 until 1959. Cerro de Pasco previous to the late 1940s refined most of its copper in the United States. Cerro then invested in a refining plant at La Oroya and built another processing plant at Yauricocha in 1948. Unionization of the mines coincided with industrial expansion at La Oroya. Cerro recognized a miners trade union for the for the first time in 1944. Within three years, 38 mine workers unions were recognized. APRA seized upon this opportunity to facilitate the creation of the *Federación del Trabajadores Mineros de Centro* (The Federation of Mine Workers of Central Peru). Despite increased unionization and labor militancy in the mining sector during the 1940s, conditions did not significantly improve in the mines. APRA legislatures were either unable or unwilling to introduce laws that would address mining conditions or wages. Cerro de Pasco operations in central Peru still accounted for 60 percent of all Peru's mining production by the late 1940s. But as production continued to stagnate and technology for processing-low grade ore advanced, major mining companies began the shift from traditional underground shaft mining to open-pit operations. Operations became more profitable, but the negative impact upon the environment was horrific.[23]

The war years witnessed the intensification of immigration of Peru's rural population to Lima that continues to the present day. Ironically, it was the strong earthquake of May 24, 1940, that may have established the formative conditions for this migration to commence. The earthquake took only 179 lives but caused extensive damage to Lima residential housing. Hardest hit were adobe structures, with at least a quarter of this type of residence being completely destroyed. Unable to find immediate temporary housing for the large number of homeless Limeños, the government tried to stabilize the existing housing situation by fixing rents and making evictions extremely difficult. These housing regulations remained in effect until long after World War II and encouraged migrants to flow to Lima and its *barriadas* or squatter communities that were emerging around Lima and extending into the coastal desert region. Once squatters had situated themselves on a piece of land, they would mark out plots and establish temporary housing rapidly. Soon the shantytowns established a good degree of infrastructure and permanence. Stubbornly resisting governmental attempts to drive them off their settlement, the barriadas, as they would later be called, slowly evolved into permanent and viable new neighborhoods of Lima. Scholars José Matos Mar Santos and Susan Lobo have demonstrated that these "spontaneous settlements" filled a housing need the government was not capable of meeting. They became part of Peru's huge informal sector that dominated the economy in the last decades of the 20th century.

Lima's expanding industrial economy and the development of the fishing industry were clearly pull factors that drew Andean migrants to the "primate" city during and after the war. Push factors were environmental events such as earthquakes, landslides, and floods. In later decades it would be terrorist activities that would force entire villages to flee their ancestral homeland.

THE CHURCH AND CATHOLIC ACTION IN PERU

The religious life of both rural and urban Peruvians during the two decades after 1930 was marked by the continuing institutional weakness of the Catholic Church. One problem more than any other marked the Church's religious role in Peru: the shortage of native-born priests and sisters to administer to the nation's Catholics. Characteristically, a high percentage of Peru's priests and nuns are foreign born. Peruvian Catholics, whether in the burgeoning cities of the coast or in the sierra, were receiving little if any formal religious instruction and infrequently attending mass and receiving the sacraments because of a shortages of priests. A careful study of Catholic attitudes in the early 1950s, for example, indicated that most Peruvians were Catholic in name only. Few had more than a passing interest in church doctrine or Catholic practice. Indigenous peoples were found to have retained a significance portion of the Quechua or Aymara beliefs as a foundation for their imperfectly learned Catholic doctrine. Most Peruvians were found to not have a profound Catholic social conscience. They related their religious beliefs to themselves personally and to their families and not to the wider social world.[24]

Before the 1960s the Church in Peru systematically opposed the populist policies of APRA and warned Catholics that the APRA party was linked to the teachings of Moscow. Sánchez Cerro was also sharply criticized for legalizing divorce in 1933 and calling for the eventual separation of church and state. Most Peruvian Catholics did not let the church dictate their political allegiances. Also, Catholic youth action groups began to emerge during the 1920s and 1930s even as the incipient APRA was attempting to make Peru a more secular state. Two prelates, Mariano Holguín of Arequipa and Pedro Pascual Farfán of Cusco, took the lead during this era in establishing a more independent church, free from direct association with the government. They sought to create a more militant Catholicism by establishing permanent laymen's associations to increase social activism and energize church membership.

This movement was launched with the highly successful Eucharistic Congress of 1935 that was attended by 100,000. The main lay speakers at the congress were the Víctor Andrés Belaúnde and José de la Riva Aguero. The congress stimulated further Catholic lay activity during the World War II years. A university component of Catholic Action, the National Union of Catholic Students (UNEC), was established in 1941 and soon 10 percent of the all Peruvian University students belonged. One of UNEC's most prominent members was Héctor Cornejo Chávez, who played a leading role organizing university students in Arequipa. He later became one of the founders of Peru's Christian Democratic party and a candidate for Peru's presidency. Association with Catholic Action seems to also have shaped the careers of Peru's two most prominent clerics of the mid-20th century, Juan Landázuri Ricketts, who would become the reformist Archbishop of Lima during the Velasco years, and Father Gustavo Gutiérrez, generally credited with playing a leading role in the Liberation Theology movement after Vatican II.[25] Gutiérrez trained for the priesthood in Europe but clearly developed his social conscience while a young man in Peru. His early involvement as a lay person in Catholic Action played an important role in his determined quest for the church to take a leading role in promoting social justice.

The eminent scholar of the Catholic Church in Peru, Jeffrey Klaiber, S.J., argues that Catholic Action during the years 1930 to 1948 developed into a "small but solid" interest group for social change in Peru. Catholic Action, according to Klaiber, was influential far beyond its listed membership, which usually did not number more than a thousand. Prominent members such as Cornejo Chávez and Landázuri Ricketts confirm this. Klaiber further argues that the reason Catholic Action did not evolve into a prominent political movement for social change was because of the broad secular and even spiritual appeal of APRA before 1950.[26] If we are to understand important components of Peru's military reformist mentality of the period from 1968 to 1975, we need to look to the roots of Christian Democracy in the Catholic Action programs of the period before 1950.

THE TROUBLED DEMOCRATIC INTERLUDE, 1945–1948

As World War II came to a close, the impulse for democratic elections and civilian government was very strong. In keeping with Franklin Roosevelt's Four Freedoms and the bloody campaigns against fascism and militarism, most Peruvians looked to the 1945 elections with hope for a more democratic future. Junior army officers, for example, were complaining among themselves that their leaders, officers like General Benavides and Ureta, were using their military prestige for political gain. They contrasted the two leaders to U.S. military commanders from World War II who were retiring from the service and quietly upholding the democratic traditions of the military in the United States. In Peru, junior officers, particularly those who formed a clique known as the Committee of Revolutionary Army Officers (CROE), seemed not to recognize that their antipolitical stance was indeed stridently political. This group, headed by an army major and Aprista, Víctor Villanueva Valencia, would be at the center of antigovernment activity with an abortive antigovernment plot at the Ancon air base in January 1945 and again in a much broader conspiracy involving officers and enlisted naval personnel in Callao in October 1948.

APRA remained illegal throughout World War II, but Haya de la Torre was given a fair amount of freedom of movement. Prado recognized that the arrest and imprisonment of Haya de la Torre could possibly lead to violence comparable the Trujillo insurrection of July 1932. Moreover, he was aware that the APRA established contact with the U.S. Embassy in Lima and that Washington felt that contact with the APRA leader would be beneficial in their anti-Axis campaign in Peru. Víctor Villanueva, who knew Haya de la Torre well, claims that the APRA leader was actually on the payroll of the U.S. Embassy to serve as a conduit for intelligence about Axis activities. Villanueva also argued that by the end of World War II, Haya de la Torre had almost completely abandoned his anti-imperialist position in favor of a pro-U.S. and later an anticommunist ideology.[27] The APRA did indeed seek to use the U.S. Embassy to try and leverage his party's legality during the war. But in the end, Prado proved to be too good of friend of the United States to risk endangering an already beneficial relationship.

Less than a week after Germany's surrender in early May, Prado felt secure enough to legalize APRA in an arrangement that would not allow the party to field a presidential candidate but would enable Apristas to be candidates for the national legislature.

In a massive rally on May 20, 1945, in downtown Lima, Haya de la Torre was reunited with his Aprista following in an open public setting for the first time in more than a decade. He stressed reconciliation rather than revenge. He outlined a moderate course for the party that differed sharply from the radical rhetoric of the 1930s. What was abundantly clear in his 30-minute address, however, was the idea, indeed the party slogan, that "only APRA can save Peru."

Peru's two most prominent military men, Marshal Oscar R. Benavides and General Eloy Ureta both sought the presidency in 1945. But, as we have seen, junior officers in the army were opposed to their candidacy. Benavides also faced the powerful opposition of the Miró Quesada family and *El Comercio*. There was a strong feeling that a candidate not involved in the intense factionalism of Peruvian politics was the best possible compromise. To this end, a distinguished jurist and diplomat José Luis Bustamante y Rivero was named the choice of the National Democratic Front, a party constructed from a agreement forged between Benavides and the APRA leadership. General Ureta built his candidacy among elements of Peru's rightist elements and the Miró Quesada clan.

Ever fearful that the 1945 elections would be rigged by Prado, APRA made yet another foray into conspiratorial politics by instigating an uprising at the airbase at Ancón March 18, 1945. At the last minute, however, the APRA leadership ordered the uprising aborted, and a number of junior army officers and members of CROE were arrested or transferred to remote garrisons. The abortive Ancón uprising was clear harbinger of indecisive ARPR leadership that would have far more dire consequences in the October 1948 Callao revolt.

With the backing of the APRA and Benavides, Bustamante defeated Ureta soundly by a two to one margin in the 1945 presidential elections. Civilian democracy seemed to have triumphed over caudillismo, but appearances were deceiving. APRA elected 64 senators and deputies to the National Congress, which was significantly short of a legislative majority. APRA would have to work with Bustamante on its legislative agenda while facing significant opposition from the congressional right. APRA's tactics during the Bustamante presidency were two fold. Its congressional representatives sought to repeal the emergency legislation of past years that had proscribed the party activities. From there the party sought to build its congressional power at the expense of the president so it could enact its legislative program.

Missing from APRA's legislative agenda was agrarian reform and other substantive social legislation that the party's rank and file hoped would be enacted during Bustamante's term. Before the election, the party promised rural workers that land redistribution would occur and that rent payments would be lowered or abolished. By 1947 only the Law of Yanaconaje (tenancy) was passed limiting evictions, sustaining the validity of contracts, and establishing improved working conditions. Exploited tenancy still remained the watchword in the sierra under APRA's new agenda. APRA did work to expand its following among urban working- and middle-class sectors by encouraging the expansion of labor unions and raising salaries for government employees.[28] The party's new position thus shifted from a "share the wealth" campaign to "creation of new wealth" by the expansion of capitalist enterprise in Peru. But this rhetorical nuance amused some members of the oligarchy, convinced U.S. diplomats that APRA was no longer a threat. However, it did not satisfy many party militants who were becoming increasingly restive.

This was the first of a number of monumental shifts in APRA's ideology since its founding in 1924. This change, however, may have been its most costly regarding the allegiance of its rank and file. For most of Bustamante's term as president there were three APRAs, the increasingly compromised and politically opportunistic leadership, the loyal but confused rank and file, and the militant Apristas who despaired as they watched the opportunity for meaningful reform slip away. The once rock-solid party discipline was eroding as Haya de la Torre and other party leaders sent mixed messages to their Aprista followers.

While carrying out it congressional agenda, the party continued to harass and intimidate its political enemies by violent demonstrations reminiscent of "radical" years during the 1930s. Known as *búfalos* (street fighters), Aprista activists reappeared during these years to reassure military and civilians alike that the party was still ready to take to the streets if necessary.

APRA, noting the advantage of its anti-Axis stance during World War II, courted Washington's support by trumpeting its anti-Communism during the first years of the Cold War. Haya de la Torre even sought to reestablish communication with the F.B.I. regarding communist activities in Peru. Reflective of APRA's increasingly conservative stance on foreign capital, the party supported a oil exploration contract in the Sechura desert by I.P.C. that many conservative nationalists in the congress opposed. The Sechura exploration legislation sounded the death knell for APRA's fundamental programmatic ideal of anti-imperialism when the party was founded in 1924. APRA's double game of legislative initiative and concurrent violence backfired in early January 1947 when the staunchly anti-APRA editor of *La Prensa*, Francisco Graña, was assassinated. Eventually two Apristas were charged with the crime. President Bustamante was forced to discharge his cabinet, which contained three

Apristas. Thereafter until his overthrow in October 1948, he came to rely increasingly on military men for advice as he struggled to control an increasingly frustrated APRA's quest for power.

Conservative opponents of APRA in the national congress finally brought matters to a climax by boycotting the senate in July 1947 thus preventing the congress from functioning under the terms of the Peruvian Constitution. With Bustamante ruling by decree and surrounding himself with a military men in his cabinet, by the end of 1947 APRA was forced to return to conspiracy and rebellion as the only path to securing full political power. Haya de la Torre, however, would discover that his policy of mixed messages to different audiences would nearly doom his party as he made yet another desperate quest for power.

Throughout the first six months of 1948, APRA stepped up its militant activities. Military leaders, especially General Manuel A. Odría, pressed Bustamante continuously to outlaw APRA. Bustamante, perhaps mindful that an illegal APRA would be even more dangerous, refused. By September 1948, three distinct groups emerged that sought to determine the fate of Bustamante's increasingly ineffectual government. Haya de la Torre and select members of the APRA leadership conspired with army general José del Carmen Marín to initiate a bloodless coup, which would install a short-term military government as a prelude to APRA's full assumption of power. Another group headed by the Aprista-hating General Odría backed by much of the army, the Miró Quesada family, and Pedro Beltan, editor of *La Prensa*, were plotting to overthrow Bustamante and establish a right-wing military dictatorship. The final faction was led by the dauntless Major Villanueva, an Aprista and a revolutionary who was quickly losing patience with Haya de la Torre and the party leadership. Villanueva planned a civil-military revolt that would begin in the port city of Callao and involve some petty and non-commissioned officers of Peru's fleet. They would be supported by some suborned air force officers, who would fly sorties from their base at Las Palmas. Aprista street fighters were to capture the Central Telephone Exchange in Lima and support attacks on naval targets in Callao. Critical to the Callao revolt's success were the coordinated operations of rebellious military personnel and Aprista supporters.

The initiation of the revolt during the early morning hours of October 3, 1948, saw rebel sailors take control of most of the ships of Peru's fleet. Soon, however, submarines manned by loyal sailors neutralized the ships before they were able to continue their bombardment of shore installations. Critical positions such as the Real Felipe fortress were captured and held for a brief time by the rebels. Soon reinforcements from infantry and tank regiments from Lima garrisons suppressed the uprising. Most importantly, Aprista street fighters were not activated as the party's leaders gave orders for all of its militants to stand down. Villanueva later argued that the revolt might have succeeded

had the party leadership supported its militants.[29] Party leader Manuel Seoane later claimed that the Callao revolt was the result of "hotheads" within
APRA's ranks. He maintained that the party did not authorize or approve
of the rebellion. Nevertheless, APRA had to face the dire consequences. The
most serious rebellion in Peru since the Trujillo uprising would quickly lead to
Bustamante's overthrow. More importantly it would have far-reaching consequences for Peru political and social affairs for decades to come.

THE ODRÍA COUP

In the aftermath of the Callao revolt, Bustamante outlawed APRA. The government arrested and interrogated 1,000 civilians and 800 naval personnel,
nearly 20 percent of the naval force. Many APRA leaders, including Haya de
la Torre, went into hiding, as the party's brief window on power firmly closed.
General Odría, who plotted Bustamante's overthrow since his removal from
the cabinet three months earlier, almost immediately laid plans for a *golpe de
estado*. Like Sánchez Cerro in 1930, Odría launched his golpe from Arequipa,
where his forces seized key installations and neutralized the local army garrison. After a radio appeal for support, Odría's revolt spread to Cuzco, Juliaca,
and Puno. Armed forces leaders in Lima, however, argued intensely before
deciding to support Odría. Air force leaders opposed the golpe but would
not use their planes against Odría's troops in Arequipa. The prestigious General Ureta argued for Bustamante's ouster. The decisive vote was cast by General Zenon Noriega, commander of the Second Light Division in Lima, who
refused to use his troops against the rebellion. On October 29, 1948, armed
forces leaders demanded Bustamante's resignation. He refused. He was then
arrested and placed aboard an airplane bound for Buenos Aires.

The Odría coup was backed by Peru's extreme right. Pedro Beltran's *La
Prensa* proclaimed in a banner headline, "The patriotic movement of the army
has triumphed." *El Comercio* and the Miró Quesada family were also part of
the movement. Upon arriving in Lima and taking power, Odría claimed in a
speech at the Limatambo airport that the "Bustamante regime has poisoned
the hearts and sickened the minds of the Peruvian people."[30] He promised
quick elections and a brief tenure in power. Most in the crowd knew that these
promises meant little. They expected tough new measures from a military dictatorship. These were the standard rules of the game in Peruvian civil military
affairs for the first half of the 20th century.

CONCLUSION

The era from 1930 to 1948 ended as it had begun, with a military golpe
estado based in Peru's southern city of Arequipa. These nearly two decades

witnessed the emergence of mass politics in Peru for the first time. It proved to be a very uneasy period of transition. APRA struggled furiously to attain political power, and in the end, the indecisiveness of its leaders cost them the allegiance of many party activists. Víctor Villanueva, who spent years in prison and exile after the failed Callao insurrection, denounced the APRA leadership in a widely read series of books for many years thereafter. Moreover, Abimael Guzmán Reynoso, the founder and maximum leader of Sendero Luminoso, pinpointed the Callao rebellion as formative experience in shaping his revolutionary views. Guzmán claimed in an *El Diario* interview, "I had the occasion to see the uprising in Callao in 1948. To see with my own eyes the people's courage, how they were brimming with heroism and how the (APRA) leadership betrayed them . . . These things exerted an influence on me. I believe, like every communist, I am a child of the class struggle and the party."[31] APRA's move to the right after 1948 created an opening for a reformist military and the radical leftist Sendero Luminoso to fill an immense void of leadership for Peru's impoverished and desperate masses.

The emergence of capitalism in the indigenous communities of the highlands certainly did not fill this void. Peru remained tied to an export-oriented economy that went hand-in-hand with dominant foreign capital in key sectors of mining, manufacturing, and agriculture.

NOTES

1. Quoted in and translated by Steve Stein in *Populism in Peru: The Emergence of the Masses and the Politics of Social Control* (Madison: University of Wisconsin Press, 1980), 68–69.

2. Peter F. Klarén, *Peru: Society and Nationhood in the Andes* (Oxford: Oxford University Press, 2000).

3. Fredrick B. Pike, *The Politics of the Miraculous in Peru: Haya de la Torre and the Spiritualist Tradition* (Lincoln: University of Nebraska Press, 1986), 167.

4. Haya de la Torre interview with the author, July 13, 1974, Lima, Peru. This interview occurred at the *Casa del Pueblo,* the APRA headquarters.

5. Daniel M. Masterson, *Militarism and Politics in Latin America: Peru from Sánchez Cerro to Sendero Luminoso* (Westport, CT: Greenwood Press, 1991), 55–56.

6. Rosemary Thorp and Geoff Bertram, *Peru 1890–1977: Growth and Policy in an Open Economy* (New York: Columbia University Press, 1978), 174.

7. Daniel M. Masterson with Sayaka Funada, *The Japanese in Latin America* (Urbana: University of Illinois Press, 2004), 41.

8. Florencia Mallon, *The Defense of the Community in Peru's Central Highlands: Peasant Struggle and Capitalist Transition, 1860–1940* (Princeton: Princeton University Press, 1983).

9. Ibid., 156–157.

10. See C. Harvey Gardiner, *Pawns in a Triangle of Hate: The Peruvian Japanese and the United States* (Seattle: University of Washington Press, 1981). The triangle of hate that Gardiner referred to in this book encompassed Japan, the United States, and Peru where race issues were paramount in wartime decision making.

11. Ibid., 159–174.

12. Oriazio Ciccareli, "Fascism and Politics in Peru during the Benavides Regime, 1933–1939: The Italian Perspective," *Hispanic American Historical Review* 70, no. 3 (1990), 405–432.

13. John Emmerson, *The Japanese Thread: A Life in the Foreign Service* (New York: Holt, Rinehart and Winston, 1978).

14. Special War Problems Division Records, Record Group 59, U.S. Department of State, "German and Japanese Nationals in Peru," March 21, 1944, Box 105, U.S. National Archives. See also Max Paul Friedman, *Nazis and Good Neighbors: The United States Campaign Against the Germans of Latin America* (Cambridge: Cambridge University Press, 2003).

15. Thorp and Bertram, *Peru: 1890–1977*, 182–187.

16. Ibid., 180–181.

17. Leon Garaycochea, *Legislación Naval de Aviación* (Lima: Imprenta Segrestan, 1940), xi, 640–648.

18. Robert L. Scheina, *Latin American Wars: The Age of the Professional Soldier: 1900–2001*. Vol. 2 (Washington DC: Brassey's, 2001),

19. G-2 Report No. 385333, June 30, 1947, U.S. Military Attache to War Department, U.S. National Archives, Record Group 319.

20. U.S. Department of State, Papers Relating to the Foreign Relations of the United States, 1944, 7, 1508.

21. Lawrence Clayton, *Peru and the United States: The Condor and the Eagle* (Athens: University of Georgia Press, 1999), 164–165.

22. David Chaplin, *The Peruvian Industrial Labor Force* (Princeton: Princeton University Press, 1967), 68–69.

23. Elizabeth Dore, *The Peruvian Mining Industry: Growth, Stagnation and Crisis* (Boulder: Westview Press, 1988), 87–143.

24. Michael Fleet and Brian Smith, *The Catholic Church and Democracy in Chile and Peru* (Notre Dame: University of Notre Dame Press, 1997), 84.

25. Jeffrey Klaiber, "The Catholic Lay Movement in Peru, 1867–1959," *The Americas* 40, no. 2 (1983), 163–164.

26. Ibid., 167–168.

27. Víctor Villanueva Valencia, *El Apra y el Ejército, 1940–1950* (Lima: Juan Meija Baca, 1977), 32–32; Víctor Villlanueva Valencia personal interview with the author, June 25, 1974, Lima, Peru.

28. Klarén, *Peru*, 292–293.

29. Víctor Villanueva Valancia, personal interview with the author, July 27, 1974, Lima, Peru.

30. Masterson, *Militarism and Politics*, 123–124.

31. *El Diario* interview. Author's transcript copy.

7

Reform to Revolution in Peru, 1948--1980

During the more than three decades after World War II, the Peruvian nation faced a reckoning regarding the social and economic forces that were in play since the War of the Pacific. Capitalism had weakened the bonds of communal traditions in the highlands, and increasing numbers of campesinos lost claim to their lands. As Lima modernized, a great flood of migrants from the highlands made the capital their new home and thus changed the demographics of Peru forever. Foreign, especially U.S, capital tightened its hold on the main sectors of the Peruvian economy, especially in the agriculture and the extractive industries. But in their haste to acquire profits these multinationals alienated important sectors of Peru's leadership, especially staunch nationalists in the army. This prompted a strong reaction by radical military reformers after 1968. Popular political parties were proscribed for much of these three decades, and they have yet to achieve an authentic viability in Peruvian politics. APRA, with it leadership in prison, confined, or in exile was unable to achieve political power in the face of rabid opposition, especially in the army and the oligarchy. Ultimately, the armed forces, led by an overly confident but well-intentioned group of radicals, tried to remake the nation in its own rather imprecise self image. It was as Fidel Castro characterized it, "Like a fire in the firehouse." The great anomaly for Peru's military radicals has yet to be fully explained. This chapter will hopefully advance our understanding to a further modest degree.

THE ONCENIO OF ODRÍA

When he seized power in late October 1948, Manuel Odría planned to rule for an extended period. He ruled as provisional president until July 1950 until formal elections were held.

The regime's first priority was to purge Apristas from the government, labor, police, and armed forces. Over a thousand Apristas were arrested and many were jailed. Very quickly most of the APRA leaders, including party chiefs Armando Villanueva del Campo and Ramiro Prialé, were also seized. Both remained in prison for extended periods in the Lima Penitentiary. Haya de la Torre avoided capture until January 1949 when he was given asylum in the Colombian embassy in Lima. He remained in diplomatic asylum in the embassy for the next five years while repeated attempts to secure safe passage from Peru failed until he was finally released in April 1953.

Frederick Pike suggests that during the years in the Colombian Embassy, Haya de la Torre grew as person, becoming less narcissistic and more accepting of the rigors of his life. He read and wrote extensively. He became a student of the English historian Arnold Toynbee. He seemingly distanced himself from the radical politics of the past and became a more contemplative person. His anticommunism grew in intensity. Despite criticism from other APRA leaders that the United States was again becoming interventionist in Latin America because of the Cold War, he held on to the belief that Washington would be APRA's champion in Peru. This was true even as the Eisenhower administration decorated Odría for his support of the United States in the Cold War struggle against communism. Haya de la Torre's isolation in the embassy in the end was a mixed blessing. Members of the ARPA intelligencia, including the poets Magda Portal, Ciro Alegría, and Alberto Hidalgo, all quit the party over differences in ideology, particularly Haya de la Torre's seeming abandonment of anti-imperialism. Magda Portal, now an intensely vocal critic of the senior APRA, complained, "Always martyrs from the working class, never from among the leaders."[1]

On November 2, 1948, the Communist Party was declared illegal as the regime wanted to make it clear to the United States that it was not going to allow a militant left to remain unchecked as the Cold War heightened. Odría clearly learned the lessons from Sánchez Cerro and Benavides regarding populist support and armed forces loyalty. He courted the Lima working classes by initiating a number of public works projects that provided jobs for the underemployed. Public housing projects were begun for the first time for Lima's growing migrant settlers. Construction projects provided jobs for

Lima's working class. Odría's wife, María Delgado de Odría became the focal point of a superficial but effective charitable foundation that was clearly modeled after that of Juan and Eva Peron's in Argentina. Along these same lines, a new Ministry of Labor and Indian Affairs was established in April 1949 to help consolidate the dictator's gains among the working class. Odría tried to shore up his support within the armed forces by the old tactic or raising salaries 45 percent within his first year in office. This was soon followed by a 20 percent salary increase for government employees. The dictator's willingness to allow poor migrants to establish squatter settlements in Lima without opposition during the early 1950s established the basis for the informal sector of Peruvian society that flourished in the decades afterward. Odría was clearly trying to undermine APRA's support among the working classes of Lima, and, to a significant extent, he succeeded.

Feeling politically secure by January 1950, Odría announced the government would hold presidential and congressional elections in July 1950. Opposition to his presidency was still significant. In response to Odría's golpe, some junior officers had been exiled or had fled Peru and settled in Panama. In July 1949 they issued a proclamation claiming the Odría had "profaned the name" of the Peruvian armed forces by his illegal golpe de estado. They called for Odría to resign and remove the armed forces its political involvement that was a "painful spectacle for the Peruvian people."[2]

The dictator controlled every aspect of the election process and could invoke a internal security law to hamstring his political opponents. Nevertheless, a group of conservative opponents put forth the candidacy of another army general, Ernesto Montagne Markholtz, a long-time rival of the dictator. The National Election Jury quickly invalidated General Montagne's candidacy, and he was arrested and deported to Argentina. A brief uprising in Arequipa protesting the denial of General Montagne's candidacy was easily suppressed. The dictator was then elected in July without opposition to a six-year term as president. These six years would be an important turning point in civil-military affairs in Peru.

THE MILITARY'S NEW PROFESSIONALISM

The 1950s witnessed the emergence of what is now called asymmetrical warfare in many diverse areas of the world. Most important for the Peruvian military are the examples of Indo-China and Algeria. These two resounding military and political defeats for the French military put the Peruvian army's training by the French in an interesting perspective. It seemed to invoke an urgency among the more intellectually oriented army leaders to seek fundamental civic, economic, and military reforms to prevent revolution along the lines of Castro's Cuba. In response to pressure that had been building among senior army leaders for nearly a decade, Odría's rubber-stamp congress created the *Centro de Altos Estudios Militares* (Center of Higher Military Studies; CAEM) in July 1950. Similar centers existed in the United States (National War College) as well as in France, Argentina, and Brazil. The primary mandate of the CAEM was to establish a national war doctrine. But what was inherent in this mission was the development of a comprehensive and sophisticated doctrine of national defense. Odría tolerated the formation of CAEM, but he was really not supportive of its mission. Named as CAEM's first director was Odría's old enemy and APRA conspirator, General José del Carmen Marín. Most of the members of CAEM first class were only a year away from retirement. CAEM during its first years was a junkyard for Odría's enemies, whom he wanted to isolate from meaningful command positions.

Still Carmen Marín, one of the army's leading intellectuals and an ardent student of French military doctrine, was determined to make CAEM an important policy-making center for the Peruvian military. Carmen Marín and his successor Colonel Marcial Romero Pardo succeeded in doing that as the Peruvian military sought to rid itself of caudillismo and become more professional in outlook. It would be simplistic to say, as some have suggested, that the CAEM was the focal point of the reformist military mentality that gave rise to the Velasco-era reforms after 1968. Velasco never attended the CAEM and neither did a number of important figures in his military government. Moreover, new military doctrines imposed from above often take root very slowly. If anything, the French military doctrine Velasco learned as a young officer and his stint in France as Peru's military attaché during the Algerian war were probably more important to Velasco's outlook than anything transmitted from the CAEM. More important to understand about the CAEM is that it raised the level of expectation of Peruvian military officers to that of guardians of the national *bienestar* (well-being) rather than simply protectors of its borders. This supposed a much higher degree of professionalism than ever before.

Countering the lingering legacy of French military theory was the expanding role of the U.S. military in Peru. The United States sold substantial amounts of World War II surplus military equipment to Peru.[3] Thus, Odría was able to maintain a good balance of expenditures for the military and the urban sector to stabilize his political power base.

What is evident from articles that appeared in the army's main service journal, *Revista Militar del Perú,* is that there was growing sentiment in the army that poverty had to be addressed as a critical national problem. Education, beginning with basic literacy training, was one of the foremost reforms advocated by the army's writers. Literacy for army recruits was seen as essential but it was also part of a grander plan of "Indian integration" that army officers were writing about since the early 1900s. Still, army writers never clearly defined what they meant by Indian integration. In a broad sense they seemed to be advocating a unified a patriotic consciousness among all of Peru's people, including the Indians. In this sense the army essayists were quite naïve in thinking that such a coherent mindset could be achieved in a nation as diverse as Peru. But certainly, by the end of the 1950s, as land invasions and peasant unrest became widespread, agrarian reform and the relief of poverty in the sierra was definitely linked to the military's increasingly sophisticated concept of national defense that joined *bienestar* (well-being) of Peru's people to the nation's security.

Meanwhile, Odría faced the continuing problem of military challenges to his regime. The dictator employed his Internal Security Law, in place since 1948 to isolate his enemies and limit civil liberties. Juan Perón's overthrow by the military in Argentina in 1955 may have alerted Odría to the possible dangers of trying to extend his term in office after 1956. Consequently, he allowed preparations for national elections to proceed. Waiting for the opportunity, as always, was Haya de la Torre now free from his confinement in the Colombian embassy.

THE 1956 ELECTIONS

The path to power for the APRA was unclear up until only a few months before the scheduled elections. It was obvious Haya de la Torre could not present himself as a candidate but he hoped his party could gain a substantial number of seats in the national congress. Fernando Belaúnde Terry, a handsome and dynamic architect, emerged as a viable presidential candidate. From a prestigious Arequipa family, Belaúnde had the support of middle-class voters, many youth groups, and large segments of the army who admired his technocratic outlook. Haya de la Torre never considered working with Belaúnde because their constituencies were similar and APRA could easily be co-opted by the young architect's growing following. Serving as an alternative candidate in the 1956 elections was former president Manuel Prado. The last of Peru's oligarchy to seek the presidency, Prado was now in his late 60s and one of Peru's wealthiest men. Nevertheless, Haya de la Torre struck a deal with Prado that gave the former president APRA's support in return for the promise that Haya de la Torre could run for president in the 1962 elections and the party's candidate could run for the national congress in the 1956 elections. Called the *convivencia* (coexistence), the political compromise angered many Apristas because of the alliance with the oligarch. Still, APRA's party discipline was sufficient to elect Prado with 45 percent of the vote. Belaúnde polled a strong 36 percent, and Hernando Lavalle, a dull lawyer and banker backed by Odría, trailed with 20 percent. Women voted for the first time in the 1956 elections swelling the electorate to more than 1.25 million. Nearly all of

Peru's indigenous peoples, however, were still prevented from voting because of the strict literacy requirements.

THE PERUVIAN ECONOMY

A skilled politician, Prado enjoyed little political opposition from military until the 1962 elections were his undoing. The military was beginning to think more institutionally and professionally, thus individual plotting in the old caudillo style was strongly discouraged. Civil military relations may have improved but unrest in the countryside became widespread. Land invasions by peasants became commonplace, and in most sectors of Peru's leadership, the feeling was that some form of land reform was inevitable. The question was how comprehensive an agrarian reform would be in its implementation. As this question remained unanswered, Peru's export-oriented economy continued to grow and be dominated by large foreign capital.

The export sector expanded dramatically during the three decades after the Second World War. This boom was helped initially by the Korea War, but it continued thereafter for a wide variety of reasons. Leading the export boom were four principal commodities: fish products, zinc, lead, and iron. Of these commodities, the fish products industry that had begun its expansion during the war years grew at an astounding rate in the 25 years after 1950. By the mid-1960s, Peru was the world's leading fishing nation (by volume); the primary export was fish meal, which was used throughout the world for animal feed (primarily swine and poultry). As with fishing nations everywhere, Peru confronted the dilemma of a profitable and heavily capitalized industry that sought maximum profits. This led to overfishing, particularly of the most important catch, the anchovy. Due to a combination of ecological policy and poor management by the military government, the industry nearly collapsed in the early 1970s, when the catch declined from 11.7 million metric tons in 1971 to only 3.5 million in 1972.[4]

In the mining sector, expansion was made possible in some measure by the U.S. policy of stockpiling strategic metals during the Cold War. Two new major corporations began operations in Peru during this period. The Southern Peru Copper Corporation began planning for the massive open-pit mine at Toquelpala, which opened in the early 1960s.

The Marcona Mining company, operating in southern Peru, became a major player in the extractive industry when the company was revitalized by major capital from the Utah Construction Company. Because it had close contacts with the U.S. steel industry, Marcona had a ready source of customers for its iron ore. Like nearly all large U.S. firms operating in Peru at this time, its profit margins were considerable. Thorp and Bertram estimate that through the early to mid-1960s, Marcona returned average annual profits of 50 percent[5] These gains far exceeded an otherwise strong growth of between 13 and 20 percent per year in the mining sector for most of the two decades following the Korean War.

The petroleum sector remained stagnant for most of this period as renewed exploration in the Sechura dessert, blocked during the Bustamante presidency, proved quite disappointing. Thus, native Peruvian oil firms had mostly abandoned their operations by the time of the Velasco golpe de estado in October 1968. In the 1960s offshore drilling soon was dominated by the foreign company Belco, which sold most of its product through the state oil company Petroperu, founded by the military government. Exploration in the Amazon region proceeded at a modest pace during this period until massive strikes were made in the Ecuadorian Amazon in the early 1970s. The Velasco government pursued this exploration with the help of Japanese investors, but again, the results proved disappointing. Petroleum was not a prominent element of the export sector for any of this period and some fields, such as those formerly held by I.P.C. were nearly played out by the mid-1970s. Just before it was nationalized in 1968, I.P.C. still enjoyed sales of $83.7 million, which was more than double its returns in 1950.[6]

Cotton and sugar production was greatly expanded in the coastal desert plain by government-sponsored irrigation projects that opened vast expanses of land to new production. Sugar production increased by 63 percent and cotton yields by 59 percent, primarily because of the opening of newly irrigated lands. As often happened in Peru, however, the continued development of new coastal irrigation networks was halted during the mid- to late 1960s because the government shifted its priorities to opening up the interior with President Fernando Belaúnde Terry's (1963–1968) "marginal jungle highway." Impeding the continual expansion of Peru's export economy in the 1960s before the Velasco government was a marked decline in domestic investment. Peruvian investors simply lost confidence in the export sector to return significant profits and turned more toward investment to real estate or investment overseas. The 12 years of military rule with its sweeping nationalizations effectively shut down domestic private investment. The distrust of Peru's potential domestic investors in their own economy was not shared by major retail enterprises such as Goodyear, B. F. Goodrich, and Sears, all of whom located in Peru during this era and did well. Still the most diversified corporate entity in Peru remained Casa Grace. The firm employed more than 10,000 Peruvians in such diverse activities as aviation, paints, paper, and of course, its original function as a steamship line. Grace owned two sugar plantations, the Paramoga paper and chemical plants, and rail and steamship lines throughout Peru. Grace was one of the top four corporations by value in Peru, and all of these were U.S. owned.[7]

In terms of social trends that influenced the Peruvian economy during this era, urbanization and the growth of the middle class were paramount. New jobs in the government bureaucracy, especially during the mid 1950s facilitated middle-sector growth, but industrialization, which opened up managerial positions, also fostered growth, and the expansion of education provided jobs for teachers at all levels of instruction. Salaries lagged in education, and teachers would become some of the most militant labor activists during this era. Lima's underemployed increased dramatically as migration exceeded the ability of the capital's economy to provide meaningful employment. Chronic underemployment of Peru's urban lower classes to this day remains a critical issue.

Thorp and Bertram have a very negative view of the process of industrialization in Peru advanced in the 1960s. They note that the nation's investment elite was never really committed to the growth of an independent group of local capitalists who could help the government plan a coherent industrial policy while committing their own resources to the process. The lack of aggressive, local capitalists opened the way for foreign multinationals, who were increasingly viewed with suspicion by many Peruvians, particularly hard-line military nationalists. The very thing some military nationalists were calling for in their planning institutes such as CAEM, an integrated economy geared to increased self-sufficiency and the development of strategic industries, was not happening. A case in point was the Chimbote steel complex, which, although funded as early as the 1940s, was still not operating by the early 1960s. Foreign capital was becoming more, not less pervasive in Peru; this trend toward further involvement of foreign capital contrasted sharply with trends in other Latin American countries such as Chile. For many reasons Peru industrialized late, compared to other Latin American countries. The process lacked effective government planning or control. At one point, for example, 13 different auto assembly plants were operating in Peru with a limited consumer base for automobiles.

Discussion of the agrarian reform imposed by the military government in the 1970s will be offered later in this chapter. Suffice it to say that much of the agricultural sector was awaiting some form of agrarian reform as early as the mid-1950s. Consequently, new investment in agriculture was often withheld as issues of future ownership were in question. The unfortunate results of this circumstance was that Peru could not produce the requisite food stuffs to avoid significant imports to feed its population. This situation reached a crisis during the military government with a further disruption in agricultural production because of the sweeping nature of agrarian reform. The Peruvian economy became increasingly troubled after the boom years of the 1950s. No governments, whether civilian or military, could stabilize the very difficult economic circumstances.

AGRARIAN UNREST

During Prado's second term, APRA mitigated discontent within organized labor by promises of future benefits once the party achieved power. Party discipline was holding but unrest within the Aprista ranks was growing. APRA was active in Peru now for more than a generation, and its rank and file were hungry for the benefits of party membership that had heretofore given them only disappointment and suffering. After a short recession in 1957, the economy, led as always by export growth, picked up again. Economic transition in the sierra reflected the course of modernization and presaged great changes in agriculture and landholding patterns. The Mantaro Valley in Junín Department and Huancayo as it commercial satellite city prospered as this region supplied the daily food needs for a fast-growing Lima. In the northern departments, profitable dairy farming was replacing subsistence agriculture among hacendados and indigenous producers alike. But the picture in the more remote and impoverished areas of southern Peru, according to Klarén, "remained in subsistence and stagnation, if not outright decline."[8] Ecological conditions, such as a severe drought that troubled southern Peru in the late 1950s worsened campesino anger that was already growing because of the increasingly anachronistic and unjust gamonale system.

Better roads and communication among the campesinos and, in the case of Pasco Department, among miners, helped the coordination of protest movements by that region's indigenous peoples during the late 1950s. Major layoffs at Cerro de Pasco's copper mines sparked a wave of strikes. An unresponsive Cerro de Pasco then confronted the invasion of its ranch lands by campesinos, mostly women and children carrying Peruvian flags and singing traditional Quechua songs. These invasions bore remarkable similarities to the methods used by squatters from the sierra as they occupied urban real estate in Lima. At first the invasions were not carefully linked to a wider world. By the early 1960s, however, Handelman shows that the rise of peasant federations (*sindicatos*) joined with student groups in the cities, trade unions, lawyers, and sympathetic political leaders to broaden the impact of their radical actions. By the end of Prado's term, rural unrest had spread to most of the central and southern sierra. Leaders such as Hugo Blanco emerged to further radicalize the peasant movement. Blanco operated in the La Convención valley in Cuzco and rose from a local peasant organizer to a major position in the Valley's peasant confederation. Blanco encouraged armed invasions of local haciendas. Finally arrested in 1963, Blanco became one of the most identifiable figures for the *sindicato* movement. Articulate and dynamic, Blanco later attracted the attention of Peru's reformist military government as a possible link to campesinos in the sierra.[9]

It can be said that by the early 1960s large land owners were anticipating that their properties would very likely be subject to some form of agrarian redistribution. Alternative proposals, such as the colonization of the selva region were being suggested, especially by Belaúnde Terry. His "marginal jungle highway" became a centerpiece of his development proposals, but it was largely a quixotic gesture that had no meaning unless the proper infrastructure, marketing, and agricultural support measures were forthcoming. And they were not. Peru met its increasing food needs by shifting from production of cotton to food stuffs as the 1960s unfolded. The 1962 elections were thus held in a time of uncertainty about many key national issues.

THE 1962 ELECTIONS

Of the seven candidates for the presidency in 1962, three had a viable chance of being elected. It was one of the most closely contested elections in Peruvian history. In fact, no candidate received the required 33 percent of the votes mandated by the Peruvian constitution. This event set in motion a process of deal making that prompted a military coup that voided the election and established a temporary caretaker military government that lasted for one year.

Haya de la Torre, as had been determined by the *convivencia* agreement with Prado in 1956, was allowed to run for the presidency in 1962. He was opposed again by the even more popular Belaúnde running under the banner of a new and active party, *Acción Popular* (Popular Action). Former President Odría, still claiming a solid popular base in Lima because of is housing and poverty relief programs during the Oncenio, was also a formidable candidate. Although the APRA had lost much of the left wing of their party due to Haya de la Torre's increasingly conservative stance on agrarian reform, U.S. capitalism, and labor activism, Haya de la Torre still was considered the favorite to win the presidency. Belaúnde, as before, appealed to youth groups, Catholic Action, women, and the progressive element of the armed forces.

Belaúnde's book *La conquista del Perú por los Peruanos* (*Peru's Own Conquest*), published a few years before the election, outlined his grand scheme for developing Peru's selva region as a cornerstone of a broad range of reforms during his proposed presidency. Belaúnde also outlined a broad ranging role for the military in his government including activities such as mapping, road building, and sanitation programs, subsumed under the term *civic action.* Such activities were being advocated strongly by the Kennedy administration. Civic action was the bedrock of the role the Latin American military was to play under the Alliance for Progress. Only Belaúnde understood and approved this for the armed forces in the minds of many military leaders.

Odría, taking another page from Perón's political play book, called himself a "socialist of the right." By now Odría was "too old and too old hat" for most military leaders. He was seen as a discredited caudillo and was equally as objectionable to the armed forces as Haya de la Torre. Some high-ranking armed forces officers, including the navy's senior officer informed the U.S. ambassador before the election that Haya de la Torre was unacceptable to the armed forces as president. The feeling expressed was that APRA was still deeply antimilitary and that its recent conservative shift was only a clever ploy to achieve power. Haya de la Torre's alleged homosexuality was also raised as a factor in the armed forces objections to the APRA chief. Right before the election the navy minister insisted to the U.S. ambassador that "APRA would destroy the armed forces within three months" if Haya de la Torre were elected president.[10]

In this troubled election climate national elections were held in early June. Ballot counting went on very slowly, and the final results were not announced by the National Election Jury until late June. Haya de la Torre emerged the leader with 558,237 or 32.98 percent of the votes cast. Belaúnde finished a close second with 543,828 votes (32.13%), and Odría trailed in this very close election with 481,404 votes (28.44%). By the barest of margins, Haya de la Torre failed to achieve the one third of the votes necessary for the election. The presidential decision was then destined to be decided by the National Congress in which APRA controlled 40 percent of the seats. Belaúnde tried to co-opt this process by rallying his supporters in Arequipa, but the movement quickly dissolved. Informed by the armed forces leadership that they would not accept him as president, Haya de la Torre turned to his old tormentor, Odría, to arrange a political deal of Machiavellian dimensions. Haya de la Torre promised to give APRA support to the old caudillo in return for the seating of the party's number two leader Manuel Seoane as vice president. Under the agreement, all elected Apristas would retain their seats in congress. In fact, Haya de la Torre informed party leader Luis Alberto Sánchez, "We have won the majority of Congress, now we will be able to control the executive and co-govern. I have lost, but not the party."[11] In fact, shortly after the APRA leader spoke these words, the armed forces implemented an institutional golpe de estado in the early morning hours of July 18, 1962, that removed Prado only 10 days from the end of his presidency. The armed forces had acted not only against their old enemy APRA but also against the old-style caudillo politics of the past in the person of Manuel A. Odría.

THE MILITARY INTERREGNUM, 1962–1963

When the Peruvian armed forces seized power in July 1962, it was called an institutional coup d'état to distinguish it from the rule of caudillos such as Sánchez Cerro, Benavides, and Odría. The military was trying to distance itself from the non-professional and individualistic actions of these dictators.

During their one-year rule, they were only partially successful in this venture. Among the reasons for the military takeover, the most important appeared to be the inability of Belaúnde to win the presidency by ballots. Certainly, the military was opposed to Haya de la Torre and APRA running the country, but they were equally distraught at the prospect of six more years of Odría. Ironically, both Haya de la Torre and Odría were too conservative, even too reactionary for the armed forces. Peru faced an eminent agrarian crisis, and most leaders of the armed forces understood that well. APRA working with Prado had produced nothing of consequence regarding agrarian reform. There was no indication it would do so working with an Odría presidency. In effect, the military declared itself a caretaker government that would rule for only one year until new elections could be held. To be sure, the military intended to establish the conditions for Belaúnde's electoral victory in July 1963. In the meantime, the military government would take limited reform measures that presaged the far more extensive changes that would be proclaimed after October 1968 when the Velasco government took power. The Junta initiated a pilot agrarian reform program in the Cuzco region, created a National Planning Institute, and built a substantial number of public housing units as a show of good faith regarding its commitment to reform. Still political divisions surfaced during it one-year rule.

During the remaining four months of the junta's rule, no new reform measures were indeed begun. The main concern was the preparation for the national elections to be held as promised in early June 1963. The armed forces controlled nearly every aspect of the election process. This and Belaúnde electoral alliance in February 1963 with the *Partido Democrático Cristiano* (Christian Democratic Party) nearly assured Belaúnde an electoral victory. The party's left were dispersed in the crackdown against the communists. With this situation, the junta felt safe enough to once again allow the candidacy of Haya de la Torre and Odría. It seems certain, however, that if either of these two old war horses had won, the military would have again intervened to abort their presidency.

National elections on June 9, 1963 gave Belaúnde a clear victory. The architect drew 708,731 votes (39%). Haya de la Torre and Odría trailed with 34.3 percent and 25.5 percent, respectively. The votes of the far left and the Christian Democrats were the key to the new president's victory. Still, Belaúnde Popular Action party fell short of a majority in congress. This did not bode well for his programs as the APRA and Odría's congressional delegates soon formed a congressional alliance that stood in the way of many of his substantive reform proposals in congress. The armed forces returned to their barracks as promised on July 28, 1963. Belaúnde's presidency began in a flush of optimism. He seemed the ideal person to move Peru forward in the spirit of the Alliance for Progress and in Peru's own image of what was necessary for the nation, Military leaders were supportive but cautious regarding the new president's ability to further their reform agenda. They would, indeed, be restless allies of the architect turned president.

REFORM TO REVOLUTION, 1963–1968

The new president had campaigned more vigorously than any previous candidate, traveling to most region of the country and paying particular attention to the highlands. He thus not only had a clear idea of the nation's problems but he was also viewed as a problem solver by a wide variety of Peruvians. Foremost among his problems was the economy and agrarian reform. Alliance for Progress funding was beginning to dry up as the United States was committed more heavily to the Vietnam War. Vietnam made things much more difficult for the new president. The armed forces were also approaching a new weapons purchase cycle, as most of their World War II–vintage surplus equipment was aging badly. This issue would cause the new administration huge problems. Migration to Lima from surged during this era as the capital's barriadas grew continuously. These issues framed the fundamental problem of Peru's economy in the mid 1960's. How would the new president confront the increasing dominance of Peru's export and industrial sector by foreign capitalists.

Because of a substantial influx of foreign capital during the Belaúnde presidency, more than half of the goods produced in Peru were in foreign hands. This did not occur mainly by foreign takeover of Peruvian firms but by new non-native companies entering the manufacturing sector. Fundamentally, this made the Peruvian economy vulnerable to sharp variations in foreign exchange rates. Moreover, it reflects the distinct unwillingness of Peru's financial elite and other potential investors to assume the role as a national bourgeoisie as similar elites were doing in Brazil, Chile, and Mexico. This unwillingness to assume an investment responsibility by the Peruvian economic elite was not lost on the military. In the minds of military leaders, foreign ownership of many critical sectors of the Peruvian economy left the nation in a very vulnerable position that threatened national security. The mining industry stands out as a venture that exemplifies this tendency. Thorp and Bertram are harsh in their criticism of Peruvian capitalists in this regard noting, "local (mining) firms, although perfectly capable of proceeding with the development of large scale mining, had preferred to stand aside and leave the task to foreign capital."[12] Perhaps the shift from underground to open-pit mining after World War II discouraged local capital from investing in a new process. Still, much of Peru's critical resource base was not owned by Peruvians.

This was not the case with the rapidly expanding fish meal industry. Fish products rose from less than a one percent share of Peru's exports by value in

1945 to nearly one third near the end of Belaúnde's presidency. Indeed, Peru was the leading fishing nation in the world as assessed by volume in 1964. Due to ecological problems associated with El Niño, and overfishing, the fishing boom would end in the early 1970s. But during its heyday, the fishing industry drew substantial new Peruvian investors, some of whom made huge profits during the productive 1960s. Tied to the increased use of fish meal for chickens and hogs the fish meal industry boasted at its peak 150 firms, most of them local, operating in Peru by the mid-1960s.

AGRARIAN REFORM: TOO LITTLE, TOO LATE

Small agriculture in Peru, which employed 8 of 10 agricultural workers, was the recipient of only a quarter of the credit distributed by the government's agrarian bank. This was also true of Peru's commercial banks, which, like the government, favored large-scale agriculture in their lending process. As already noted, the pervasive impression that agrarian reform was inevitable discouraged many large landholders to continue capitalization of their properties. Much of the capital that would have been invested in agriculture was thus diverted to urban construction and real estate. Understandably, agricultural production declined during Belaúnde's presidency.[13] Never fully understood, however, was the consequences of agrarian reform once it had begun. This made the president and advisors very conservative in their approach to this critical issue. In effect then, their agrarian reform program could be characterized as too little and too late.

The agrarian reform law was introduced into the Peruvian congress in August 1963. Belaúnde's initial caution was reinforced by the Aprista–Odriista alliance in Congress, which effectively blocked much of the president's reform agenda. This was done even though agrarian reform was justified and greatly anticipated by Peru's campesinos. Still, the Belaúnde regime made good initial progress with the construction of 2,600 kilometers of new roads, 500 hundred new schools, and 2,000 community buildings. Many of these structures were built by students under a program called *Cooperación Popular* (Popular Cooperation), a program akin to a domestic Peace Corps for Peru.

But the government faced a daunting task. At least one of three agricultural families were without any land. Peru had one of the lowest per capita landholding quotients in the world. This, of course, had much to do with its rugged terrain, non-irrigated lands, and vast tracts of rain forest lands. But it was a fact that the nation's pre-Columbian civilizations made more efficient use of the land than was the case in 20th-century Peru. By the mid 1960s, one quarter of Peru's GNP was supplied by agriculture but 6 of 10 Peruvians workers toiled in this activity. Significantly less than 1,000 hacendados and corporate giants like Grace dominated landholding in Peru. Even more troubling were the work obligations that many campesinos were held to on local haciendas. These extended to personal service for the hacendado and his family in their household and even at times to their home in Lima. Feudalism continued and its associated rigid class system remained pervasive in Peru's highlands as the anachronistic vestige of Peru's colonial past. Peru's political leaders during Belaúnde's presidency were unwilling or unable to confront this huge historical problem. This failure alone may have been sufficient to bring down the Belaúnde presidency. In the end, a good deal of the land expropriated under the Agrarian Reform Act of 1964 was taken in the Departments of Pasco and Cusco, where land invasions and guerrilla activity was most prominent. Nearly 600,000 families gained title to 1.43 million acres of land. But much of this was de facto government recognition of land already occupied by campesinos. What was lacking was a systematic approach to move farther into other parts of Peru that had not yet been touched by agrarian reform.

The most visible failure of the agrarian reformers was their unwillingness to expropriate the vast holdings of the Cerro de Pasco Corporation. Acquired under infamous circumstances in the 1920s, the Cerro Corporation's lands should have been the most subject to expropriations since so many claims by campesinos had been filed against the corporation. Watered down by legislative compromise, the agrarian reform law was filled with exemptions that allowed hacendados to escape wide-scale expropriation. Article 25, in particular, benefited the already more developed agricultural units by assessing different values of irrigated, dry, and pasture lands. From the beginning, the agrarian reform was underfunded and enforcement of its codes was haphazard.

It should be understood that Belaúnde's first priority for the agrarian problem was not land redistribution but rather the opening up of new lands in the selva. His marginal jungle highway project would link Peru with its neighbors, open new arable land in the *ceja de montaña,* and help curb the massive flow of sierra migrants to Lima. Funds for this project were insufficient, and it was never completed. Ironically, what infrastructure that was put in place aided the development of drug trafficking in the Upper Huallaga Valley in the 1970s. In the end, only 1,900 campesinos were given clear title to their land under the auspices of the agrarian reform program. This represented 0.1 percent of the landless and *minifundistas* (very small plots) in Peru.[14]

I.P.C. CONTROVERSY

The inability of the Belaúnde to initiate effective agrarian reform frustrated legitimate civilian and military reformers. But his failure to resolve the long-standing issue of I.P.C.'s tax and legal status in Peru, proved to be far more damaging politically. Peru, like Mexico and other Latin American companies did not legally recognize I.P.C.'s claims to subsoil rights or oil reserves that had not yet been tapped. Such a dispute had led the Cardenas government in Mexico to expropriate most foreign oil holding in 1938. The same action was taken in Peru in 1968. The government maintained that I.P.C. had systematically avoided paying proper taxes in the amount of $600 million since the 1920s. The company countered that it was the leading taxpayer in Peru and that had been a good corporate presence in the Talara region. Hard-liners on the I.P.C. issue, especially Luis Miró Quesada, editor of *El Comercio*, felt that I.P.C. should indemnify the Peruvian government for the petroleum extracted that was never paid for. Taxes were not enough, he insisted, because the valuable mineral was lost forever to Peru. As pressure by the Peruvian government intensified on I.P.C., the company in fact prepared for its exit from Peru by repatriating its capital to the United States in the form of amortization allowances. The estimated value of its holdings in Peru dropped from $70 million to $20 million in the period from 1960 to 1967. Moreover, much of the petroleum reserves in the La Brea Parinas had been tapped by the time of I.P.C.'s expropriation in 1968. Contract negotiations between I.P.C. and the government consumed much of Belaúnde's last months in office. They also cost him United States Agency for International Development (U.S.A.I.D.) from Washington, as Undersecretary of State Thomas Mann felt withholding such funds would speed the negotiations. In fact it served to weaken Belaúnde. The controversy became the catalyst for the president's opponent's of all political persuasions to gather against his government. Most of all, I.P.C. represented the delayed nationalist reaction in Peru to protect the nation's own resource base. Bolivian leaders nationalized foreign oil in 1937; Mexican President Cardenas did the same in 1938. The supreme populist Juan Perón expropriated the British-owned railroads in 1945. When a bizarre dispute over a missing 11th page of I.P.C.-government contract hit the newspapers, the Peruvian military were prepared to make their own nationalist statement.

ARM AND POLITICS

Of all Peru's political leaders, Belaúnde more closely identified with the armed forces than any other politician in Peru. Odría was rejected by most of the more progressive leadership as a reactionary caudillo. Belaúnde's bold ideas for building Peru's infrastructure drew the military's attention, but the president also had to attend to the armed forces' material needs. Foremost on the list were more modern aircraft. In early 1967 Peru tried to purchase Northrup F5A fighters. Argentina had just recently bought Skyhawk fighter bombers from the United States, and Chile had purchased Hawker Hunter attack fighters from Britain. Members of the U.S. Congress opposed sale on the grounds such a sale promoted militarism and were inconsistent with Peru's development needs. In the midst of the controversy the United States enflamed the dispute by blocking the sale of six Canberra bombers by invoking an obscure provision of the Marshall Plan. Under extreme pressure from the air force and the senior leadership of the military, Belaúnde turned to France and quickly purchased 12 Mirage V fighters, one of the most sophisticated and expensive airplanes in the world at that time. U.S. Congressional oversight of the weapons purchase controversy certainly backfired. In the process, military relations between Peru and the United States deteriorated. Since 1967, with the exception of naval purchases, Peru's military has avoided the United States as a source of its major weapons purchases.

GUERRILLAS 1965

The armed forces confronted their first rural guerrilla threats in 1965. Two distinct guerrilla forces were mobilized. The *Movimiento de Izquierda Revolucionaria* (Revolutionary Left Movement; MIR), was led by Luis de la Puente Uceda. He was a former member of APRA who broke with the party over its swing to the right. He was trained in Castro's Cuba and was confident of Castro's foco theory of revolution. The foco was a small revolutionary band that would build support from peasants in the countryside to mount a revolutionary campaign. De La Puente Uceda's openly public campaign for support in Lima exposed him to infiltration by Peruvian military intelligence and was eventually his undoing. Héctor Béjar led the other guerrilla front that called itself the *Ejército de Liberación Nacional* (National Liberation Army; ELN). Both guerrilla groups, operating in central Peru, planned to coordinate their armed efforts, but they never succeeded. They began operations in early June 1965 attacking local haciendas in the La Convencion valley and guardia civil columns in the Department of Junín. Although Belaúnde belittled these preliminary operations, the armed forces took them very seriously. Civil liberties were suspended for 30 days throughout Peru, and a special contingency fund of $9 million was quickly created to fund counterinsurgency operations. The MIR units made the huge mistake of establishing a guerrilla base on the Mesa Pelada plateau in the La Convención Valley, thereby becoming isolated by Peruvian army troops soon after their initial campaign began. Facing overwhelming opposition from Peru's 4th army in early October 1965, MIR units withdrew to the plateau where Peruvian air force bombing, including napalm, decimated their ranks and caused considerable damage to the countryside. Béjar's units continued operations in the Ayacucho region until they were eventually ambushed by army troops in mid-December 1965 near Tincoy. Béjar escaped but was later captured and imprisoned. Ironically, he was released during the Velasco government and later became an official advisor to that military regime.[15]

The 1965 counterinsurgency had a great impact on Peru's military mentality. The ease at which it was suppressed produced a false sense of confidence

within the military ranks, which very likely contributed to the muddled strategy of the initial campaign against the Sendero Luminoso insurgency. On the
other hand, progressive military leaders saw the uprising as an indication of
the potential explosiveness of the agrarian sector. Reports by some such as
Rogger Mercado claimed that hundreds of campesinos died as a result of the
Mesa Pelada campaign. This troubled progressives in the armed forces. They
felt that the military was maintaining a bad image as a repressive force.[16]

THE INFORMAL SOCIETY

Hernando de Soto argues persuasively that an alternate or informal society
was created in Peru's capital after World War II by indigenous migrants the
changed the nature of the city forever.[17] Others put it more bluntly by noting
that even the formerly exclusive Lima suburbs of Miraflores and San Isidro
have been "cholofied." During the mid- to late 1960s urban communities were
taking shape on the hillsides and coastal desert lands on the outskirts of Lima
that would grow into significantly larger than cities such as Grand Rapids,
Michigan, or Peoria, Illinois, in the United States.

These barriadas or *Pueblos Jovenes* (New Towns) as they were called during
the Velasco government started as primitive squatter settlements, and over
time, as their inhabits improved their individual housing, the community acquired basic service and established an governing organization. A sustainable
community then emerged. In *A House of Our Own,* Susan Lobo describes remarkably well how the residents of Ciudadela Chalco in Callao evolved as a
squatter community with roots as far back as the 1940s. Housing, originally
made of *esteras* (woven reed matting), were remolded using wood planking
and eventually bricks and stones gathered from construction sites or from
paving stones in public sidewalks. Lobo notes that residents of the barriadas
can actually benefit from earthquakes as the tremors make more construction
material available.

Many of Lima's middle-class neighborhoods had begun this way during
the Odría era. But during the 1960s the sheer number of migrants added enormous pressure to transportation systems, schools, hospitals, and the labor
market. Thus, small operators began jitney services throughout Lima. The
number of street vendors exploded to a point where it was difficult to walk on
many of Lima's downtown streets. The informal economy, which is defined
by De Soto as an alternate economic system that exists outside of legal capitalism, responded to everything from housing to heath care. It was a response by
intelligent and creative Peruvians to provide for themselves what their government could not. Of course, informalism does not only exist in Lima but
also thrives in Rio de Janeiro, Mexico City, Cairo, Lagos, and most other large
cities of the Third World. The poor, in the case of Peru, adopted very well.

BELAÚNDE DEPOSED

Fernando Belaúnde Terry's presidency, which began with such high hopes in July 1963, was overthrown by yet another golpe de estado in the early morning hours of October 3, 1968. The president's stature had fallen to such a point in late September that his Acción Popular fragmented, and party members engaged in a violent struggle for control of party headquarters on September 24, 1968.

The armed forces leadership was restive for most of Belaúnde's last two years in office. The I.P.C. controversy, the political paralysis of the congress, and Haya de la Torre's announcement that he would once again be a candidate for president in the 1969 intensified the military's discontent. Belaúnde's fate was debated by military men during group meetings and private conversations. The senior commander of the army, Division General Juan Velasco Alvarado, held the key to the president's fate. Velasco was convinced that Belaúnde could no longer govern effectively nor could Peru's civilian politicians in general. Without gathering the support of all the armed forces leadership, the rebel general conspired with a select group of approximately 12 officers to overthrow the government and establish a long-term reformist regime that would transform Peruvian society. In this sense Velasco and the military golpe differed fundamentally from other military regimes in South America. In Argentina, Brazil, and Chile, abject repression and violence against the nation's perceived leftists was the standard course of action. Peru would adopt a very different course.

Juan Velasco Alvarado was born in Castilla, near Piura, in northern Peru on June 16, 1910. He had 10 siblings, and his father made a precarious living as a medical assistant. He made his way as a young man living in what he termed "dignified poverty." often making money as a shoeshine boy and doing well in school. Velasco may well have been subjected to a degree of racial prejudice because of his dark-skinned, Indian features. During his army career his nickname was El Chino. As with most nicknames in the military, it may not have been bestowed with the best intentions, nor received with them.

Like Sánchez Cerro, Velasco sought to use the army as a vehicle for self advancement. Without any apparent army mentors he could not gain entrance into the Chorillos Academy. He thus enlisted in the army as a private in April 1929. He then took the entrance exam for Chorillos, wrote the top entrance exam, and went on to graduate first in his class in 1934. Moving steadily through the ranks with disruption, Velasco attained the rank of brigade general by 1955. Despite his high marks at Chorillos, Velasco was not a military intellectual as were a number of his close colleagues. He seemed to be more a man of action than complex ideas. It is important to note that he did not attend CAEM and that the military think tank did not play a prominent role in his military government. Velasco had some battlefield experience, having served briefly in the 1941 Ecuador War, but the general did at one time or other held every major command post in the army. He also had valuable foreign experience as the Peru's attaché to France and a member of the Inter-American Defense Board in Washington, D.C.

What sets Velasco apart from many of his military colleagues is his deep social sensibility. He was passionate about his social beliefs. He was also personally honest when a number of his colleagues in the military government were not. A retired navy admiral who differed sharply with Velasco over the legitimacy of the armed forces role in social and economic reform nevertheless felt that Velasco was truly "seeking to end many of the injustices in our society." A U.S. military officer who knew Velasco confirmed the general's dislike for Peru's oligarchy. Velasco also believed strongly in the real need for effective agrarian reform.[18] Velasco grew up in relatively humble circumstances not far from I.P.C. holdings, and his strong feeling about the company may have originated from his experience there.

It is critical to understand one important aspect of the October 1968 golpe. It had only the tacit approval of the armed forces leadership. Indeed, most of the navy's leadership opposed it in principal. They felt the armed forces was not mandated to guide the nation through such fundamental changes in society. The navy leadership felt Velasco's program divided the military and subjected it temptations of corruption and misconduct. In reality, only about a dozen officers were involved in the planning and execution of the golpe. Of these 12, the most important were clearly General Edgardo Mercado Jarrín, who was the army's intellectual leader and very likely the author of a number of its reforms. He would remain influential as a retired officer into the 1990s. General Alfredo Arrisueño, commander of the armored division, and General Alberto Maldonado, commander of Lima's second division, backed Velasco's takeover. These officers held the most powerful posts in the army, and it was very difficult to oppose them. A number of progressive colonels who commanded key units were also brought into the plot. Among those, Colonels Jorge Fernández Maldonado and Enrique Gallegos Venero both made their voices heard regarding progressive reforms in Velasco's government. And it was Velasco's government. He ran it like a caudillo, sometimes leading tumultuous meetings with his service pistol before him on the table. These were men who felt a particular urgency to change Peru. Velasco had been to France, where he had come to admire DeGaulle leadership style, but he also was keenly aware of the near political demise and repeated assassination attempts on the French leader because of the terrible Algerian War. The Tet offensive and the tumultuous summer of 1968 in Paris, Chicago, and Mexico City could not have been far from his mind. Velasco and his fellow plotters put the train of reform in motion quite quickly. The newly dubbed Revolutionary Government of the

Armed Forces needed allies outside the military to validate its reform program even within its own ranks. From the beginning, its most important support came from the Peruvian Catholic Church.

THE CHURCH AND THE MILITARY

Cardinal Juan Landázuri Ricketts, Peru's leading churchmen and a figure of immense importance the nation's church for a third of a century, was a staunch supporter of the Velasco government reforms through the formative stages of the regime. Considered a moderate, he led the Peruvian church through a re-thinking of its mission in society. Landázuri played leading roles in the Latin American Bishops conferences in Medellín, Colombia, in 1968, and in Puebla, Mexico, in 1979. He was the official face of the powerful reformist ideology known as Liberation Theology. Liberation Theology argues that spirituality is indeed tied to material conditions and that lessening the suffering of the poor can enhance the state of grace of both the givers and the receivers. Articulated by a fellow Peruvian priest Gustavo Gutiérrez, Liberation Theology swept through Latin American Catholic Church from the mid-1960s until it was opposed by the Vatican in the 1980s. Educated at the University of Louvain in Belgium, Gutiérrez founded the concept of Liberation Theology to apply the lessons of the Second Vatican Council (1962–1965) to social and economic conditions in Latin America. Influenced by Mariátegui, among others, this reformer priest focused much of his attention on the poor. Gutiérrez and his colleagues encouraged the clergy to leave their traditional surroundings and take their ministry to the poor. Bishop Luis Bambarén was given the assignment of caring for the spiritual lives of those living in the *pueblos jovens.* This was an enormous task given the rapidly burgeoning populations of these new housing settlements.

There were very personal links between the Peru's Catholic Church and the Velasco government. The Minister of Interior, General Ernesto Montagne, was Cardinal Landázuri's brother-in-law. A number of ranking officers in the government were members of the *cursillos de cristianidad* (Short Courses in Christianity). These officers were committed through further Catholic education to help spread the Church message.[19] At the other end of the spectrum parish, priests and nuns facilitated the growth of community organizations in Lima and elsewhere by providing meeting spaces and some directions to grassroots organizations, which were mushrooming during the early reform period. In order to fully understand the impact of the Catholic church's support for the initial reform agenda of the Velasco government, it should be understood that the thrust of the Liberation Theology Movement in the rest of South America was not reform but a desperate effort to mitigate the severe repression of the continent's other military regimes. The Bishop of Recife, Dom Helder Camara, another pillar of Liberation Theology, did much to bring attention to the poor in Rio de Janeiro's *favelas* (slums) and the grinding poverty of Brazil's northeast. For his opposition to violent methods of the Brazilian military dictatorship (1964–1985), he was labeled a communist by conservatives. One of Dom Helder's young clerical followers was brutally murdered.

Political support for the military government reforms was also forthcoming from Peru's small Christian Democratic Party and its leader Héctor Cornejo Chávez. The Communist Party of Peru, following Moscow's line closely, also backed the regime. This connection may have facilitated the major Soviet weapons purchases by the Velasco government in the mid 1970s. The alliance with the Communist party signaled a major shift in Peru's foreign policy that could best be characterized as nonaligned.

By any definition, the Revolutionary Government of the Armed Forces was politically antidemocratic. Political parties were banned, the congress and the supreme court were closed. The press was granted a measure of freedom until July 1974 when they were expropriated by the government. Thereafter there was very little official opposition to the government. This was a revolution led from the barracks where soldiers were accustomed to being obeyed.

THE CHARACTER OF THE VELASCO REGIME

The breath and complexity of the Velasco regimes reforms can only be summarized within the limits of this study. It is important to state at the beginning that the reforms seemed at times to be ambiguous in character. The Velasco government has been described as populist, corporatist, institutionalist, and even communist by members of the armed forces themselves. In truth, it had elements of all these tendencies. Its character defies precise description because the reform process was a fluid response to various factions within the military, the efficacy or lack of certain reforms, and the loosening grip on leadership as General Velasco's health declined in the mid-1970s.

The Revolutionary Government of the Armed Forces made a concerted effort to make it appear that this was a regime that welcomed full participation by the people in the reform process. It quietly enlisted the support of Peru's Moscow-line Communist Party to help the regime establish at least the rhetoric of the far left. This collaboration by Peru's Communist Party contributed to the splintering of the far left during the late 1970s, clearing the way for the appearance of Sendero Luminoso. But in the final analysis, the Velasco regime was in fact a revolution from above. The revolution was decreed by military men who were distrustful of civilians and particularly the consequences of uncontrolled mobilization. The *Sistema Nacional de Apoyo a la Movilización Social* (National System to Support Social Mobilization; SINAMOS), was created by the regime in 1971 to channel popular support for the regime. It failed.

One of the driving forces behind SINAMOS was the Velasco regime's principal civil advisor, the anthropologist Carlos Delgado. Rather than be conduits for citizen participation, this agency largely functioned a social control mechanism particularly in the *pueblos jovenes* in Lima. It would be an exaggeration to say the SINAMOS was Peru's equivalent of the Committees for the Defense of the Revolution, Fidel Castro's neighborhood watch agencies in Cuba. It is clear, however, the intent of both programs was the same. SINAMOS existed to determine and, when necessary, mitigate opposition to government policy. There was always the possibility that SINAMOS could have been the vehicle for the creation of a permanent military-dominated political party along the lines of Mexico's early National Party of the Revolution (PNR) and its successor the Institutional Revolutionary Party (PRI). That never happened largely because of divisions within the military over long-term military rule.

NATIONALISM AND FOREIGN AFFAIRS

Many of Velasco government's reforms sought to encourage nationalism and break the bonds of dependency of foreign, particularly U.S. capital. The military government also wanted chart a new foreign policy that was more independent of the United States. The architect of this policy was Foreign Minister General Mercado Jarrín. CAEM position papers from the early 1950s onward warned of the dangers to Peru's national defense capabilities as long as large components of the nation's agriculture and extractive industries were in foreign hands. Peruvian military intelligence confirmed this fact. Indeed, Peru lagged far behind most major Latin American nations in laying full claim to its critical resources base. Velasco established the direction his government would take in this area by expropriating the I.P.C. without compensation as the first major act of his administration.

Such was the sentiment against I.P.C. that the military regime immediately gained a good measure of legitimacy in the minds of many Peruvians. When Washington responded to I.P.C. expropriation by ending economic aid to Peru under the terms of the Hickenlooper Amendment, the door was open for the Velasco government to seek economic aid and trade agreements beyond the hemisphere. The military government was clearly seeking new allies, and it was determined to distance itself from Washington. This policy was taken over the vocal objections of the navy leadership whose working relationship with the U.S. navy was still very close. The radicals within the military government pushed the regime farther away from the United States and eventually to the decision of purchasing Soviet weapons. This led to inviting Soviet technicians to Peru and to sending 800 army and air force officers to Russia for training. With these developments the navy became completely estranged from the Velasco government.

As with the Mirage jet controversy during the Belaúnde regime, when Peru sought a major weapons upgrade in 1973, the government first approached the United States, France, and Israel. Washington refused to respond, and the armaments from France and Israel were to costly. General Jorge Fernandez Maldonado later confirmed that the military government negotiated an arms pact with the Soviet Union primarily because Moscow gave Peru the best price and financing. The decision was without ideology, General Fernández Maldonado insisted.[20] Nevertheless, the weapons purchase from the Soviet Union was the largest by any Latin American nation other than Cuba in the history of the region. It also changed the balance of forces in the Andean regime and marked a major setback for the United States in the cold war. The first purchases in 1973 and 1974 were for the army when 350 Soviet medium tanks were acquired. Later substantial purchases of Soviet fighter bombers were made.

Clearly the Velasco government was intent upon making a major upgrade in the Peruvian military's weapon systems when it was most opportune to do so. But it definitely raised the perceived threat level regarding a possible war with Chile. It also hardened relations with the Washington, which had, nevertheless, blundered its way into allowing the Soviet Union a major bridgehead in South America. Peru accomplished what it set out to do, end dependency upon the U.S. arms sources. The downside was that Peru 's military arms profile was one of the most diverse in the world. Weapon systems coordination would be a nightmare. Also, who could predict the collapse of the Soviet Union in less than two decades? Again, the navy abstained from these Soviet weapons purchases, instead looking to Italy and Germany for its technical needs. By 1976, Velasco's successor, General Francisco Morales Bermúdez Cerruti, was deploying his new tanks and aircraft on the borders with Chile and Ecuador seeking to drown out internal dissent with his policy with a nationalist diversion. No hostilities occurred with Chile on the 100th anniversary of the beginning of the War of the Pacific in 1879. Still, a conflict with Chile had been anticipated by many.

Peru's foreign policy took a completely new direction. The Soviet Union was diplomatically recognized in 1968. The next seven years saw a 10-fold increase in the volume of trade between the two nations. When humanitarian assistance was needed during a massive earthquake and mudslide on May 31, 1970, the Soviet Union provided substantial aid. Indeed, 70 Soviet medical personnel were killed when their plane crashed in the North Sea en route to Peru.

The massive quake of May 1970 was situated in Peru's Department of Ancash in the long valley known as the Callejón de Huaylas. Most of the towns of Huaraz and Yungay were obliterated. The residents of Yungay suffered the worst when an avalanche of mud, ice, and rock from Peru's highest mountain Huascán inundated the city. Many of its residents were buried alive. The final death toll numbered in the range of 70,000 with 500,000 homeless.[21] This was the most destructive earthquake in Peruvian history, and one of the worst natural disasters in the history of the Southern Hemisphere. Once again the seismic instability of Peru's Andean range had taken its toll. The emergency response of the Peruvian government was significantly aided by Soviet helicopters and medical teams. The United States also sent substantial aid and First Lady Patricia Nixon visited the earthquake side to express her support for the victims. Interestingly, when the military government began the rebuilding effort in the Callejón de Hauylas, they planned not just for the restoration of housing, roads, and public buildings. Rebuilding was done with a plan of making the area, one of the most beautiful in Peru, into a tourist destination. The military government often had an agenda that was never publically announced before action was taken.

Peru soon opposed the economic embargo on Cuba while establishing diplomatic relations with the island nation. Fidel Castro then whimsically characterized the Peruvian military government as a "fire that started in the firehouse." Like Cuba, Peru became a member of the Group of 77 or the Non-Aligned movement. Additionally, Peru became a charter member of the Andean Pact or Common Market in an effort to diversify its trade. In the mid-1960s Peru's navy began aggressively enforcing the declared 200-mile territorial and resource zone to protect its fishing rights. The arrest, fining, and detention of U.S. tuna boat crews led the United States to suspend military aid to Peru. Velasco responded by expelling the entre U.S. military mission, breaking a military partnership that dated to the 1920s. Efforts were made to forge trade agreements with France, China, and Japan. Except for Japan, which invested heavily in oil exploration, these efforts to diversify were not very successful. Facing the agrarian crisis inherited from the Belaúnde administration, the Velasco government was determined to enact a sweeping land reform program that would alter the character of labor and landholding forever. The primary goal of the agrarian reform, however, was pragmatic. Intense discontent among Peru's landless campesinos was to be defused to avoid an agrarian war that had been looming since the colonial era. Not withstanding the Sendero Luminoso terrorist campaign, to a significant degree this was accomplished.

AGRARIAN REFORM

When Velasco announced the agrarian reform program, he echoed the words Tupac Amaru II, "Peasant, the landlord will eat no longer from your poverty."[22]

There was no common model for the Peruvian agrarian reform as there was, for example, in Mexico with the *ejido* (communal landholding). The structure of Peruvian agrarian reform drew on the ayllu and the Andean indigenous communities for inspiration and leadership only minimally. Eastern European collectivist models and a dominant policy-making role by government-appointed *technicos* were the fundamental reality of agrarian reform. It can be said that the military government did not trust the Peruvian campesinos to make the transition from tenants to productive landholders on their own. The hope for the agrarian reform program was two fold: it would end injustice in the countryside while also increasing agricultural production because more land would be cultivated than under the supposedly inefficient hacienda system.

The highly efficient coastal sugar estates, some foreign owned, were expropriated first. This signaled that the government was not avoiding the tough decision to seizing efficient and highly profitable commercial estates. What immediately proved troublesome, however, was the question of who would these properties would pass to, permanent tenants or their seasonal workers who lived away from the land. It was easier and more efficient to grant ownership to the permanent workers, and this was done. The *yanaconas* (seasonal workers) were left out of the benefits of reform. Perhaps the military planners were worried about conflict if they tried to include them in the reform. Too much subdivision of the land was another possible concern, but seasonal workers in both the coastal estates and the sierra carried their discontent long after the military government ended in 1980.

Reform in the highlands saw the elimination of the hacienda system for the first time since the 16th century. With the demise of the hacienda system the feudal labor obligations that were associated with the system for hundreds of years were abolished. The granting of land to Peru indigenous masses was extremely important. But abolition of labor obligations that were really a thinly veiled form of slavery was of monumental importance. Agrarian reform gave many campesinos their lives back. Labor obligations, which often ran a high as 200 or more days per year, were now at an end. Most scholars overlook this key development when they describe the Velasco government's agrarian reform program as largely a failure.

Among the factors that severely mitigate the success of the agrarian reform was a lack of investment. The government was the sole source of investment and its financial capabilities declined significantly by the mid-1970s. The technicos were often agronomists who spoke little Quechua and were not familiar with the serrano way of life. Yet the technicos were given primary decision-making authority. This produced significant tension at time in the agrarian cooperatives. Problems also arose between the Indian residents on former haciendas and those in nearby Indian communities where both laid claim to disputed lands. At the beginning of the reform, government planners projected that agricultural production would increase over 4 percent for the period from

1971 to 1975. This was overly optimistic to say the least. Hacendados would be compensated for their lands in 20- to 30-year government bonds that could be amortized more quickly if they were invested in industrial enterprises. This plan was also a failure. If the former agricultural elite continued to invest in Peru, it was likely to be in urban real estate, not in industry. The point has been made numerous times thus far that there was no vitality to Peru's nascent industrial bourgeoisie. In the end, agricultural production stagnated during the Velasco government as it often does during major agrarian reform. With Lima's fast-growing population, Peru began importing substantial amounts of foodstuffs (even potatoes) and subsidizing these imports to keep prices down.

What can be said about the scope of the agrarian reform. It was massive in scope and nearly unprecedented in its pace. Sources differ on the exact details, but a careful and reliable assessment by Fernando Eguren states that 15,826 properties were expropriated between June of 1969 and June of 1979 in all regions of Peru. The land redistribute totaled approximately 23 million acres to 370,000 beneficiaries.[23] These totals would be equivalent to the size of the state of Indiana in the United States. Peru's agrarian reform ranks as one of the most comprehensive ever attempted in Latin America, even surpassing that of Mexico or Cuba. The pace of the reform was very swift. Much of it was completed before Velasco left office and all was in place at the end of the military regime in 1980. Mexico, on the other hand, was not redistributing land in a substantive way until a quarter century after the revolution began in 1910.

NATIONAL DEFENSE AND THE ECONOMY

The I.P.C. expropriation in October 1968 was followed by similar actions against the major foreign firms in the extractive sector. Eventually, Cerro de Pasco Corporation, Southern Peru Copper Company, and the Marcona became Peruvian owned. This occurred by either direct sale to the Peruvian government or expropriation with compensation. Grace was another corporation whose huge assets and long history in Peru could not convince the Velasco government to abjure from seizing its holdings. Compensation for these properties was a central issue regarding negotiations between the United States and the Peruvian governments. Eventually, in February 1974 an agreement was reached by a Manufacturers Hanover Vice President James Green and the Peruvian government. The Green agreement allowed for the renewed flow of funds from the International Development Bank and World Bank funds, which had been held in abeyance as a result of the deadlock. The Velasco government did not want to create a statist economy on the Soviet model. Rather, important economic sectors such as the extractive industries were deemed too important to remain in the hands of foreign capital. Revenue from basic economic sectors such as minerals, sugar, and fish products were seen as an essential engine of economic growth that would be diverted to industrialization. This would make the Peruvian economy even more diverse and more under the control of Peruvians. The Velasco government was thus acting on the strategy outlined in military journals as early as the 1930s calling for economic autonomy and self-sufficiency. The problem with this strategy was that the usual reliable mineral and fishing sectors suffered through periods of low world prices and poor fishing harvests.

Also, the Velasco government was forced to deal with the major dilemma of a lack of foreign or private domestic investment in Peru. Significantly, foreign corporations and Peru's former elite may have been frightened away by the pace and uncertain direction of reform, but foreign bankers were not. Peru's mineral resources attracted banks such as Wells Fargo and the nation's foreign debt rapidly soared five fold from $1.1 billion in 1968 to $5.5 billion in 1976. In effect, Peru was replacing most investment in the private sector with foreign borrowing. This period is the beginning of a debt cycle that reached paralyzing proportions in the late 1980s. The government did move aggressively in oil exploration under the auspices the new state oil company Petroperú. Eighteen foreign oil companies were granted service contracts to search for oil in the selva region. Firms in Ecuador located major oil deposits in the same region thus encouraging Peruvian exploration. But no significant oil reserves were located, and the companies packed up and left Peru by the end of the Velasco era. This was just one of a number of economic setbacks suffered by the Velasco government.

Peru's nationalized fishing industry fell into crisis in 1973 and 1974 as a result of massive overfishing of the Humboldt current's anchovy stocks combined with substantially reduced numbers of anchovies due to environmental conditions. The fish meal industry collapsed in 1972 and revenues fell from a high of $331 million in 1970 to only $136 million in 1973. Responding to the crisis the government nationalized the fishing industry in 1973 and took upon itself a failing enterprise. These economic difficulties might have been mitigated somewhat if revenue from domestic sources had been greater. Thorp and Bertram, however, argue that the military government's refusal to address tax reform was one of its greatest mistakes.

With no significant new petroleum discoveries in the early 1970, the world oil crisis of 1974 caused Peru additional hardships by driving up the cost of imports. Government salaries suffered as a result and Peru began to confront labor unrest and increasing discontent with the Velasco government. At this point one of the most radical measures adopted by the military regime was put forth. It was clearly an attempt to quiet social unrest and confirm the reformist legitimacy of the government.

LABOR AND SOCIAL PROPERTY

Seeking to co-opt APRA's labor strength and other established labor unions, the military government attempted, without much success, to establish its own urban and peasant labor organization in order to co-opt the existing labor agencies. The nation's poorly paid teachers proved to be the most militant of all labor groups during this era.

One of the Velasco regime's most ambitious reform initiatives was its social property laws. Of his intentions for this measure Velasco said as early as 1972 that it would be an integral component of the enduring Peruvian revolution. Announced in April 1974, the long-awaited social property initiative introduced the concept of worker participation, in which worker's would be included in management decision making and profit sharing for new firms created in Peru. Anticipating that existing firms would be subject to social property laws, businessman in Peru held off making new capital commitments to their companies. Thus the protracted wait for the government's policy on this critical issue further contributed to the low level of domestic investment in the industrial sector. The Velasco government was now actually being whipsawed by conflicting policies regarding industrialization. Although agrarian reform bonds given as compensation for expropriations could be directed toward investment in industrial enterprises, few were willing to do this while social property measures were still being contemplated.

THE REVOLUTION FALTERS

The strong leadership provided by General Velasco was badly weakened when he suffered an abdominal aneurism in February 1973. The subsequent amputation of his right leg, his absence while being treated in Washington, D.C., and his two-month convalescence clearly left a leadership vacuum. Velasco never really recovered, yet he stayed on as head of the government until August 1975 when he was deposed. Waiting to take over the leadership of the government was General Edgardo Mercado Jarrín, the most capable officer within the regime and a man sympathetic to most of Velasco's agenda. Yet Mercado Jarrín was allowed to pass into retirement while Velasco refused to step down. This decision had significant implications for the course of the military government from the time of Velasco illness until the military returned to the barracks in 1980.

The navy as an institution had never supported the Velasco regimes reforms. Arguing that the sweeping role of the military in changing Peru's society was a gross violation of professionalism, the navy increasingly expressed it's vocal resistance usually in service meetings such as the navy's Mother's Club. By mid-1974 the situation reached a crisis and the navy's senior officer, Vice Admiral Luis M. Vargas Caballero, was expelled from the government. He explained his position years later in this way: "I believe no group is prepared for such sweeping reforms in such a short time. The armed forces are not prepared for political action; they should help the government but within its own field."[24] At this point, there was widespread sentiment within the navy officer corps that the service, along with the naval infantry and marines should oppose the continuation of the Velasco regime through armed resistance. The seizure of the port of Callao by the marines and the subsequent blockade of the port by naval vessels was part of the general plan of operations. Vargas Caballero, however, opposed this course of action on the grounds of its potential high cost in lives both military and civilian.[25] After May 1974, the navy was effectively cut out of the Velasco government. Then in July the Velasco government nationalized the nation's newspapers, thus further stifling dissent. More trouble was soon to follow.

In early February 1975 a strike by the Guardia Civil (the national police force) was met with force by the government. The new Soviet tanks were sent against the Guardia Civil headquarters in Lima. In one of the worst riots in Lima's history, there was widespread arson and looting, much of it directed against the SINAMOS headquarters and military installations, and 86 people died and 155 were wounded.

A SHIFT TO THE RIGHT

General Velasco's rapidly declining health and the tense political climate following the February riots in Lima made it clear to most members of the military government that a change at the top was necessary. With the retired Mercado Jarrín out of the picture, attention turn to the conservative and capable Minister of Defense, Division General Francisco Morales Bermúdez Cerruiti. He orchestrated Velasco's peaceful removal from office in early August 1975. A severely ill Velasco lingered two more years before his illness took his life in 1977. In my extended interview with Morales Bermúdez in May 1990 he stressed that his main objectives were to slowly remove the military from Peruvian politics while at the same time trying to consolidate those reforms that were most substantive and repeal those that had proven disruptive to the economy. But when Morales Bermúdez took power in August 1975, he claimed that the "Revolution" would not vary "one millimeter" from the Velasco Government's policy. In fact his years in power were a "Thermidorian Reaction" during which much of the Velasco government's reforms were dismantled as the military government moved sharply to the right.[26]

The problems confronting the new regime were many. Peru's foreign debt was at record levels (above $4 billion) and it needed to be financed. The

International Monetary Fund (IMF) was pressuring the government to cut expenditures. Thus subsidies for food and many other daily needs common with the previous military government were cut back. The Peruvian sol was also devalued by 44 percent. These measures brought a violent reaction and unrest within the armed forces. Morales Bermúdez was compelled to purge pro-Velasco members of the officer corps. Very quickly the sacred cows of the Velasco reforms were slaughtered. The Social Property initiatives were scrapped, SINAMOS was closed down, the Communist Party's connection with the government was ended, and government-sponsored labor unions were cut loose without financial support.

The year 1977 was very difficult for Peru and the Morales Bermúdez governments. Strikes and protests against the austerity program were constant. Unemployment nearly doubled in the five-year period after 1973, and underemployment, a common fate of Peru's informal sector, accounted for one of every two Peruvian workers. This was a period in which the Left, always weak and disorganized in Peru, was making significant organizational headway. With increasing reports of scandals within the military government involving weapons purchases and the administration of state agencies, the armed forces, once respected as leaders of change, were now viewed as the same kind of opportunists as the civilian politicians of the past. How serious was the problem of corruption during the military government? A senior naval officer in 1990 claimed that there was a "large cartel of corruption" within the armed forces during the 1970s, particularly regarding Soviet Weapons purchases. It must be recognized that the navy was estranged from the other services and did not participate in these weapons purchases. Still, as much as $250 million was expended and ample opportunities for kickbacks must have occurred.[27]

Given all these problems and his own conservative view of the armed forces mission, Morales Bermúdez was determined to take the military out of politics as soon as feasibly possible. However, he needed a political vehicle to accomplish this transition. Moreover, given the massive changes in public policy initiated by decree by the Velasco government, a new constitution to establish a legal foundation for civilian government was necessary. The government opened negotiations with APRA and parties of the right to establish the basis for elections to a constitutional assembly as a prelude to general elections for congress and the president. The political Left and Belaúnde Terry, who had been living in Peru and teaching in Washington, D.C., refused to participate in the talks. This solidified Belaúnde Terry and his party Acción as the main opposition party to the military government. As the economy deteriorated and austerity measures continued to be imposed, Acción Popular benefited from this broad-based discontent.

Elections in early June 1978 for the constitutional assembly reflected a substantial shift of the Peruvian electorate to the left. Thirty-six percent of the vote went to parties of the Left and their representatives gained 34 seats in the assembly. APRA drew, as it always had, about one third of the electorate (35 percent) and seated 37 of its party members. Haya de la Torre led all the candidates for the assembly with 230,000 votes. The main party of the right *Partido Popular Cristiano* (Popular Christian Party; PPC), polled 24 percent. Acción Popular at Belaúnde's direction boycotted the elections and thus APRA was the majority party. Haya de le Torre was elected president of the constitutional assembly and thus held public office for the first time in his long career in Peruvian politics.[28]

At age 83 and in the slowly dying of lung cancer, Haya de la Torre finally became the statesman his APRA followers always thought he would be. Exhibiting the "patience of a grandfather," Haya de la Torre was an effective conciliator throughout the complex work of establishing the assembly. After 11 months of deliberation, the new constitution was completed.

Haya de la Torre lived long enough to sign the final document from his deathbed. With his passing, one of the most well-known and controversial political leaders in 20th-century Latin American history left a political heir that would achieve what Haya de la Torre could never do, attain Peru's presidency. Alan García would keep the APRA alive, when no one else could.

In the June 1980 general elections, the first held in Peru since 1963, Alan García was still only an aspiring newcomer in the APRA leadership. Old-guard leaders Armando Villanueva del Campo and Andrés Townsend Ezcurra sought to fill the vacuum left by Haya de la Torre but could not. The left, splinted among a number of parties as always, still generated significant support. Belaúnde, back from Washington and running on a campaign very similar to his of 1963 seemed a far more personable candidate than the APRA's Villanueva del Campo or the Popular Christian party's Luis Bedoya Reyes.

Belaúnde won his second term as president with a substantial 45 percent of the vote. APRA's poor showing of 27 percent was a reflection of the loss of Haya de la Torre and the lack of appeal of its aging old-guard leadership. The most important aspect of the 1980 elections was that illiterates, mainly Quechua- and Aymara-speaking Indians, were allowed to vote for the first time in Peru's history. This aspect of the 1980 constitution changed Peruvian politics forever. From this point onward, the electorate will become more unpredictable, more volatile, and interestingly less prone to support traditional political parties. The charisma of political candidates such as Alberto Fujimori and Alejandro Toledo was far more important than party affiliations. On July 28, 1980, the military left politics and returned to the barracks, where they have remained ever since.

CONCLUSION

This era in Peru's history witnessed the passing of rule of the oligarchy as vast demographic changes reshaped Peruvian society and politics. Migration from the sierra to the coastal cities, mainly Lima, changed the capital city and other cities such as Trujillo and Arequipa fundamentally. These migrations were sparked by a modernizing economy that was still very much oriented toward the export market. Coastal agriculture, especially sugar and cotton, fared quite well until the mid-1960s. Still, these activities were dominated by large producers supported by a significant resident and seasonal labor force. The mining sector was still dominated by foreign multinational and plagued by labor unrest. The biggest deficiency marking the Peruvian economy was the failure of native investors to support industrialization. This void was so great that industrial investment was the primary priority of the Peruvian military government under General Velasco.

The APRA, divided and driven underground by the failed Callao naval revolt of October 1948, made a significant ideological shift to the right in order to establish a viable coalition to achieve national power. This avenue was denied to the party until General Morales Bermúdez reached an understanding with APRA before the 1978 Constitutional Convention elections. In the interim, land invasions, guerrilla activity, and the worldwide lessons of the Algerian War for independence, the Vietnam War, and most of all the threat from a Soviet-backed Cuban regime convinced the military that they had forge changes that would preempt seemingly eminent social revolution.

The military *Docenio* (12-year rule) witnessed the first systematic attempt to alter the economic and social structure of Peru since the arrival of the Spanish in the 16th century. Fundamentally, the Velasco regime's initiatives were doomed from the beginning because popular participation without true decision-making capability is meaningless. Yet the agrarian reform abolished the injustices of the centuries-old hacienda system.

The attempt by the Velasco government to became the sole managers of the Peruvian economy was, in the final analysis, very naïve. Perhaps more than any member of the military government, Finance Minister Morales Bermúdez knew the limitations and capabilities of the military managers. Accordingly he was a restraining but still a moderate force under Velasco. He, of course, abandoned much of the revolution foundations once he became head of government in August 1975. Still, the Velasco government ended the domination of foreign capital in the extractive sector and commercial agriculture in just little more than half a decade. No previous government had been able to do that during the entire 20th century.

There was political repression during the Docenio. However, it was nothing like the brutal violence perpetrated on the peoples of other South American nations as military leaders thwarted the need for change by some of the worst systematic repression in Latin American history. Among the core leaders of the Velasco regime Peru, there was a deep concern for social justice and *bienestar* (well-being) for the Peruvian people. The leaders simply tried to do in seven years what had not even been seriously attempted in Peru's entire republican history. Optimists and visionaries, these generals certainly were; realists, they definitely were not. Still, the enormous contrast with the jails and torture chambers of the military regimes in Argentina, Brazil, and Chile must always be remembered.

NOTES

1. Magda Portal, quoted in Fredrick B. Pike, *The Politics of the Miraculous in Peru: Haya de la Torre and the Spiritualist Tradition* (Lincoln: University of Nebraska Press, 1986), 238.

2. *Manifesto a los institutos armados y el pueblo del Perú*, signed by Major Jorge Tejada Lapoint,, Captain German Guerrero, Major Carlos Meza Navarro, and Captain Jorge Rosas Burgos, Panama July 1949. in Colleción de Volantes, 1949 folder, Biblioteca Nacional del Perú.

3. The destroyer escorts were U.S. 1943 vintage; the submarines were purchased from the Electric Boat Company in the United States. *Janes Fighting Ship, 1954–1955* (London: 1955), 281–283.

4. Rosemary Thorp and Geoff Bertram, *Peru 1890–1977: Growth and Policy in an Open Economy* (New York: Columbia University Press, 1978), 242–247.

5. Ibid., 217.

6. Thorp and Bertram, *Peru, 1890–1977*, 226–229.

7. Lawrence Clayton, *Peru and the United States: The Condor and the Eagle* (Athens: University of Georgia Press, 1999).

8. Peter F. Klarén, *Peru: Society and Nationhood in the Andes* (Oxford: Oxford University Press, 2000), 310–311.

9. Howard Handelman, *Struggle in the Andes: Peasant Mobilization in Peru* (Austin: University of Texas Press, 1975), 120–125.

10. Former Ambassador James I. Loeb interview with the author, December 17, 1973, Cabin John, Maryland.

11. Pike, Politics of the Miraculous, 257.

12. Thorp and Bertram, *Peru, 1890–1977*, 287.

13. Ibid., 281–285.

14. James F. Petras and Robert LaPorte, *Cultivating Revolution: The United States and Agrarian Reform in Latin America* (New York: Random House, 1971), 95.

15. Héctor Béjar, *Peru, 1965: Notes on the Guerrilla Experience* (New York: 1970)

16. Rogger Mercado, *Las guerrillas del Perú* (Lima: Funda de Cultura Popular, 1966).

17. Hernando de Soto, *The Other Path: The Invisible Revolution in the Third World* (New York: Harper and Row, 1989).

18. Personal interview with Vice Admiral (ret) Luis Vargas Caballero, May 6, 1985, Lima, Peru, and personal interview with Colonel (ret) James Aikens, June 28, 1985, Hampton, Virginia.

19. Michael Fleet and Brian Smith, *The Catholic Church and Democracy in Chile and Peru* (Notre Dame: University of Notre Dame Press, 1997), 94.

20. Personal interview with General Jorge Fernández Maldonado with the author, May 30, 1990, Lima, Peru.

21. Barbara Bode, *No Bells to Toll: Destruction and Creation in the Andes* (New York: Charles Scribner and Sons, 1989).

22. Fernando Eguren, Editor, "Reforma Argraria y Desarollo Rural en el Perú," in a book of the same title. (CEPES: 2006), p. 12.

23. Juan Velasco Alvardo, *La voz de la Revolución: Discursos de General de División Juan Velasco Alvarado* (Lima: Ediciones Participación, Oficina Nacional de Difusión del SINAMOS, 1972), 55.

24. Questionnaire response from Vice Admiral (ret) Luis M. Vargas Caballero, to author, May 13, Lima, Peru.

25. Personal interview with Vice Admiral (ret) Luis M. Vargas Caballero with the author, May 13, Lima, Peru.

26. Daniel M. Masterson, "Peru's New Leader," *The Christian Century 42* (1975), 1112–1113.

27. Personal interview with a Peruvian naval officer, June 16, 1990, Lima, Peru.

28. Klarén, *Peru,* 363.

8

Terror and Renewal, 1980–2008

Much of the last quarter century in Peru has been deeply traumatic. Terrorism and government repression during the war against Sendero Luminoso claimed tens of thousands of lives in the period from 1980 to 1995. The 1980s were one of Peru's worst decades economically. Burdened by a large foreign debt, crippling inflation, and the destruction of much of the country's infrastructure, this era rivaled that of the War of the Pacific as a period of national crisis. Yet Peru has witnessed a remarkable recovery since the year 2000 with high economic growth, peace in the countryside, a booming tourism industry, and a widespread feeling of hope within the populace. The nation is now in the midst of longest sustained period of civilian political rule in its history. Civilian political institutions such a the judiciary, civil service, and a wide variety of NGOs are gaining more legitimacy. However, Peru's congress still lacks credibility in the minds of many Peruvians who are content to place their hopes in the hands of one strong leader in the caudillo tradition. For them Alberto Fujimori (1990–2000) met many of their needs, albeit at significant cost in civil liberties.

AFTERMATH OF THE DOCENIO

A number of critical developments stemming from the reforms of the Docenio soon became apparent during the second Belaúnde administration (1980–1985). The new Constitution of 1978 codified the agrarian, labor, and education reforms enacted by the military government.

The term of the presidency was shortened from six to five years with no reelection permitted. Very significantly, articles 273 and 278 redefined the role of the military as the mission of "guaranteeing the independence, sovereignty and territorial integrity of the Republic." The 1933 Constitution stipulated that the armed forces must maintain "public order" and "guarantee the constitution and laws of the Republic." This wider mandate in 1933 opened the way for the three golpe de estados by the armed forces since 1933. Legal restraint was not all what kept the military from intervening over the past quarter century. The terrorist war against Sendero Luminoso gave the armed forces ample justification to do so, but they held back. Rather it was the fundamental divisions that long-term rule had created in their ranks that kept them in the barracks. Also, many highly professional officers felt, as did Admiral Vargas Caballero, that it was not the military's function to rule. Clearly, politics for the armed forces was too corrupting and divisive. Attempting to finally deal with the indigenous rights, the framers of the new constitution gave illiterates (many of whom were indigenous) the vote for the first time in Peru's history. True mass politics now determined the course of Peru's political future. One would think this would have been the prelude to the flourishing of new and vibrant political parties; however, except for the parties of the left, this was not the case.

The Docenio also speeded the process of centralization of Peru's civilian political institutions. During the Velasco government the prefect for a department was appointed by the military. This official administered the department nearly unilaterally. Whatever autonomy local and regional governments were able to achieve from the 1930s to the Velasco era were largely eroded thereafter. With a strengthened Guardia Civil in many parts of rural Peru, prefects, court officials, and the police became increasingly more powerful and often corrupt. It is likely that the decline in institutional autonomy at the local and regional levels aided Sendero Luminoso's initial operations in highland Peru. It certainly was a factor in the relatively poor intelligence that armed forces were burdened with before 1990. The centralization of Peruvian governance is still a fundamentally important issue in present-day Peru. Anthropologists argue that citizenship only became more a fact of life in Peru after illiterates could vote. This process, however, produced a dilemma. Citizenship is based upon a "unitary national consciousness" that ultimately diminishes unique cultural and ethnic difference between peoples as assimilation occurs. Indian integration, always a controversial topic in Peru, is still an open question. The violence of the 1980s and early 1990s actually facilitated this assimilation by forcing refugees from the sierra to Lima in search of personal safety. Cultural adaption to Western ways, especially for the children and grandchildren of migrants from the sierra ,was usually pervasive.[1]

The political left, always marginalized in Peru before the 1970s, gained considerably from the expansion of the electorate. Previously badly splintered over ideology, the parties of the left decided to form a coalition in 1980 and seek power through elective office. The driving force between the coalition was Alfonso Barrantes, who as a former Aprista knew a good bit about political organizing as well as compromise. Drawing on the voters of Lima's barriadas, Barrantes created a new party, *Izquierda Unida* (United Left; IU). He was elected Lima's first Marxist mayor in 1983. IU candidates did well in southern Peru and gained 30 percent of the vote overall. This was one of the best performances of the left in any modern Peruvian election. APRA revived after a poor showing in 1980 but still was limited to its nearly inevitable one third of the electorate with 34 percent. The radical left, represented most infamously in the 1980s by Sendero Luminoso, disdained electoral politics from the beginning in favor of violence and terror as a means to power.

As Belaúnde's political power eroded, he seemed incapable of making the adjustments that would make his government more legitimate and productive. A handsome, articulate, and intelligent man, Belaúnde still lacked political and social acumen. An architect by trade, the president promised regional development projects more sensible than his marginal jungle highway of his first administration. But with a debt-ridden economy he could not deliver on these projects or many of the country's other social services, which were curtailed by the IMF-directed austerity measures.

In June 1984 the president of Peru's Central Bank, Richard Webb, epitomized the complexity of the nation's economic dilemma. Belaúnde had just given in to the enormous pressure from the working classes and initiated subsidies on gasoline and food. This undercut negotiations for debt relief with hard-liners from the IMF. Webb criticized the president for his decision but at the same time lamented that the IMF's monetary schedule for servicing the growing debt was unacceptable. He projected that over half of Peru's export income for the rest of the decade would have to be earmarked for interest on the debt at present IMF schedules. This enormous debt burden gave Alan García his principal campaign issue for the presidential election of 1985.[2] The debt crisis gravely affected the ability of Lima's poor to cope, and the nation's inflation was becoming nearly intolerable as the decade wore on.

Still, Peruvians found ways to endure the crisis. Particularly in Lima's squatter settlements but elsewhere in rural Peru, spontaneous organizations usually led by women provided meals, child care, and array of support for the poor. Indeed, women began to assert their political power during the 1980s as times became increasingly more difficult. In a fundamental way, the communal traditions of the sierra communities were transmitted to a new and difficult way of life in Lima.

The labor sector was mobilized by the Velasco government because the military badly needed its support. Yet, Peruvian labor groups, especially those affiliated with APRA, was difficult to control. For example, the nation's teachers become sharply more militant after 1975. Their wages were frozen from 1967 to 1972 ,and subsequent raises were considered too small. Still, in general labor's expectations were raised by Velasco. Thus, much of labor was unwilling to accept the austerity measures imposed during the later stages of the military government and during the Belaúnde presidency. During the 1980s Peru confronted an incredible average of 670 strikes and 18.5 million lost "man hours" per year. This was a period when Peru's external debt grew substantially and the nation's labor movement was often at odds with the dictates of the IMF guidelines for austerity and debt refinancing. Belaúnde showed no talent whatsoever in establishing a dialogue with labor. As a result, both the legitimate and radical left were given openings that were exploited, ultimately weakening the Peruvian state.

Two often opposing elements of the Peru's urban population gained their momentum during the Belaúnde and Alan García (1985–1990) administrations. The industrial middle class, still allied with foreign capital, began to become more assertive in its investment policies. However, economic challenges such as lower commodity prices and strict austerity policies imposed by the IMF soon checked their enthusiasm. The widespread privatization of Peru's state-owned industries, a legacy of the Docenio, did not occur until the 1990s. At that point, Peru's infrastructure was badly damaged by terrorism and the investment climate was at rock bottom. Foreign investors ultimately returned to Peru from all over the world and once again became the primary owners of Peru's industrial and extractive base industries. Accordingly, the vibrant industrial middle class is only now beginning to come into its own in Peru.

With the government's official sanctioning of the barriadas during the Docenio, the informal sector exploded in the Lima/Callao metropolitan area during the 1980s and early 1990s. Contributing substantially to the capital's growth were refugees from the war in the sierra. By the early 1980s more than half of all Peruvians lived in Lima. Historically rural farming people were becoming urbanized squatters with few marketable skills and little education. Their communities when first established had no facilities associated with modern urban areas. Clean water often had to be purchased from tanker trucks and there were no sewer systems. Electricity could only be supplied by illegal taps on the city's centralized power lines. Informals lived by their wits as small-time wholesalers in street markets selling anything and everything.

For example, within the communities such as Chalco, the tailors, barbers, and appliance repairmen often found sufficient work to keep them in the community without looking for work outside. Some factory work was also available. Women did domestic service, labored as seamstresses, or worked in their communities in a cooperative way to construct better lives. Making the lives of the informals increasingly difficult during the 1980s was inflation.[3]

Much of the migration from the sierra to Lima was done in the chain pattern. Initial migrants from a village or small locale in the highland established households in a certain barrio or neighborhood of a barriadas. Soon the word was passed to the home village that more *paisanos* (kinsman) would be welcome. A enlightening study of this process is *Taquile en Lima,* which examines the lives of migrants from one of the islands in Lake Titicaca after they settle in one of Lima's barriadas. Lobo notes that Andean social patterns serve them well in Lima: "the built in flexibility of the highland kin and alliance systems serves the migrants well in their adaption to urban life."[4] These alliances and kin relationships would be tested severely once Lima's squatter settlements became the target of Sendero Luminoso terrorists. The remarkable cohesiveness of such relationships in the face of many hardships attests to the strength of the Andean peoples, who had been enduring difficult times for many centuries.

Belaúnde's major difficulties during the first years of his administration beyond the debt burden were the huge government bureaucracy inherited from the Docenio and the crop damage associated with a particularly destructive El Niño event in 1982 and 1983. This occurrence was one of the most destructive in the late 20th century and caused $2.2 billion in damages worldwide. A number of other policy decisions also contributed to the virtual ineffectiveness of the Belaúnde government by the late 1983. Belaúnde left the Peruvian people to their own devices to confront a growing economic crisis of monumental proportions. As we have seen, the informal sector was the only recourse for many. At this time, Peru's cocaine economy was emerging in the Upper Huallaga Valley, the very area that Belaúnde had earmarked for colonization and development during his first administration. Little would be done to the quickly growing threat from narcotraffickers in the 1980s. Sendero Luminoso emerged from its underground period in 1980 to begin its brutal war against the state. Belaúnde originally met this terrible threat with disdain and indifference.

THE ORIGINS OF NARCOTRAFFICKING

The cultivation of coca shrub began on the eastern slopes of the Andes more than 2,000 years ago. Coca was chewed as a mild analgesic by people of Peru's coastal plane only a few hundred years after. This suggests the rapid emergence of a product that became an integral part of the Andean peoples' lives to the present day. Chewed to lessen the effects of *soroche* (altitude sickness) and hunger, coca leaves also have become part of the Andean economy and played a central role in religious practices in token forms of sacrifice. With the shift of the drug trade in Latin America from the Caribbean to South America in the 1960s, there was an increasing demand for cocaine as heroin shipments to the major industrial countries were steadily being interdicted. Colombia became the epicenter of cocaine processing and shipment to the United States and Europe because of its location between the Caribbean and the main suppliers of Peru and Bolivia. Cocaine consumption in the United States increased substantially in the 1970s and the basis for a coca-based economy in Peru's Upper Huallaga Valley was laid.

During the first Belaúnde administration (1963–1968) the government tried to colonize the province of Leonico Prado as part of the marginal jungle highway project. Tingo Maria in the early 1980s was the main urban center that was reached by a partially completed road that would soon be used primarily by drug traffickers. The peasants in the region grew coca at altitudes of 2,000 to 6,000 feet on the eastern slops of the Andes in northeastern Peru. Picked, dried, and processed into bales (*arrobas*) of 25 to 50 lbs each, the peasants often bartered the coca leaves for wheat, broad beans, dried pork or lamb, hardware goods, and small amounts of cash. The highest paid laborers in the coca plantations were the "two feet jackasses" of the cocaine industry who carried as much as 100 lbs of processed coca leaves on their backs up the steep trails to the remote processing areas. For their labor, these young and strong peasants could earn as much as $10 per trip or about $250 per month. This was substantially more than a migrant from the Tingo Maria area could make as a laborer in Lima. These type of wages captured a labor base in the Upper Huallaga Valley, where Peru's cocaine-based economy was consolidated by the mid 1980s.

In these remote areas of the Upper Huallaga valley there was plenty of opportunities for ambitious local coca producers to get into the business of processing the coca into cocaine. Then the sale of the product or *pasta* usually involved bribing local police or circumventing road blocks as the pasta was transported to Lima and other coastal cites for transshipment to Colombia or directly to foreign markets. The underground commercial movement of cocaine pasta is controlled by middle-class mestizos. These might be small businessmen, government employees, or managers working in commercial agriculture. By the late 1980s profits from the cocaine trade attracted Peruvians of many callings. What is perhaps most disturbing about the early phases of the coca trade in Peru's eastern Andes is the high incidence of cocaine use among the young peasants of the region. Contrary to most scholarship, the proliferation of processing labs in the region allowed for a significant amount of the final product to be available to the local peasantry, and sadly, it was being consumed.[5]

Peru has long had a legal trade in coca leaves. Coca farming is also far more profitable than any alternative form of agriculture when the end product is cocaine. These have been complicating factors in dealing with cocaine trafficking. In 1975, a decade after the colonization project in the Upper Huallaga Valley began, 4,000 metric tons of coca leaf were produced in the region. By 1980 the amount rose to 18,000 metric tons. After more than decade of the terrorist war waged by Sendero Luminoso, coca leaf produced in the Upper Huallaga Valley escalated to 80,000 tons.[6] Much of Sendero Luminoso's success after 1985 was due to its alliance with drug traffickers in the Upper Huallaga Valley. Senderistas were paid to protect the drug traffickers in the region. This bankrolled the terrorist front and allowed them to purchase modern arms to better combat the Peruvian military. Moreover, it allowed Sendero to remain independent of foreign sources of funding that often came with ideological strings attached. Since the 1980s the absolute priority of U.S.-Peruvian relations has been the reduction in narcotics trafficking. President Ronald Reagan declared "a war on drugs" in 1982 and every U.S. president has followed suit since then. By the mid-1980s the military's ability to combat drug trafficking was limited as it confronted one of the most brutal insurgencies ever endured in Latin America.

DESCENT INTO *CHAQWA*

As we have seen, Peru has witnessed many Andean resistance movements from the Taki Onqoy sect in the 1560s to the Hugo Blanco–led hacienda invasions of the early 1960s. But only the Tupac Amaru II uprising in the 1780s could compare in violence and in scope with the self-styled peoples war of *Partido Comunista del Perú en el Sendero Luminoso de José Carlos Mariátegui* (Communist Party of Peru in the Shining Path of José Carlos Mariátegui). Referred to commonly as *Sendero* or *SL*, this movement had little to with the communal Marxist theories of Mariátegui.

The Quechua term *Chaqwa* means chaos or the world turned upside down. That is why most campesinos loathed Sendero. The insurgency was not primarily peasant-based as many earlier commentators believed. The use of the name of Peru's most venerable Marxist seems to have been an attempt to associate Sendero Luminoso with an indigenous brand of Marxism that had not been corrupted by Moscow or compromised by political alliances with military dictators like Odría or Velasco. In many ways Sendero Luminoso resembled the early APRA with a highly secretive cell structure, rigid party discipline, vocal attacks on imperialism, an unquestioned messianic leader, and the use of violence for political ends. But it would be foolish to take this analogy too far, for APRA leaders never thought in the absolutist terms of Sendero's leaders. In fact, Sendero's founder, Abimael Guzmán Reynoso, commented many years later that Haya de la Torre's betrayal of the militant wing of his party during the early hours of the Callao Naval revolt of October 1948 convinced him of APRA's lack of legitimacy as a revolutionary party.

More than any other belief system, Abimael Guzmán Reynoso drew on Maoist teachings as guidelines for his campaign in Peru. Guzmán, like Ho Chi Minh in Vietnam and Pol Pot in Cambodia, was a disaffected intellectual who sought ideological inspiration abroad. Ho Chi Minh and Pol Pot did so in France, while Guzmán travelled to Communist China during the especially violent Cultural Revolution in the mid-1960s. His writings and oratory overwhelmingly make reference to the Maoist experience as his model for Peru. A brief look at Guzmán's early life will help put his thinking in a clearer perspective.

Guzmán was born in Mollendo, near Arequipa in early December 1934. The illegitimate son of a local merchant of some financial means, Guzmán received a good early education at Catholic private schools and later at San Augustín National University in Arequipa. Reclusive and shy, Guzmán completed his graduate studies with a dissertation examining Emanuel Kant's "Theory of Space." He was then hired by the provincial university in Ayacucho, San Cristóbal de Huamanga, to teach philosophy. The university had only just been reopened after a long absence and pilot programs in vocational education were begun for the region's young people. Graduates of these programs had only modest success in finding employment in desperately poor Ayacucho and its environs. Significantly, the Ayacucho region was barely touched by the Velasco regime's agrarian reforms. Thus there was great discontent among what some have called the semi-peasantry or the sons and daughters of peasants who were frustrated because of a lack of opportunities even with a legitimate education. Ayacucho was thus an ideal place for Guzmán to begin laying the groundwork for his "people's war." In San Cristóbal de Huamanga as a professor and later an administrator he began recruiting students and faculty for his cause.

Little of substance is known about his activities in China during the mid-1960s, but it appears he was schooled in small-unit tactics, the use of explosives, party discipline, and certainly the absolute necessity of extreme violence in "the people's war."

Guzmán's visit to China corresponded to the beginning of Mao Zedong's Cultural Revolution in which he purged his enemies in the Communist Party and throughout the government by using youngsters know as the Red Guards. These school children were instructed to be violent as a matter of course. Students in a Beijing girls school, for example, attacked and killed their headmistress. Later decorated by Mao himself for their actions, they renamed their school, "The Red Violent School."[7]

Viewing purges of apocalyptic proportions certainly may have heightened Guzmán's belief that only a movement that replicated such violence could succeed in Peru. Violence as a cleansing or renewing experience is a central tenet of Marxist/Maoist thought. As the Peruvian writer Gustavo Gorriti commented on this idea of transforming violence, he noted that Guzmán also owed much to Stalin. By the late 1970s the Sendero leader now was convinced that "to kill gave life, that war brought peace, (and) that the most extreme tyranny brought the greatest freedom."[8] By this time Guzmán had been underground for number of years, planning his campaign and training his cadres in the highlands. He later claimed that the exit of the military from politics in July 1980 was an opportune time to strike. He correctly assumed that military was discredited, professionally divided, and exhausted after the Docenio.

Sendero opened its nearly cataclysmic campaign to destroy the Peruvian state in May 1980 when hooded Senderistas burned the ballot boxes for the national elections as a show of protest against the democratic process. During the initial phase of Sendero's operations in Ayacucho, the movement presented itself as a moral force in the highland meting out vigilante justice against cattle rustlers, corrupt village officials, even unfaithful husbands or wives. Belaúnde at first refused to take the insurgency seriously at first referring to them as "cattle rustlers." Initially, the Guardia Civil's counterinsurgency units known as the *Sinchis* were given the task of combating Senderistas. With poor intelligence the Sinchis performed badly between 1980 and 1983, and human rights abuses against serranos soon began to become commonplace. Retaliation against villages that had been visited by Sendero columns was commonplace. One serrano woman, a native of Chuschi, lamented at this time that the Peruvian campesino was caught "between the sword and the wall," in their struggle to survive the nation's war forces.

Recruitment for Sendero combined propaganda produced by its "generated organisms" or support groups. These generated organisms were most active in Lima's universities and in the pueblos jovenes. Many supporters of Sendero early on were not fully aware of the insurgency's ideology or intentions. They were simply fed up with Peru's economic and social conditions and not enthusiastic advocates of democracy. In the highlands recruitment was often done by force with Senderista-armed columns entering villages at night and taking both young boys and girls forcibly into their ranks at ages as young as seven. This recruiting pattern emulated the Khmer Rouge in Cambodia and the Viet Cong in Viet Nam. The young recruits would be indoctrinated, trained, and vetted into the insurgency. The vetting involved the killing of a public official, a village leader, or if in Lima, a policeman. More likely it was a member of the peasant self defense brigades that were forming in the sierra by the mid

1980s. It was not unusual for both a father and a son to be dragooned into Sendero. This forced recruitment was a vital factor in alienating Peru's campesinos during the 1980s. Still, eyewitness accounts by armed forces personnel of the fanaticism of young Senderistas is a strong testament to the strength of their commitment to their cause. In some cases mortally wounded prisoners would died rather than give information with a promise of medical aid.[9] Guzmán and Senderistas often talked about the quota or the sacrifice in lives and blood the insurgency would have to make before it could achieve victory. Like every revolutionary leader from Lenin to Eamon de Valera, Guzmán dragged up the worn cliché about "crossing the river of blood" to achieve victory. Senderistas jailed in the capital's prisons may have been trying to meet the insurgency's quota when they rioted simultaneously at Lurigancho, Santa Barbara (a women's prison), and the Naval Prison at El Frontón in mid-June 1986. The rioting at El Frontón was met with massive force by Peruvian marines. More than 300 prisoners died in the riots with reports that many were executed after they surrendered. The prison riots and their suppression hardened Sendero reputation as a tenacious foe. It also gave the movement the martyrs that revolutionary movements need to develop their ethos.

The standard Senderista-armed column usually numbered no more than 20 or 30 fighters. Often they were commanded by leaders who were older, usually in the late 20s or early 30s. These were the core of the Sendero armed forces. Some were likely trained in North Korea, China, or Cuba and were known as *responsible politicos* (political officers). They were similar in a general way to the commissars in the Soviet Army. They stayed constantly in the field gaining intelligence and planning operations. Usually their targets were government installations such as electrical towers, bridges, agricultural stations, or anything that represented the power of the state. One of Sendero's goals, among others, was to destroy Peru's infrastructure as a prelude to cutting off Lima from the rest of the country. The Peruvian armed forces had the advantage in weaponry throughout most of the conflict in the 1980s, but this changed when Sendero forged an alliance with Peru's narcotraffickers after 1987. Once Sendero began operating in the Upper Huallaga valley, revenue and training was forthcoming from the narcotraffickers. Better arms such as AK-47 automatic rifles and rocket launchers made the insurgency a tougher foe for government forces. Sendero tactics added to the military difficulties.

Guzmán created the *Ejército Guerrillero Popular* (Popular Guerrilla Army; EGP) in 1983 as the official military element of the party. As they gained confidence and strength, their tactics became bolder and more brutal. One veteran of two separate sierra campaigns against Sendero in 1983 and 1985 stated that the insurgency would often herd campesinos taken from nearby villages in front of a Sendero column to shield their fighters when the engaged with army or marine units. Government forces were required to combat an insurgency over an incredibly vast and rugged terrain. As in Vietnam, Peruvian forces conducted operations from firebases in remote areas of the interior. Length of patrols was limited by altitude and the rugged nature of the landscape. Hampering government operations more than any single factor was the lack of good intelligence. As in any war against a clandestine insurgency, whether it be Algeria, Vietnam, or Peru, poor intelligence usually assures high levels of civilian casualties. Peru was no exception. As the terror war escalated, killings and retribution on both sides caused casualties in the tens of thousands.

As the Sendero campaign evolved in the 1980s, it became increasingly clear that they could not recruit, forcibly or otherwise, sufficient numbers of fighters to win the war against government forces in the sierra. Either through a fundamental misunderstanding of indigenous communal values and practices or arrogance, Sendero's leadership never gained the lasting support of the peasantry.

Forced recruitment, of course, alienated many peasant villages from Sendero. Later assassinations of village leaders, very similar to the tactics of the Viet Cong, aroused campesino hatreds. But mostly it was a fundamental disregard for the welfare of the campesinos that doomed Sendero. In an effort to strangle the cities in Maoist fashion, Sendero tried to limit agricultural production or completely curtail the external market. Destruction of a peasant-owned milk processing plant or the mass slaughter of cattle and alpaca herds are other examples of these tactics. In Chuschi, where the "peoples war" began Sendero tried to completely remake village economic and social patterns that had been in place for centuries. Alcohol and fiestas were banned, campesinos were not permitted to sell their products in at the weekly market, and a planting system was put in place that had no relation to the complex reciprocity, kinship, and moiety structures that had always directed village activities.

Sendero Luminoso's organizing and recruitment program was more calculated and restrained in Lima's pueblos jovenes. Targeting the huge settlement of Villa El Salvador south of Lima that contained 260,000 inhabitants, the insurgency first tried to undermine support for the legal left IU. There tactics included participation in local councils, participating in new land invasions, and more mundane activities such as establishing a water and electricity committee as well as women's groups. Senderistas also gained sympathy with residents by eliminating thieves and other dangerous members of the community that civil authorities could not reach. Guzmán referred to Lima's shanty towns as "iron belts of misery." They were, indeed, the key to bring the people's war to the capital. But like Sendero's campaign in the sierra, terror soon replaced collaboration in Guzmán's war strategy.

Claiming falsely that Sendero had attained "strategic equilibrium" in the sierra, Guzmán ordered in late 1990 a campaign of assassinations and bombings in Villa El Salvador and subsequently in metropolitan Lima. One of the victims of Sendero's terror was Maria Elena Moyano, the extremely popular mayor of Villa El Salvador who had publically denounced the insurgency on numerous occasions in the press. Moyano was assassinated and her body dynamited in full public view of hundreds of witnesses. Of all Sendero's assassinations, Moyano's was the most outrageous as she had worked tirelessly with women's groups and then residents of Villa el Salvador to build better lives. Mary Jo Burt effectively argues that Sendero never really tried to gain popular support in Villa el Salvador. That would have taken too long and required too much patience. Instead the insurgency sought to exploit divisions within the community and its political leadership to encourage the erosion of participatory government in the community.[10] When faced with resistance in 1990 with the emergence of *rondas vecinales* (neighborhood defense committee), Sendero responded with terror. But the ultimate result was the alienation of the inhabitants of these "iron belts of misery." The insurgency confronted these same rondas on a much larger scale in the sierra.

Anthropologist Orin Starn has written extensively on peasant resistance to Sendero Luminoso in the sierra. He makes emphatically clear the insurgency was not a peasant-based movement. He argues that Sendero "was begun by privileged intellectuals in the city of Ayacucho." He further maintains that the movement mirrored the rigid hierarchy of race and class that it claimed it sought to destroy. "Dark-skinned kids born in poverty filled (*Sendero's*) bottom ranks under a leadership composed mostly of light-skinned elites.[11] The myth of a peasant-based Sendero is countered most effectively by the experience of the *rondas campesinas* (peasant self-defense committees) that came into being in the Andes as a response to Sendero terror. Some of the rondas developed at the behest of the military, who could not contest the insurgency throughout the Andes with its limited manpower. They were also formed spontaneously by the campesinos as a desperate attempt to defend themselves when the military could not.

The army followed a policy after 1983 of relocating villagers in war zones into *agrupaciones* (nucleated settlements) to better control peasant movements and enhance monitoring of the insurgency's activities. This caused substantial hardship for campesinos who were taken away from their land and communal environment. Still it provided a measure of protection for remote villages that were vulnerable to the insurgency's activities. As indicated earlier, during the early 1980s peasants suffered equally at the hand of the military and Sendero. Much of the counterinsurgency theory studied intensively at Peru's war colleges was not applied as commanders faced little accountability for their actions in a war in which the enemy was not easily defined. It will be recalled that the guerrillas on the Mesa Pelada near Cuzco in 1965 were obliterated with napalm. This was hardly a classic counterinsurgency operation.

What the Peruvian army was doing before 1985 in the Sendero war was rep-
licating the tactics of French paratroopers in Algeria (1954–1962), who often
followed a scorched-earth policy with furious reprisals against rebel villages.
Poor intelligence led directly to large numbers of casualties. As Sendero's campaign of terror was countered by rondas campesinas, intelligence drawn from
the peasantry improved and human rights abuses by the military declined.
This led directly to the rapid appearance of rondas committees, mainly in the
poorest departments of Andahuaylas, Apúrimac, Ayacucho, and Junín. In
these areas war casualties declined by nearly one third by 1990. The Peruvian
government was so convinced of the effectiveness of the rondas campesinas
that in 1991 it took the unprecedented step of distributing 10,000 Winchester
model 1300 shotguns to peasants rondas throughout the war zones. Never
had a Spanish colonial or Peruvian republican government distributed firearms to campesinos. It was both a measure of the desperation of the Peruvian
government but also its growing confidence in the capability of the rondas
campesinas to successfully combat the insurgency. By 1990, there were as many
as 300,000 rondas campesinas patrolling the highlands and forcing the leadership of Sendero to escalate the war in Lima before the Maoist imperative of
encircling the capital had been achieved. Some of the most effective resistance
was in the Apurímac River Valley, where peasants were motivated often by
protestant evangelicalism. These highly religious campesinos were often targeted by Sendero for particularly violent abuse. Reacting to this, the peasants
responded with a form of holy war that identified Sendero as the anti-Christ.
Identifying Sendero in Andean mythical terms, the peasants claimed that the
terrorists "eat human flesh and suck human blood."[12] Interestingly, the rondas
Apurímac used Sendero tactics against the Senderistas. More than half of the
valley's economy was composed of the coca trade. Colombian drug dealers
were thus charged a tax of up to $5,000 per airplane flight in the early 1990s.
The money was used to buy arms and ammunition to fight Sendero.[13]

It can be said that Sendero failure to win the war in the sierra was due to a
deeply flawed strategy because of a misunderstanding of the peasantry. Disregard for traditional Andean ways by Sendero's leadership is not be surprising.
Guzmán's hero, Mao Ze Dong, exploited the peasants remorselessly throughout his 27 years in power. Jung Chang and Jon Halliday demonstrate in their
carefully researched biography of Mao Ze Dong that the Chinese leader was
never interested in the welfare of the peasantry. Rather what consumed him
was the gaining and holding of power, largely through terror. His "superpower" program in the 1950s, for example, was aimed at making China the
military equal of the United States and the Soviet Union. In order to pay for
the cost of militarization Mao Ze Dong starved the peasantry so that food
could be sold overseas to pay for arms. Because of the government's forced

food requisitioning program in early 1955, many Chinese peasants were reduced to eating tree bark. Mao reportedly told his inner circle to prepare for
deaths in 100,000 villages. Heartlessly he gave them assurances that the food
requisitioning campaign would not jeopardize communist rule. He noted that
such a program had worked well for the Japanese occupiers of Manchuria. It
had not threatened the brutal Japanese hold on their captured colony.[14]

But Mao Ze Dong was dead by 1976 and Sendero's people's war deviated
from his strategy of strangling the cities by opening a terrorist campaign in
Lima, even as the insurgency was being defeated in the sierra. By 1990 the
capital was plagued by street crime brought on by an overworked police force
that was constantly the target of Sendero assassins. Over 150 police were killed
on Lima's streets by Senderista gunmen. Hard economic times and an undermanned police force made Lima one of the most dangerous cities in Latin
America during the early 1990s. Sendero tried to exploit the turmoil by bringing its terror campaign to a climax in mid-July 1992 with a series of bombings
in Lima and Callao. A police station and a television station were targeted.

The deadliest of these attacks was the car bombing of an exclusive Lima
suburb of Miraflores in July 1992. Said to have the explosive equivalent of
1,800 pounds of dynamite, the ammonium nitrate and fuel oil (ANFO) bomb
killed 22 and injured 250. An entire city block was leveled with 183 residences,
400 businesses, and 62 parked cars destroyed. Some commentators noted after
the car bombing that this was the first time residents of Lima's affluent communities had come face-to-face with the war. Many had stopped traveling
into center city Lima years before thus avoiding the jammed streets and petty
crime that plagued the capital.

Less than two months after the car bomb offensive, when many felt Sendero
was capable of winning the battle for Lima, Guzmán was captured by a special police unit in Surco, a posh suburb of Lima. Peru's national intelligence
police known as DINCOTE conducted an extended campaign of surveillance
that finally located Guzmán's hideout. For years he had been traveling in the
trunks of cars, never being seen in public and only issuing communiqués. In
his own right, he developed a mystique similar to Osama Bin Laden. Captured along with Guzmán were members of Sendero's metropolitan committee and computer files, which were invaluable to police. Guzmán was quickly
tried by a military court and sentenced to life in prison without parole. He
was housed in a specially constructed jail cell in specially constructed prison
in Callao. Guzmán was at first defiant in his courtroom appearances but relatively soon he was calling for his Senderista followers to stand down, so
negotiations could begin with the government. Guzmán seeming surrender
after such a short time in prison deeply divided his followers. Most of the
movement's senior leadership supported their leader and argued the 50-year
people's war was entering yet another phase. Guzmán's bitter critics argued

he was only negotiating for better prison conditions. He was also unfavorably compared with Nelson Mandela, who suffered long years in South Africa's Dobbins Island prison without ever renouncing his ideals.

The son of a former army general, Oscar Ramírez Duránd, known as Comrade Feliciano, continued to command Sendero's increasingly weak resistance to the government from bases in the Upper Huallaga Valley drug zone. Government amnesty programs prompted many Senderistas to turn in their arms and abandon the armed struggle in the mid-1990s. Ramírez Durán was captured by the army in mid-September 1999 and imprisoned in the same El Frontón facility as Guzmán. Sendero now seems to have morphed into a narcotrafficking mode and has little of the mystic of the insurgency of the 1980s. But at the same time the Sendero Luminoso over the past year has sought to conciliate its fierce image among the peasantry. In a recent incursion at the Pukatoro mining camp in Ayacucho province a Sendero column dressed in black and wearing body armor addressed the minors assuring them that "they were not going to commit the same acts of violence like they did in the past." Nevertheless, the army is seeking to establish two or three new firebases in the Upper Huallaga Valley in the second García government's effort to eradicate Sendero Luminoso once and for all.[15]

Sendero Luminoso did not operate alone during the last decades of the 20th century. Another terrorist group known as the *Movimiento Revolucionaria Tupac Amaru* (MRTA) drew militants to its ranks as well. Here only brief summary of its activities is warranted. MRTA began operations in 1984 and was a primarily urban-based guerrilla terrorist front with ties to Cuba. Like many Peruvian political organizations, revolutionary or not, they took their name from Tupac Amaru II, the rebel leader who had very nearly defeated the Spanish in the early 1780s. MRTA was never peasant-based and recruited students and people of lower middle-class status. It relied on bombing of high-profile U.S. and Japanese holdings in Lima. Those Limeños who had a taste for Kentucky Fried Chicken (now KFC), for example, satisfied it at their own risk.

MRTA conducted its most brazen operation when 14 militants took control of the Japanese ambassador's residence in Lima in December 1996. The militants detained 72 members of the Peruvian government and diplomatic corps for four months before special units of the army stormed the building in April 1997 releasing all hostages except one who died of a heart attack. Following an unwritten policy involving terrorist in hostage situation, the army assault group took no prisoners among the 14 MRTA operatives in the residence. MRTA has dwindled to less than 100 activists over the course of the last decade. It has undertaken no significant operations since the April 1997 confrontation with the Peruvian army.

What can be said about Peru's terrible period of violence from 1980 to the mid-1990s? Peru's Truth and Reconciliation Commission headed by Dr.

Solomón Lerner Febres interviewed 17,000 witnesses and were given unprecedented access to military documents for a two-year study beginning in 2001. The commission concluded that 69,280 died or disappeared during the two decades after 1980. The vast majority were Quechua-speaking indigenous peoples of the highland. Lerner's group concluded that at least 50 percent of the deaths and disappearances were caused by Sendero. At least a third were attributed to the military's reactive violence. Other deaths were attributed to smaller guerrilla groups or militias. In the latter case, the commission may be attributing some of the deaths to the rondas campesinas, which were accused at times of vigilantism and vendetta killings under the guise of defending their villages against Sendero. Critics of the Lerner commission claimed that a flawed methodology inflated the number of suspected deaths, but no one seriously challenges the war's cost in continued physical and emotional suffering more than a decade after its supposed conclusion.

Upon submitting his report to the president of Peru in August 2003, Lerner claimed, "The report contains a double outrage: that of massive murder disappearance and torture, and that of indolence, incompetence and indifference of those who could have stopped this humanitarian catastrophe and didn't."[16] Despite these telling comments, a mechanism for establishing a mechanism for the adjudication of crimes against humanity still has not been established in Peru.

Two Peruvian commentators, one a former rebel and another a distinguished scholar best characterize Peru's descent in *Chaqwa* at the end of the 20th century. Héctor Béjar, who fought the Peruvian government as a guerrilla in 1965 and later advised the Velasco's government, lamented that those in the armed struggle knew why they were fighting but not what they were fighting for. He argued that what we have today is a confusing mix of guerrilla fighting, sabotage, terrorism, propaganda, and intimidation; clean fighting and dirty war; revolution and vengeance over social resentment. Above all, social resentment was the key. Carlos Ivan De Gregori argues similarly that the violence of the late 20th century stemmed from the anger of "young people without hope" channeled by intellectuals who themselves were scorned by a racist society. In any event, it was a reckoning that was both feared and anticipated by many Peruvians who were sensitive to the nation's injustices.

DEMOCRACY WITHOUT PEACE

During the last years of the Belaúnde administration, the armed forces remained in the barracks despite one of the greatest threats to national security in the 20th century. There were a number of reasons for this. The divisive legacy of the Docenio was still fresh in the minds of officers who now knew they were not prepared to lead a nation and conduct a counterinsurgency campaign at the same time. Argentina's defeat in the Malvinas War was a powerful lesson to the Peruvians. The Belaúnde government loaned 14 fighter jets to the Argentines in an effort to bolster their allies campaign against the British. Of course, Peru was really more concerned with how Chile would take advantage of a weakened Argentina at Peru's expense. Nevertheless, the collapse of the Argentine military government and then subsequent prosecutions of perpetrators of the Dirty War was not lost upon Peru's military leadership.

Belaúnde and his presidential successor Alan García Pérez (1985–1990) also gave very wide latitude to the military commanders in the field in the campaign against Sendero Luminoso and MRTA. This was particularly true in the early 1980s when the military intelligence was poor, and frightened inexperienced troops committed the most egregious human rights abuses of the war. Much of Peru by the late 1980s were declared emergency zones. In essence, democratic rights were suspended and military rule was the order of the day. Peru was a democracy in name only. Of course, this was true of neighboring Colombia as well, but the basic framework of democracy survived in the form of elections and a functioning congress.

As he had during his first presidential administration, Belaúnde firmly supported the military border defense operations. When a brief fire-fight between a Peruvian helicopter and Ecuador troops occurred in the long-disputed Cordillera del Condor region occurred in late January 1981, Belaúnde rushed to the area in conflict, posed with Peruvian troops, and declared the Ecuadoran operations to be a "macabre masquerade." He vowed that Ecuador would face "grave consequences" if it did not cease operations. Belaúnde's tough stance helped him retain the support of the military at this critical time. The Cordillera del Condor conflict was not resolved, however, flaring again in 1995.

Confronting a mounting foreign debt and IMF-austerity measures that engendered increasing popular dissent, Belaúnde still bent to the wishes of the air force and purchased Mirage 2000 interceptor fighters from France and Hind helicopters from the Soviet Union. Incredibly, the Mirage jet purchases followed the pattern of earlier arms negotiations with the United States. F-16 General Dynamics fighter, easily one of the best fighter planes ever built and the workhorse for the U.S. air force and navy for a generation, were available to Peru at a lower price than the Mirages. Yet the deal could not be consummated. By the mid-1980s Peru's military budget reached a staggering 30 percent of national expenditures. Still, another issue remains to be explained. Why was Peru's air force buying sophisticated fighter aircrafts when what it needed were far more helicopters to fight an extremely dangerous insurgency in remote areas of the country?

THE GARCÍA DEBACLE

Because of his adept or, one could say, solicitous dealings with Peru's armed forces, Belaúnde was able to serve his full five-year presidential term. This was indeed no small accomplishment. Even more unusual was the election of an APRA candidate to the presidency in June 1985. García was only 36 years old when elected. He had been Haya de la Torre's personal secretary, and he best represented the youth wing of an aging party. He was educated in Paris and Spain, where he reportedly paid for part of his studies as a café singer. He headed a party group known as the Bureau of Conjunctions that formed a bridge between the APRA old guard and young turks. Garcia was very young, intelligent, charismatic, and politically astute. During his presidential campaign he built a coalition of the informals in the barriadas campesinos and the remnants of APRA's old labor coalition to forge a victory over the UI's candidate Alfronso Barrantes and two other candidates. Nearly 9 out of 10 eligible voters cast their ballots in a vital expression of democracy in a very troubled land. García polled nearly half of the largest electorate in Peru's history. Finally, APRA exceeded its perennial one third of the popular vote.

President García immediately adopted a strongly nationalist stance by announcing that debt payments by Peru would not exceed 10 percent of the nation's exports. This position was popular with the poor because Belaúnde had followed the IMF's hard line by not protecting them against Peru's punishing inflation. Nevertheless, such a tactic put Peru on a collision course with the international lending community. García's economic plan involved shifting the resources saved by cutting back interest payments on the debt in order to energize the domestic economy by channeling subsidies, financing tax credits, and manipulating export duties and exchange rates. This policy actually brought solid results in the first three years of his administration with GNP growth averaging nearly six percent yearly. Manufacturing and construction, two of the government's main targets, grew a spectacular 19 percent and 30 percent respectively. Plans for a community development program in the sierra with a $640 million price tag never materialized as they were overtake by economic events during García's last three years in office.[17]

The Achilles' heel of the government's economic program was a Peru's tax system, which was woefully inadequate and riddled with fraud. Simply put, far too many businesses and individuals avoided paying taxes and thus government revenues declined even as economic growth surged. By one report, tax fraud amounted to nearly five percent of Peru's GDP. In response to the government-declared limit on debt payments, the IMF blocked any further loans to Peru. The foundation of an immense crisis in the Peruvian economy was thus laid.

With a decision that had little basis in sound economic policy, in July 1987 García nationalized the remaining 20 percent of the nation's banks that remained in private hands. As other nations in Latin America were moving increasingly toward the free market, this was an extreme measure that proved to be a major political misstep. In the immediate aftermath of this decision, inflation raged out of control to nearly 3000 percent for the year 1989. The *Inti*, the new Peruvian monetary unit, was devalued repeatedly between 1987 and 1989. Peru had never experienced inflation of this magnitude. By the end of García's presidency, many Peruvians were living in a barter economy. This was not quite Weimar Germany in the early 1920s, but the misery certainly was equal to that stricken society. As Klarén notes, 7 out of 10 Peruvians were either unemployed or underemployed by 1990. Food may have been available, but most could not afford it.

García took a much more interventionist policy toward the armed forces and police than his predecessor. In February 1986 legislation combined all of Peru's diverse policy agencies into a single national police force. This allowed García to purge 1,800 police personnel accused of corruption. The Guardia Civil responded by striking in May 1987, but the violence of the February 1975 strike against the Velasco government was avoided. The president then ordered significant salary and benefit increases for the for the police both in an effort to mollify the strikers and to gain the loyalty of new policy personnel. These measures were met with suspicion and hostility by the armed forces. The police and the armed forces never have had a professional bond in Peru. President Leguía, it will be recalled, used the Guardia Civil as an ally against the army during the 1920s. That sense of rivalry still remained. At the heart of the armed forces suspicion was that García might well be trying to mimic Leguía by using the reformed national police as his ally against the armed forces.

The young president also ambitiously took on the task of unifying the armed forces under a *comando conjunto* (joint command), which would be represented by a single defense minister in the cabinet. This command structure, similar to the U.S. joint chiefs of staff, would exclude the individual service ministers who had previously represented only their services interests. Very likely the minister of defense would be a civilian, and this caused a great deal of angst within the armed forces senior leadership. Still, this measure was adopted in April 1987. It reflected the military's restraint even against an increasingly unpopular civilian government. Again, when García cut Belaúnde's Mirage fighter purchase by half (from 26 to 13) in September 1985, the armed forces remained largely restrained save for a poorly supported protest by an air force general at the Las Palmas air base. But for all his boldness with the military, García failed profoundly as Peru's president from 1985 to 1990. After his nationalization of the banks, the political right, all but invisible in the 1985 elections, was revived. Riding the horse of free market economics, fiscal responsibility, and strong support for the armed forces' counterinsurgency campaign, the-world renowned novelist Maria Varga Llosa entered politics. A resident more of Europe and the United States in the decades preceding the 1990 election, Vargas Llosa presented an urbane and polished presence to the

Peruvian electorate. In March of 1990, as wreckage of the García years was visible everywhere in Peru, there seemed to be no other viable candidate than the impressive figure of gifted novelist. Then the unpredictability of Peru's expanded and diverse electorate became manifest to all: a completely unknown candidate with Japanese ancestry emerged from near obscurity with no formal political backing to contend for Peru's presidency.

THE FUJIMORI DECADE

As a resident of Lima in 1990, as was the author of this book, Fujimori confronted a society in profound stress. PeruvianInti notes often had had a bewildering number of zeros. Money changers lining the streets in Lima's suburbs were a regular fixture. Police and security personnel were everywhere. Banks sometimes were guarded by as many as 15 police or hired security personnel. Private security guards were in evidence nearly everywhere in Lima's more affluent suburbs. Travel to Peru's interior was both dangerous and difficult because of the condition of the roads as well as concerns for security. Water and electricity supplies were tenuous at best. Not surprisingly, Latin America's most severe cholera epidemic of the modern era struck Lima in 1991. Tens of thousands were sickened and nearly two thousand died. The disease was spread by a public water system that was in bad disrepair. Yet Limeños endured with a quiet tenacity that one could only admire. Still after a decade of civilian rule, most Peruvians were far worse off than when they were ruled by military strongmen. Peruvians were looking for a strong, competent experienced candidate who could appeal to their values and understand the needs of the poor. That candidate was Alberto Fujimori, a former rector of Peru's Agrarian University at La Molina on the outskirts of Lima.

Because of his importance to contemporary Peruvian events, some extended background on Fujimori is warranted. Born in Lima in 1938, Fujimori was the son of parents who had migrated from Kumamoto Prefecture in southern Japan. His father Naoichi arrived in Peru in 1920 to work on a cotton plantation in Paramonga. He struggled economically nearly all his life and never achieved the comfortable lifestyle of most other Japanese immigrants. Fujimori's mother, Matsue, was married to Naoichi in an ceremony marriage in Kumamoto in 1934. By all accounts she was a strong and resourceful women who was a major influence in the future president's life. Fujimori's birthday is reportedly July 28, 1938, Peruvian Independence Day. Pragmatically, his parents registered his birth with the Japanese Embassy in Lima. This made him potentially eligible for Japanese citizenship.

His early life was marked by hardship as the family barely avoided deportation to the United States during World War II. Naoichi Fujimori did suffer the loss of his tire repair business as it was confiscated by the Prado administration. Very likely he was not deported because the family did not participate actively in Japanese community affairs. Naoichi's economic status also kept him off the Peruvian government black list of potential deportees.

Alberto Fujimori received a solid education and eventually enrolled in the agricultural university at La Molina in the late 1950s. After graduation and a brief period of study in France, Fujimori became a faculty member in mathematics at La Molina. In the early 1970s he was invited to attend the University of Wisconsin at Milwaukee to earn a master degree in mathematics. There he studied under the guidance of Professor Gilbert Walter, whom he had met at La Molina. Fujimori actually lived for a year in Walter's home while completing his second year in the masters program. Professor Walter has characterized Fujimori as a resourceful and intelligent man who has a real sense of his own competence. He has said that Fujimori gave the appearance of being shy but was able to mix well with other university students and made a number of friends including women. Walter noted that Fujimori was quite ambitious but that he clearly wanted to succeed not as a Japanese-Peruvian but as a Peruvian. On the other hand, Walter noted that Fujimori's ambition did not really extend to the academic profession. He chose not to continue in a Ph.D. program in mathematics because it didn't seem relevant to his future life. As to Fujimori's character, Walter maintained that Fujimori felt he was the only person who could solve Peru's many problems. Fujimori tended to resent the oligarchy, not so much for their callousness, but for their "incompetence."[18]

From the beginning of his presidential campaign, the Japanese community in Peru tried to distance themselves from Fujimori. Their reasons were straightforward. The Nikkei did not know Fujimori very well and tended to consider him as an outsider. They were also fearful that his candidacy would raise the profile of the Nikkei community, which had been barely visible since World War II. At a time of terrorism and instability, the Nikkei did not want to be targets of violence as they had been in the past. Peru's 50,000-member Nikkei community was actually more in sympathy with the economic policies of Mario Vargas Llosa, who wanted to exert the necessary measures to restore stability to Peru's inflation-ravaged economy. At one point in the campaign, Japanese students actually demonstrated against the Fujimori candidacy. The alienation between the Fujimori and the Nikkei community was substantial.

There are some who feel that Fujimori did not really have presidential ambitions when he registered as a candidate to the 1990 elections. The Peruvian constitution of 1979 allowed a candidate to file for both a senate and a presidential campaign. That is what Fujimori did. Perhaps hoping his quixotic bid for the presidency would help him get elected to the senate, Fujimori's campaign caught fire in March 1990. He campaigned as a man of the people, a man of color who represented competence and honesty and the famous work ethic of the Japanese. He rode a bike or a tractor through the barriadas and rode a mule wearing a poncho in the sierra. He drew sharp contrasts between himself and the urbane Vargas Llosa, who seemed detached from the Peruvian electorate. Vargas Llosa also called for tough austerity measures to confront Peru's economic problems and to mend fences with the world lending community. Fujimori never hinted on his intentions on this issue.

In the preliminary elections round in April 1990, Fujimori qualified for the final round by finishing only slightly behind Vargas Llosa. Fujimori polled 25 percent to Vargas Llosa's 28 percent. The APRA candidate garnered only 19 percent and this put Fujimori in an advantageous position to appropriate the APRA votes in the final election in June. Fujimori's political vehicle for his election, *Cambio* 90 (Change 1990), was a political party in name only. Fujimori had to depend upon his populist appeal, the support of APRA, and also an understanding with the armed forces. These is a strong possibility that Fujimori was given access to military intelligence data by order of president before he was elected. This put him in a strong position with regard to national security issues during the final election round. In the final election round Fujimori's left-of-center alliance with APRA and his enormous appeal in Lima's shanty towns and in the sierra carried him to a resounding victory over the FREDEMO coalition of right and center-right parties that was backing Vargas Llosa. The margin of victory was 62 to 38 percent.

FUJISHOCK AND THE "DELAGATIVE DEMOCRACY"

Nearly immediately after his inauguration in July 1990 Fujimori confronted the crisis of the Peruvian economy by initiating the sweeping austerity measures he had attacked Vargas Llosa for proposing. The new president faced a monumental task of reestablishing Peru's international credit rating, encouraging future foreign investment, rebuilding the nation's shattered infrastructure, and defeating the Sendero Luminoso insurgency. Remarkably, most of these tasks were accomplished within his first term as president by a process termed *delegative democracy* by social scientist Guillermo O'Donnell. This process is by definition has a "hyper-presidential system characterized by few checks or balances to executive power and weak civil liberties."[19]

Fujimori's austerity program was dubbed Fujishock (from shock therapy) by the Peruvian populace. Dramatically reducing government subsidies and initiating a sweeping program of privatization that deconstructed the state capitalism of the Velasco years, Fujimori adopted whole cloth the economic package of his opponent Vargas Llosa. Immediately, the price of basic necessities rose dramatically. The price of gasoline, for example, rose 3,000 percent. Unemployment increased significantly as well, but interestingly these was only limited protests from Peru's population. Instead, in Lima's new towns, cooperative soup kitchens and the continuation of the *vaso de leche* (glass of milk) programs for children from the García years helped Limeños endure and improvise in order to get by. Still, Limeños confronted yet another challenge in 1991 with the outbreak of a cholera epidemic brought in the bilges of ships from the Orient. The city's outdated water and sewage system clearly contributed to the deaths of more than 2,000 people and the sickening of another quarter million more.

Fujimori's tough measures brought results. Inflation fell from 7,650 percent in 1990 to just 15 percent in 1994. By 1994, Peru's GDP growth rate was 12.4 percent, one of the highest in the world. But the nation was still making up for so much regression in the 1980s. The IMF and international investment community, however, were returning to Peru. Chilean investment was strong in food and beverage industry and Chinese investment was targeting the extractive industries.

In his relations with the armed forces, Fujimori had an important ally: Vladimiro Montesinos, a former army officer who had been expelled from the army for suspected espionage. Specifically, he was thought to have attempted to pass information about Soviet weaponry to the CIA during the Docenio. Later, as a lawyer, he defended a number of prominent drug traffickers and apparently made contacts in Peru's underworld.

Montesinos was a shadowy, Rasputin-like figure who became invaluable to Fujimori in many ways. As a legal advisor he helped the president through a constitutional referendum and two reelection campaigns to perpetuate Fujimori's hold on the presidency. He became head of Peru's National Intelligence Service (SIN) that gathered information on civilian and military personnel as well. SIN served more as a political tool of Fujimori than as a system of domestic intelligence gathering for national security purposes.

Had Montesinos stayed in the army, he would have been of the same generation of officers who were in command positions when Fujimori was elected president. Thus he had a first-hand knowledge of the character and personality of many of these men and that clearly helped him coach Fujimori in his dealings with the armed forces. The tough-minded president gained the support of the armed forces by granting them virtual autonomy in the counterterrorism campaign. He insisted, however, on absolute loyalty and senior command positions were granted on this primary criteria. Some of the navy's senior officers were thus forced into retirement because of their support for Vargas Llosa.

Very much like Leguía in the 1920s, Fujimori heavily politicized the armed forces and undermined its professionalism during his decade in power.

Fujimori's delegative or authoritarian predilection was made quite clear when after the Peruvian Congress failed to pass a number of emergency measures designed to substantially increase government powers in the counterinsurgency campaign. Fujimori closed congress on April 5, 1992 and proceeded to rule by decree. With his popularity hovering about 70 percent, president felt he was taking a safe step. Polls indicated that Peru's poor had little sympathy with congress. However, the international community quickly put great pressure on Fujimori to reverse his *auto-golpe* (self coup). The first Bush administration in Washington took the lead and suspended economic assistance to Peru. A number of countries followed suit. Fujimori responded by pledging to rewrite the 1979 constitution and hold elections for congress within the year.

In that interim, the Sendero Luminoso–leader Guzmán Reynoso was captured in September 1992, thus boosting Fujimori's popularity even more. Despite Guzmán's capture, Fujimori purged the judiciary as he had the leadership of the armed forces by the end of 1992. Special military tribunals were also established to try terrorist suspects and broader definitions of crimes against the security of the state were decreed. If the Belaúnde and García era were "democracies without peace" then the Fujimori era was fast becoming a delegative democracy without political liberties. Still, the material condition of the Peruvian people was slowly improving, For many, this is what mattered most. When the constitutional congress presented the document in October 1993, its most prominent component was the reelection of the Peruvian president. Now Fujimori was eligible for another five-year term. It also shifted even more administrative power to the presidency, enacted even more counterterrorism laws, and further centralized an already dominant national government. The death penalty was reactivated as well. The constitution was approved by only four percentage points in a national referendum, suggesting the wariness that Peruvians were beginning to have with Fujimori. In retrospect, they should have been alarmed because the 1993 constitution facilitated the demise of Peru's traditional political parties. The Docenio left Peru's political parties weak. The Fujimori decade damaged many of them beyond repair. During the last two years of his initial term, Fujimori was able to increase social spending from revenues Peru gained from the sale of state-owned companies. This sell-off would continue for most of Fujimori's decade in office and would provide very substantial revenues for development programs and unfortunately for corruption. The level of corruption and the specifics as to who benefitted await legal and historical assessment, but it seems likely that Fujimori's decade in office will compare with Leguía's Oncenio with regard to the magnitude of graft and public malfeasance.

Given his careful engineering of the constitutional and electoral process in 1995, it is not surprising that Fujimori handily defeated his two presidential rivals, the diplomat Javier Peréz de Cuellar and the Stanford-educated populist Alejandro Toledo, with 64 percent of the vote. Soon, the Fujimori would be tested by international events that he would have less control over. But for the next five years, Fujimori would be the elected caudillo who seemed to be morphing into a paradigm for other politicians in Latin American to follow. The cult of *continuismo* (continuism) was gaining new members. Soon, however, international events shook the steady structures of the Fujimori regime.

CONFLICT IN THE CORDILLERA DEL CONDOR AND ALTA CENEPA

As we have seen, conflict and border tensions between Peru and Ecuador were persistent from the early republican era to the mid-1990s. Ecuador renounced the 1941 Rio Treaty in the early 1960s. Still, nearly all the borders were mapped and marked by a U.S. army aerial team known as the McBride Commission, named after the professor who led the team. The only portion of the border not definitively marked was the Cordillera del Condor. A previously uncharted river, the Upper Cenepa, and the rugged nature of the terrain prevented this final section of the border to be marked. It totaled 50 miles. This small border section was the scene of many border incursions since the 1940s. In the early 1990s while Peru was occupied with the counterinsurgency campaign, Ecuador used the opportunity to strengthen its position in the area of the Upper Cenepa River Valley. After the 1981 border clash with Peru, Ecuador began an arms purchasing initiative that included shoulder fired anti-aircraft missiles and Israeli Kifir aircraft. Ecuador moved troops to the high ground in January 1995. There they were able to defend their positions with mortars, rockets, and small arms fire. When Peruvian forces tried to dislodge them, they took significant casualties. Ecuadorian troops reportedly shot down two Sukhoi-22 fighter bombers, one A-37 aircraft, and a Canberra bomber. Five Peruvian helicopters were reported downed, but this has never been confirmed.

Smarting from this major setback, the Peruvian air force put enormous pressure on Fujimori for a quick material fix for their losses. The government acted quickly. In April 1996, Peru purchased 16 single-seat MiG-29s from the former Soviet republic of Belarus. This make of airplane was one of the most advanced fighters in the world. They are comparable to the U.S. F-18 Hornet or France's most advanced Mirage-2000. In addition two MiG 29UB Fulcrum two-seat aircraft were also acquired by Peru. The later serves as trainer for the MiG-29s but can also play a combat role. The cost of these purchases was never announced but it was estimated to be in the range of $24 million per aircraft. This amounts to a price tag of more than $400 million. One can argue that the air force once again overreached in a technological leap that cost the nation dearly in a time of economic recovery. But just as much to the point with regard to civil-military relations in Peru is that the air force was drawing a vastly disproportionate share of Peru's weapons purchases in the later decades of the 20th century. The navy, and particularly the army, was witnessing its weapons system deteriorate badly. Would replacement for the 1970s-era

T-55 tanks be needed as Ecuador and Chile developed better relations with Peru? This remains an open question.

During the period from 1995 to 1998, Argentina, Brazil, Chile, and the United States were the original guarantors of the 1941 Ecuador-Peru peace settlement. They took up this task once again in an effort to resolve this tenacious conflict. Troops from Latin American nations were inserted into the disputed area as peacekeepers and were largely successful, despite some minor skirmishing between small pockets of Peruvian and Ecuadoran troops. High-level peace talks were carried on in Brazil and the United States over the course of the next three years. Finally an imaginative peace process was finally completed with the signing of a treaty in Brasilia in late October 1998. Both nations agreed that their common border in the disputed border area would follow the peaks of the Cordillera del Condor range. Peru granted Ecuador a plot of land within the Peruvian territory known as Tiwinza as the private property of the Ecuadoran government. The hill, encompassing 250 square acres, would still remain under the sovereignty of Peru. A road connected this plot of land to Ecuador was to be built by Peru as part of the agreement. Two ecological parks contiguous to one another were also to be constructed in the area. Park rangers, not military or police, would have responsibility for these parks. Most important of all, Peru granted navigation and port concessions to the Ecuador government to facilitate their access to the Amazon River basin. Peru also pledged to seek foreign development funds for Ecuador's economic enterprises in the area. This treaty marked one of the most successful multilateral diplomatic efforts in 20th-century Latin America. The stakes were very high in this conflict. The area in dispute may be extremely remote, but the possibility of gold, oil, and uranium deposits in the area made it much more important than a mere nationalistic conflict over useless landscape.[20] Fujimori dealt with the negotiations quite well. He needed a boost at this point because, once again El Niño had wrought a destructive swath across coastal Peru and set back the government's economic recovery program.

EL NIÑO AND THE CAUDILLO'S DEMISE

The 1990s saw Peru endure some of the most pronounced El Niño events of the 20th century. The 1995 El Niño was the culmination of one of the longest ocean-warming events on record. It will be remembered that that the El Niño's most damaging effect in Peru is flooding. Areas that had not received rain in decades along Peru's coastal desert were inundated. Tens of millions of dollars in damage to crops, roads, houses, and other aspects of the infrastructure occurred during the 1990s. A giant El Niño occurred during the 1997–1998 season that altered weather patterns around the world and killed 2,100 people. The El Niño warming effect heated a range of the ocean the size of Canada off of South America's west coast. Seas in some places were 10 inches higher than normal and were heated to a remarkably warm 86 degrees Fahrenheit. In some places along Peru's north coast it rained as much as five to six inches a day. The Piura river overflowed it banks and wiped out small settlements. Much the same form of flooding took a heavy toll in the region of Chiclayo. The runoff from these floods formed a vast inland lake in the Sechura Desert, which had seen little precipitation in decades. In isolated areas, the water pooled and formed inviting habitat for malaria-carrying mosquitoes. In the Piura area alone, 30,000 cases of malaria were reported. By the late 1990s scientists were beginning to understand the age-old El Niño/La Niña phenomenon far better, but the people of Peru's coastal regions, nevertheless, face the daunting task of rebuilding their lives as there ancestors had done for more than two millennia.[21]

Some Peruvians referred to Fujimori's 1990 election and his first years in power as the Fujimori Tsunami. Near the end of his decade in office, the political manipulation, obvious corruption, and authoritarian nature of the regime had soured many Peruvians who initially admired the Nikkei's ability to resolve many of Peru's monumental problems. Two violent insurgencies were largely defeated. Inflation was brought under control. Peru's international credit standing was restored. Tourism was thriving as never before. The government's high profile attempt to alleviate extreme poverty had mixed results, but Fujimori continued to give his program to combat poverty significant attention in government discourse. Still, many of these accomplishments seemed distant memories to many disenchanted Peruvians when the "perpetual president" began laying plans for his reelection bid in 2000.

Legal engineering through a Fujimori-controlled supreme court again paved the way for the caudillo's continuing hold on presidential power. In Latin America, the continuation of power is known as *coninuismo* (continuation). It stems from hubris, love of power, and a belief in one's singular ability to direct a nation's affairs. Clearly Fujimori possessed all three of these qualities. He may also have been fearful of what post-Fujimori investigations into the workings of his presidency might have revealed. In any event, the Nikkei again ran for the presidency in April 2000. Peru's political parties had all but disappeared by this time. Accion Popular and Izquierda Unida no longer existed and the APRA was barely surviving as a party. The only candidate standing in the way of Fujimori's reelection was Alejandro Toledo Manrique, a child of the Andes and a Ph.D. graduate of Stanford University in economics. Toledo had become the focus of opposition to Fujimori since the mid-1990s.

The first round of elections saw Fujimori and Toledo dominate the returns with the incumbent receiving nearly 5.5 million votes or 49.83 percent of the votes cast. Toledo gained 4.4 million votes and 40.32 percent of those cast. No other candidate received more than three percent of the vote. The APRA candidate, Abel Salinas Izaguirre, received a mere 150,000 votes or less than two percent. Fujimori's politics had indeed undermined the vitality of party-based democracy in Peru. His maneuvering to eliminate Toledo from the second round became a big political misstep. Amid reports of computer malfunction in the first round, Peru's electoral body still proceeded with an early date for the final presidential runoff. Toledo, protesting the possibility of a fraudulent election scheduled for May 28, 2000, withdrew from the presidential race and asked that a new date be set.

Running as the sole candidate for his third term as president in late May 2000, Fujimori won a pyrrhic victory. Facing a fine of $33 if they did not vote, Peruvians "spoiled" nearly one of three ballots in apparent protest to Fujimori's electoral bid. With his name still on the ballot, Toledo received 26 percent of the votes to 74 percent for the incumbent president. This time Fujimori did not face triumphant crowds in his post-election celebration. Highly destructive riots broke out in central Lima, Chimbote, Cuzco, Cajamarca, and Trujillo. Even as he began his third term in office in July 2000, Fujimori's days as president were numbered.

Vladimiro Montesinos, Fujimori's shadowy operative proved to be the Nikkei president's final undoing. When a videotape showing Montesinos being bribed by a Peruvian congressmen, the wheels quickly came off Fujimori's government. First Montesinos fled the country to avoid prosecution. Then the president left Peru ostensibly to attend an Asia-Pacific summit in Brunei in November 2000. During a supposed one-night stopover in Tokyo, Fujimori faxed his resignation to the Peruvian Congress. That body rejected his resignation and instead impeached Fujimori. The former president then spent the next five years in Japan where he married again and lived a relatively quiet life all the while harboring ambitions to return to Peru. This he tried to do in October of 2005 when he travelled to Chile in hopes of making final passage to Peru to participate in the 2005 presidential elections. Instead, Chilean authorities detained Fujimori and eventually extradited him to Peru. At the moment, Alberto Fujimori is standing trial on charges of a variety of charges for crimes during his presidential term. One of these charges links him as an "indirect perpetrator" in collusion with a army death squad known as La Colina, which operated against alleged terrorists in the mid-1990s. The former caudillo faces a prison sentence of up to 35 years.

Montesinos, the main witness against Fujimori during the 2008 trial, was captured in Caracas, Venezuela, in June 2001. He was subsequently tried in 27 cases since his capture. He reportedly stole huge sums during his years in the Fujimori regime. He faces an extensive prison sentence for his crimes. At this point, Fujimori has been convicted of one crime against a political opponent and sentenced to six years in prison.

The dictator Augusto Leguía was deposed and ended his days in prison. His fall from power was complete. We still await the fate of one of Peru's most powerful men of the 20th century. Despite his alleged crimes, he still has many supporters in Peru.

Fujimori's legacy in Peru is, to say the least, mixed. Political democracy and particularly the party system was weakened considerably by his authoritarian measures. The congress became largely a rubber stamp confirming in the minds of many Peruvians its lack of utility in the democratic process. The military became heavily politicized and arguably deeply divided by those officers who tolerated corruption and those that did not. Salaries remained low during the 1990s, and many younger officers in all the services could no longer afford to make the military a lifetime career. This situation has not changed materially since Fujimori fled Peru in disgrace. Human rights were greatly abused during Fujimori's decade in power as indicated by Peru's Truth and Reconciliation Commission report in 2003. Beyond leaders such as Fujimori and Montesinos, there has not yet been a full judicial accounting of many of these human rights violations.

On the positive side, Fujimori helped establish the economic structure for a recovery of the Peruvian economy from the chaos of the period from 1986 to 1990. Peru's foreign debt crisis was resolved, and new investment was solicited particularly in the extractive industries.

Peru's state-owned industries were privatized as was true nearly everywhere in Latin America. Funds from these sales funded many aspects of Peru's economic growth but also was the source of significant corruption. Perhaps, most importantly, Peru became a safer country with the near demise of Sendero Luminoso. The demise of the Sendero opened all of Peru to tourism, which has become an enormously important source of foreign exchange and the livelihood of many poor Peruvians in nearly all parts of the nation. An indication of Fujimori's lingering popularity is the election of his daughter Keiko and his brother Santiago to the Peruvian Senate in 2006. Keiko received the most votes of any senatorial candidate.

DEMOCRACY WITH PEACE

This study will close with an overview of nearly eight years of sustained economic growth and political peace in a country that has had very little of both for most of the past century. The 21st century began with the demise of a Japanese-Peruvian president who was elected in 1990 as a "man of color." After a short interim as a caretaker president following Fujimori resignation, Alejandro Toledo Manrique became Peru's first truly indigenous president when he was elected in April 2001. Toledo was born on March 28, 1946, in

Cabana, Ancash, a remote village at 12,000 feet in the sierra. He was 1 of 16 children, 6 of whom died before reaching adulthood. The family moved to Chimbote on Peru's north coast. There his father worked as a bricklayer and his mother was a fishmonger. Contacts with the Peace Corp led to a one-year scholarship at the University of San Francisco. By means of a soccer scholarship and part-time work pumping gas he graduated with a B.A. Continuing his education, he entered a Ph.D. program in economics of human resources. He completed the Ph.D. in the mid-1970s and subsequently worked at the United Nations, World Bank, Harvard University, and at ESAN, Peru's leading business school in the 1990s.

As we have seen, Toledo was a leader in the opposition to Fujimori, which positioned him well to run for president in 2001. Still the race, primarily against former president Alan García, was close and ugly. Toledo lacked a true political organization. His *PeruPossible* (Peru Possible) has slight organizational experience or discipline. García, on the other hand, had revived a moribund APRA to challenge Toledo. The APRA leader accused Toledo of immoral behavior, and Toledo responded with charges of García's corruption and incompetence. Lourdes Flores Nano, a professor at Lima's Catholic University, revived the conservative right in the first round of the elections by claiming 24.3 percent of the vote. In the second round Toledo won the presidency with 53.1 percent to 46.9 percent for García. The elections were contentious but fair. A team of international observers headed by Jimmy Carter assured this. Peru has thus taken an important step toward reestablishing democratic institutions. Toledo's task was to make progress toward social democracy.

The new president was hindered by a lack of a political organization and a poor management style. Despite his extensive experience as an economist, very little of his background was in management. Rumors of immoral behavior dogged him. His wife Elaine Karp, a Belgian-born anthropologist, was his staunch but often tendentious advocate. Despite his indigenous appearance, he did not identify as well with Lima's poor as had Fujimori. Until the very end of his presidency Toledo's approval ratings were very low, at one point reaching just 10 percent. But public approval did not reflect a level of accomplishment that was indeed quite remarkable.

Throughout Toledo's five-year presidency, Peru's economic growth rate averaged over six percent. This marked Peru's longest and most substantive growth since the 1920s. Even more stunning was the nation's low rate of inflation, averaging less than two percent for most of Toledo's presidency. One of Toledo's primary initiatives, reducing poverty, showed less spectacular results. The national poverty rate fell during his presidency six points from 54 percent to 48 percent of the population. This small drop certainly did not reflect the consistent expansion of the economy. Rural poverty, as high as 77 percent in 2001, dropped only to 68 percent. The number of Peruvians living on less than $1 per day declined from 24 percent to 18 percent. Designed to deal with Peruvian poverty, Toledo created the *Juntos* (together) program. The program is a conditional cash transfer process aimed at women heads of households in rural areas. Begun in 2005 it was funded with 120 million soles ($40 million) for 100 thousand families. It was designed to reach three times that number before Toledo left office.

Following in the footsteps of Fujimori's globalization initiatives, Toledo aggressively sought a free-trade agreement with the United States. The agreement was signed with the Bush administration in April 2006 and ratified by the U.S. Congress two years later. Expanded trade with the United States will allow Peru's burgeoning agro-business enterprises to flourish. Using advanced techniques such as drip irrigation systems in Peru's arid coastal region, agricultural crops for export have expanded dramatically in the last decade. Food products from avocados to asparagus are now being shipped to the United States. With expanded investment in the agricultural sector, Peru has the possibility of being the dominant agricultural nation on the west coast of South America.

Peru's chief source of export revenue is mining. And the mining sector is now primarily in private hands. By the year 2000, 90 percent of all of the nation's mining ventures were in private hands. Since 1990 over 100 foreign firms have entered the Peruvian mining sector, with the Chinese playing a very significant role in iron ore investments. Prices for copper and precious metals are approaching record-high price levels and competition for Peru mining products dramatically are increasing with Chinese consumption. Yet, revenue levels from mining that should be directed back into development and anti-poverty programs are no where near what Peru needs to address it long-standing problems. On a positive note, 70 percent of the firms in silver mining are of medium size. This percentage contrasts directly with the years before 1968 when Peruvian mining was dominated by such firms as Cerro de Pasco, Marcona, and Southern Peru Copper Company. In sum, the Toledo presidency were years of economic growth, relative political peace, and certainly an era that saw the political system open to democratic debate.

Still an area of deep concern in Peru and, of course, the United States was the illegal narcotics trade between Peru and the United States that had flourished for more that 40 years. Efforts to eradicate coca, replace it with alternative crops, and interdict the coca paste at its source have never been fully successful. The primary producing area in the Upper Huallaga Valley and near Tingo Maria is still an active narcotrafficking area. What remains of Sendero Luminoso is headquartered in the Upper Huallaga Valley. There are problems in the Apurímac Valley as well. As late as June 2008, Peruvian marines engaged in firefights with narcoterrorists in that region and suffered casualties. U.S. counter-narcotics aid was cut substantially to Peru in 2004 from $722 million to $443 million to help pay for the war in Iraq. Counternarcotics has been the cornerstone of U.S.-Peruvian diplomatic and economic assistance for more than a generation. Not only has it produced few results, but it has directed both countries attention away from more substantive economic programs that might divert peasants away from growing coca.

DEMOCRATIC TRANSITION: THE 2006 ELECTION

Having no political party of consequence that could provide a vehicle for his successor, Toledo allowed the political process to unfold without any of the manipulation so characteristic of Fujimori. The presidential race drew 20 candidates for the first round of voting in April. Emerging as the favorites were again the candidate of the right Lourdes Flores Nano. Ollanta Humala Tasso, a radical populist and former army officer with a violent past and connections to Hugo Chavez in Venezuela, drew important support with his fiery populist rhetoric. Humala Tasso actually won the first voting round with 30.6 percent. The APRA leader Alan García, making his third bid for the presidency trailed at 24.3 percent. Flores Nano barely lost out to advance to the final round with 23.84 percent. In the final round, many Peruvian voters shifted their support for the once-failed president because of their fear of Humala's radicalism. García thus won the presidency by 700,000 votes.

The 2006 election says a great deal about the Peruvian electorate. Few presidents have failed more completely than Alan García during his 1985–1990 tenure. Yet, he was the candidate of the only viable political party left standing in Peru after the Docenio and the political deconstruction of the Fujimori presidency. Peru is now a political democracy aligned with personalities not parties. Most Peruvian voters are quite young and have little if any memory of the early García years. There is a history of presidents who have resurrected themselves in Peru, including Leguía (1908–1912 and 1919–1930) and Belaúnde (1963–1968 and 1980–1985). García was also older, more contemplative than his opponents. In any event Peru is now being guided by a man who clearly seems to have matured as a politician and leader.

During the first two years in his second term in office García abandoned the anti-United States populist line that characterized his first presidency. He upheld the Free Trade Agreement that was negotiated by Toledo. The U.S. Congress ratified the treaty in mid-2008. There is now be a greater flow of good between the United States and Peru than at any time in history. García has also established close relations with President Uribe of Colombia; this relationship will help in the area of counternarcotics. In an effort to establish closer ties with Brazil, García encouraged Peru's national oil company *Petroperú* to sign an agreement with Brazil's country's state oil company *Petrobras* that will help modernize oil refining capabilities. In addition, Peru has voiced it support for a inter-oceanic road to connect Lima with the Bolivian cities of Sao Paulo and the eastern terminus. Significantly the Peruvian president established good relations with Chile president Michelle Bachelet. By so doing, Peru now has the best circumstances for peace with its neighbors in its entire republican history. There are still touchy issues regarding Chile and Peru's definition of maritime jurisdiction to be resolved, but diplomatic Peru's relations with its Andean neighbors with the exception of Venezuela are in good order.

ISSUES ON THE HORIZON

Peruvians have much reason for hope today. Yet there are major issues that remain unresolved that can certainly cloud the nation's future. Foremost is poverty. The poorest Peruvians are people of indigenous origins living in remote regions in the southern sierra.

In this region three of four people, mostly Quechua or Aymara speakers, live in poverty. This amounts to five million people. Rural women suffer the most. Nearly 70 percent of rural women in Peru are extremely poor. Women hold down the rural households tending livestock, working in agriculture, and weaving for the family and the regional market. This allows their husbands to migrate in search of seasonal work.

The roots of rural poverty in Peru have proven deeply resistant to reform. They include high rates of illiteracy, particularly among women; a lack of essential services, such as clean water, electricity, and educational opportunities; poor infrastructure, mainly roads; low levels of research in agriculture and animal husbandry; and inconsistent government funding for rural development programs.

The lifespan of people born in Peru's highlands is 20 years less than those born in Lima. Those living in Peru's larger cities can earn more than 30 times what a rural farmer draws from the sierra's rocky soils. So long as this disparity continues to exist, then rural migration to Lima will remain a fact of life in Peru. As we have seen, essential services in Lima have never kept pace with rates of migration from the highlands. Peruvians have really only adapted to urban life by means of the informal sector and strong communal bonds in the barriadas. The mandate for the Peruvian government is clear. Substantial funding most be earmarked for rural development and educational programs for the foreseeable future. The most conservative element in Peruvian society, the armed forces, has been advocating this initiative since the 1930s. They could aid in the construction of schools, roads, and other elements of the infrastructure.

Another important issue is the future mission of the armed forces. Peruvian national security analyst Alberto Bolívar addressed these issues in a recent essay. Among his key points were that in the wake of the Sendero campaign, the Alta-Cenepa conflict with Ecuador, and the corruption trials following the Fujimori government, the armed forces must assess its material condition in light of whatever mission it defines for itself in the coming decades. Even more importantly, Bolívar argues that the armed forces' professionalism has been diminished by the political interference and corruption of the Fujimori years, the human rights problems of the 1990s, and the setback at Alta Cenepa. Bolívar maintains that the armed forces must be "reinstitutionalized" and the National Police overhauled as well. He warns that a lack of attention to national security issues can have enormous costs. Narcotraffickers and a latent threat from still not completely subdued Sendero Luminoso are reminders of Peru terrible pain from 1980 to 1995.[22]

The armed forces is now restive in Peru. In an extraordinary manifesto released on June 28, 2008, to the Lima press, 54 retired senior officers of the army, navy, and air force complained forcefully of the poor material condition of the armed forces and lamented the underfunded state of the pension system, which does not allow a sustainable living for retired officers. Among those signing the memorandum was former president Francisco Morales Bermúdez, the leading strategist in the Peruvian military Edgardo Mercado Jarrín, and four for members of the Velasco government. The generals and admirals argue that the armed forces are not prepared materially to defend the nation. They are correct, if one thinks in conventional terms of border defense. Much of Peru's Soviet-build tanks and aircraft are long since obsolete. But border tensions are as low with Peru's neighbors as the have been in memory. Peru's military and civilian government must resolve the question of the armed forces mission and allocate funds accordingly between poverty reduction and national defense. These need not be mutually exclusive objectives.[23]

PERUVIANS ABROAD

The nation's social and economic turmoil before 2000 prompted at least 2.5 million Peruvians to migrate overseas. The primary receiver nations for these migrants, were the United States, Japan, Spain, Chile, and Argentina. What distinguishes Peruvian migration patterns from those of other Latin American nations is its heterogeneity. Peruvians of all classes and ethnic background are included in the diaspora or dispersion. In the United States, the primary sites of Peruvian settlement are Miami, Los Angeles, and Patterson, New Jersey. A lesser, more affluent community exists in the Washington, D.C., area that has its roots in the diplomatic and professional community dating to the mid-20th century. In Spain the locus of settlement is Barcelona; in Japan it is Tokyo, Yokohama, and Isesaki. As one would imagine it is Buenos Aires in Argentina, and in Chile, it is Santiago. The motives for the "dispersion of Peruvians are diverse but in the end they are primarily economic in nature."[24]

During the 1990s large numbers of Japanese Peruvians migrated to Japan after that nation modified its strict immigration code to allow for people of Japanese ancestry to attain temporary guest worker status. Japanese Peruvians and much larger numbers of Japanese Brazil left their homes to work in Japanese factories for hourly wages that were as high as any in the world. It was common for Nikkei from Peru to earn as much as $23 per hour, many times what they could earn in Peru or Brazil. This wage seeking led to both promise and problems. Portions of wages could be remitted to families in Peru to significantly alleviate their economic distress, but, inevitably, family life was disrupted and a secure future was denied because of time limits on work visas. A cycle of return and remigration to Japan began and many Nikkei became migrants without a country. Criteria for Japanese citizenship is very strict, and immigration oversight has become demanding after significant numbers of "false *Nikkei*" entered Japan in the early 1990s.[25]

Indeed, many Peruvians living abroad are doing so illegally. As one would imagine, this uncertain status places tremendous pressure on Peruvian migrant families. They are often relegated to lower skilled jobs, denied health care, and can not pursue many educational opportunities. Still, through the strength of community, so much a part of the Andean tradition, these Peruvian migrants are prevailing. In Paterson, New Jersey, for example, there is a Peruvian community numbering nearly 30,000. In New York City and the surrounding New Jersey suburbs, as many as there are 150,000 Peruvians have established permanent residence. Paterson is a magnet city whose industries attracted Peruvian immigrants in the early decades of the 20th century. Now the community has soccer leagues; the *Congreso Peruano Americano* (Peruvian American Congress), which facilitates the attaining of U.S. citizenship; Peruvian Independence parades; and a Catholic Brotherhood that is linked to others in the northeastern United States.

Permanent return rates for Peruvian living overseas are not available.[26] But Peruvians do return for periodic visits to their native land reasonably frequently. As most immigrants do, they are recreating the culture of their homeland in their enclaves overseas. Only time will tell if the improving economic and social conditions in Peru will persuade many of these migrants to return permanently.

CONCLUSION

Peruvians have not always been well served by their leaders. But their reserves of emotional strength have allowed them to endure with a sustaining hope for a better day.

In some of Peru's darkest times it has been women who have carried their burden with great courage. María Elena Moyano, the murdered mayor of Villa el Salvador, was one such women. She stated emphatically that "the primary work of women continues to be their families and the priority of women from poor classes is survival."[27] During the days of Sendero terror in Villa el Salvador, Moyano became the target of many threats because of her vocal opposition to the insurgency. When asked if she was fearful she replied, "There are people who ask if I am afraid. Yes, at times, I am, but I am very firm and have moral strength. I have always been ready to surrender my life, I have faith."[28] Many Peruvians gave their lives for the defense of their communities in the years from 1980 to 1995, one of the most violent in all of Peru's history. But reciprocity and community are the bedrock qualities of the Andean people, so the ability to withstand tremendously hard times is certainly admirable but very much within their cultural traditions. The rondas campesinas banded together for their own protection again terrorism when all they had was themselves. Women's groups in Lima's pueblos barriadas kept their communities together through community solidarity.

A visitor to Peru in 2008 will see a country vastly different from even a decade ago. It is now one of the leading tourist destinations in the world. Wonderful roadside cafes are emerging in some of the more remote areas of the highlands. Peruvian agricultural products are appearing in stores in Europe and North America. Peru's satellite cities such as Arequipa are thriving in an expanding economy that is attracting investment as never before. Is the stolid faith of Peruvians in a better future justified? In the midst of all her turmoil in Villa el Salvador, María Elena Moyano believed that it was. In February 1992, not long before she died, Moyano wrote:

My God, how I have lived,
Thank you for giving me so much!
Love, the opportunity to give my all—
Everything.[29]

NOTES

1. David Nugent, "Building the State, Making the Nation: The Basis and Limits of State Centralization in Modern Peru," *American Anthropologist* 96, no. 2 (1994), 350–353.

2. Latin American Weekly Report, June 29, 1984, 9.

3. Lobo, *A House of Our Own* (Tucson: University of Arizona Press, 1981) 51.

4. Ibid., 176.

5. Edmundo Morales, "Coca and Cocaine Economy and Social Change in the Andes of Peru," *Economic Development and Cultural Change* 35, no. 1 (1986), 143–161.

6. Lawrence Clayton, *Peru and the United States: The Condor and the Eagle* (Athens: University of Georgia Press, 1999), 276–277.

7. Jung Chang and Jon Halliday, *Mao: The Unknown Story* (New York: Knopf, 2005), 517.

8. Gustavo Gorriti, "The Quota," in Orin Starn, Carlos Iván DeGregori and Robin Kirk, editors, *The Peru Reader: History, Culture and Politics* (Durham: Duke University Press, 1995), 319.

9. Personal interview with anonymous armed forces officers who commanded units in Ayacucho in 1983 and 1988. May 11, 1980, Lima, Peru.

10. Mary Jo Burt, "Shining Path and the Decisive Battle in Lima's Barriadas: The Case of Villa El Salvador," in Steve J. Stern, editor, *Shining and Other Paths: War and Society in Peru, 1980–1995* (Durham: Duke University Press, 1998), 267–306.

11. Orin Starn, "Villagers at Arms: War and Counterrevolution in the South Central Andes," in Stern, *Shining and Other Paths*, 229.

12. Ponciano del Pino, "Peasants at War," in Orin Starn, et al. Editors, *The Peru Reader: History, Culture and Politics* (Durham: Duke University Press, 1995), 379–381.

13. Ibid, 380.

14. Chang and Halliday, *Mao*, 393.

15. Personal interview with retired Peruvian naval officer and marine, Annapolis, Maryland, September 20, 2008.

16. Comisión de la verdad y Reconciliación, *Press Release*, August 28, 2003.

17. Peter F. Klarén, *Peru: Society and Nationhood in the Andes* (Oxford: Oxford University Press, 2000), 388–389.

18. Personal interview with Professor Gilbert Walter, May 20, 2005, Milwaukee, Wisconsin.

19. O'Donnell, quoted in Catherine M. Conaghan, *Fujimori's Peru: Deception in the Public Sphere* (Pittsburgh: University of Pittsburgh Press, 2005), 7–8.

20. A good review of the historical and diplomatic background to the conflict is David Scott Palmer, "Peru-Ecuador Border Conflict: Missed Opportunities, Misplaced Nationalism, and Multilateral Peacekeepers," *Journal of International Studies and World Affairs* 39, no. 3 (1997), 109–148.

21. Curt Suplee, "*El Niño/La Niña:* Nature's Vicious Cycle," *National Geographic*

22. Alberto Bolívar, "Problematica de la Seguridad y Defensa Nacional el Peru, 2008," unpublished manuscript, Lima, Peru, July 2008.

23. Pronunciamento a La Opinión Pública, June 28, 2008. Press release on material and fiscal needs of the Peruvian armed forces. Signed by 54 retired senior officers of the armed forces.

24. Karsten Paerregaard, *Peruvians Dispersed: A Global Ethnography of Migration* (Oxford: Berg, 2008), 1–37.

25. Daniel M. Masterson, with Sayaka Funada, *The Japanese in Latin America* (Urbana: University of Illinois Press, 2004), 265–271.

26. Paerregaard, *Peruvians Dispersed*, 60–63.

27. María Elena Moyano, *The Autobiography of María Elena Moyano* (Gainesville: University Press of Florida, 2000).

28. Ibid., 63–64.

29. Ibid.

Notable People in the History of Peru

Atahualpa. One of two brothers contesting for control of the Inca Empire. He was the Inca emperor at the time of the arrival of the Spanish. He contested for control of the empire with his brother Huascar. He benefitted from a strong military following. He was captured by the Spaniards in November 1532, then held for a huge ransom and finally executed.

Víctor Andés Belaúnde. Peruvian diplomat, educator, and intellectual. Born in Arequipa and the uncle of Fernando Belaúnde Terry, he took a conservative approach to Peruvian social conflict advocating a quest for *Perunidad* (Peruvianness), which stressed conciliation and a unified national vision.

Susana Baca. Internationally known Afro Peruvian singer. She has been instrumental in reviving Afro Peruvian music particularly with the release of her 1995 CD *The Soul of Black Peru* featuring the prominent song "Maria Lando." Her accompanying musicians often play Afro Peruvian instruments to accompany her folk ballads.

Jorge Basadre. Peru's most esteemed and prolific 20th-century historian. Best known for his seminal *Historia de la república del Perú, 1822–1933,* he began teaching at the University of San Marcos in Lima in 1928 and later was director of Peru's national library. He was honored by many foreign universities. His work, *La promesa la vida de la Peruana* seeks to answer the often asked question of how Peru will realize its great promise as a nation.

Micaela Bastidas. The mestiza wife of José Gabriel Condorconqui (Túpac Amaru II), who played a leading role in her rebel husband's campaign against the Spanish in the early 1780s. Bastidas was the mother of three sons by the rebel leader and played a critical role in the execution of the attack on Cuzco. Captured along with her husband when the campaign faltered, she was brutally tortured and executed by the Spanish as a prelude to Túpac Amaru II's own execution.

Fernando Belaúnde Terry. A native of Lima, he hailed from a famous Peruvian family. Educated as an architect at the University of Texas, he was twice elected to the Peruvian presidency. His first term (1963–1968) was shortened by a military coup and his second term (1980–1985) was marked by economic decline and the rise of terrorism. His prized development scheme, the Marginal Jungle Highway was never completed.

Oscar R. Benavides. Peruvian army officer from an elite family who served as Peru's president in 1914 after a coup d'état ousted civilian president Guillermo Billinghurst and again from 1933 to 1939 following the assassination of President Luis M. Sánchez Cerro. He held conservative even pro-Fascist beliefs during his second presidency but his regime was only mildly authoritarian. He made one last failed bid for the presidency in 1945 before his death in that same year.

Andrés A. Cáceres. Late 19th-century military man who distinguished himself during the War of the Pacific by his well-led irregular warfare against occupying Chilean forces after the fall of Lima in 1881. He went on to dominate Peruvian national politics until he was defeated in a civil war by the opposition civilian leader Nicolás de Piérola in 1895.

Ramón Castilla. Peru's leading military caudillo of the mid-19th century. Was twice president of Peru (1845–1851; 1855–1862). Presided over a period of economic prosperity made possible by the guano boom. Castilla brought a decree of unity to faction-ridden Peru and sought to strengthen respect for constitutionalism. His most important social initiative was his abolition of African slavery in Peru in 1854.

Lourdes Flores Nano. A prominent attorney, educator, and legislator, Flores Nano has been a candidate for Peru's presidency in 2001 and 2006. Representing the conservative wing of the Peruvian political spectrum, Flores Nano has retained ties with the Christian Democratic movement in Peru and Latin America.

Alberto Fujimori. Japanese Peruvian president of Peru from 1990 to 2000. His parents were immigrants from Japan, and he vaulted to prominence in April 1990 after a career as a mathematics professor a Peru's agrarian university. His presidency is marked by great success in ending terrorism, stabilizing the economy, and resolving border conflict with Ecuador. But the human rights and corruption abuses during his presidency along with his manipulation of the constitution to perpetuate himself in power turned the people against him. He was forced him to resign the presidency while in Japan in 2000.

Alan García. Originally the protégé of APRA leader Víctor Raul Haya de le Torre, this young politician was elected president of Peru in 1985 in the midst of a terrorist war and rampant inflation. After some initial successes, his erratic policies on the economy and counterterrorism brought Peru to the brink of collapse at the end of his term in 1990. Elected again in 2006 to the presidency he has moved cautiously as he has inherited a strong economy and a peaceful nation that is progressing better than expected.

Miguel Grau. Peruvian naval officer and fallen hero in the War of the Pacific. During the early months of the war, Grau conducted bold raids on the Chilean fleet and shore installations from his flagship *Huascar.* He was finally caught and killed by a superior Chilean naval force off Angamos in October 1879.

Gustavo Gutiérrez. Peruvian priest who was educated in Belgium and was active in Catholic Action during his early years. Considered to be one of the founders of the Liberation Theology movement in Latin America that encouraged the Catholic Church to minister to material as well as the spiritual needs of the poor.

Abimael Guzmán Reynoso. A former philosophy professor who founded the terrorist front Sendero Luminoso in the 1970s. Guzmán, remained underground during the height of Sendero-led terror campaign likely spending most of the time in comfort in Lima. He was captured in September 1992 and sentenced to life in prison in a Navy prison in Callao.

Víctor Raul Haya de la Torre. Founder and long-time chief of the APRA party. The main party of the left in Peru until it began a pronounced shift to the right beginning during World War II. Somewhat of a philosopher and prolific writer, Haya had charisma to maintain the party's leadership despite pragmatic changes in party philosophy to enable the APRA to achieve national power.

Huascar. Claimed the Inca throne in the early 1530s along with his brother Atahualpa in a dispute that divided the Inca empire at the time of the arrival of the Spanish. After Atahualpa's capture by Pizarro's forces the captive Inca ordered the death of his brother to prevent Pizarro's from ruling through Huascar.

Juan Landázurri Rickets. Archbishop of Lima and the Catholic Primate of Peru from 1955 to 1988, the archbishop embraced a social mission for the church with special attention to the nation's poor. He supported the Liberation Theology movement within the Latin American Bishops Conference (CELAM) and was a quiet ally of the Velasco regimes reforms during the 1970s.

Augusto B. Leguía. Civilian caudillo who dominated Peruvian politics as president of Peru from 1914 to 1918 and for the *Oncenio* (11-year rule) from 1919 to 1930. Originally a leader in the Civilista political coalition, he later ruled with the support of U.S. dominated economic investment and the support of the Guardia Civil and Guardia Republicana.

Manco Inca. Son of Huayna Capac and brother to Huascar and Atahualpa, Manco Inca was used by the conquering Spaniards as a puppet during their early days of rule in Peru. In response to poor Spanish behavior, Manco Inca rebelled and established a stronghold at Villacamba. He eventually met his death at the hands of the Spanish.

José Carlos Mariátegui. The foremost intellectual of the Left of 20th-century Peru. Advocated a form of hybrid indigenous socialism based on Andean traditions. A prominent writer and intellectual, his most important work was *Seven Interpretive Essays on Peruvian Reality*. Mariátegui was a founding member of Peru's Socialist party. His early death in 1930 deprived the Peruvian Left of its most dynamic and original thinker.

Clorinda Matto de Turner. Born in Cuzco in the early 1850s Matto de Turner became an influential writer and editor of literary journals. She published a trilogy of novels in the mid 1890s that won her a wide readership but also enmity because of the novels' biting social criticism. The most important of these novels *Torn from the Nest* was published in England in translation and achieved significant recognition. Forced into exile in Argentina because of her views, Matto de Turner's works are now regarded in Peru and abroad as not only the work of an important feminist but of a world-class talent as well.

Maria Elena Moyano. One of the leading community activists in Lima's *barriadas,* especially Villa el Salvador during the 1990s. Led community self help movements such as the vaso de leche (glass of milk) programs during the difficult days of the first Fujimori regime's austerity programs and the Sendero Luminoso war. Bravely opposed Sendero's infiltration of Villa el Salvador and was assassinated by the terrorists as a consequence.

Manuel A. Odría. Army general and caudillo who ruled Peru for eight years (1948–1956) after overthrowing the elected government of Bustamante y Rivero. Tried to style his politics after Juan Peron in Argentina, who appealed to the urban working classes. Mass migration to Lima began in earnest during the Odría years. Armed forces reform began as well with an emphasis on the articulation of a national defense mission. Odría was an important element in Peruvian national politics until the early 1960s.

Javier Pérez de Cuellar. An experienced and highly regarded Peruvian diplomat who served as the fifth Secretary General of the United States for two terms in the 1980s. Pérez de Cuellar was a member of Peru's first delegation to the United Nations in 1946 and many key posts in the organization until being selected Secretary General. He has been awarded honorary doctorates by many of the world's leading universities. He has also been a candidate for Peru's presidency after his retirement in the 1990s

Nicolás de Piérola. Leader of a prominent Arequipa family, Piérola he twice served as president of Peru (1879–1881; 1895–1899). He led Peru during the final defense of Lima during War of the Pacific and ended the caudillo rule of Andrés Cáceres in a civil uprising in 1895. Not terribly different from the Civilistas in outlook, his political style, however, did foreshadow the leadership style of civilian autocrats August Leguía and Alberto Fujimori in the 20th century.

Francisco Pizarro. Leader of the Spanish expedition to Peru in the early 1530s that captured Atahualpa as a prelude to subduing the defenders of the Inca empire. Pizarro's campaigns in Peru were aided immeasurably by disease and Indian allies opposed to the ruling factions in the Inca empire. In the end Pizarro was killed in internecine strife between competing conquistadores.

María Rostworowski de Diez Canseco. Considered Peru's most respected and prolific modern historian of the nation's ancient cultures. Of Polish heritage, she was educated at the University of San Marcos and worked with Raúl Porras Barrenechea. Her most recent general history of the Inca is available in English under the title *A History of the Inca Realm.*

Luis M. Sánchez Cerro. Ambitious and daring Peruvian army officer who toppled the long-standing Leguía regime in 1930. His brief tenure in power (1930–1933) was marked by violence and civil war as populist politics emerged to challenge existing oligarchic rule during the first years of the depression. Sánchez Cerro was assassinated in April 1933 as he tried to lead Peru into an unpopular war with Colombia.

Túpac Amaru. The last of the Inca emperors from the royal line. He was the third son of Manco Inca and ruled briefly in the rebel redoubt of Villacamba resisting Spanish rule in the early 1570s. Captured by the Spanish after Villacamba fell, he was executed in Cuzco main square. Over the years, rebel groups in Peru and elsewhere have taken his name as a symbol of resistance to the established order.

Túpac Amaru II. With the actual name of José Gabriel Condorcanqui, this larger than life figure initiated the great Andean Revolt of 1780–1783 that nearly expelled the Spanish from the Andes. A descendent of the original Túpac Amaru, the rebel leader sought to enlist the vision of Incari, or the recreation of the Inca empire, in leading Peru's Indians against the Spanish. He built on enormous Indian resentment against the mita and reparto systems. Divisions within the Indian cacique leadership and firm opposition from the creole classes eventually led to his defeat and execution.

Mario Vargas Llosa. This Arequipa-born writer is now regarded as one of Latin America's greatest writers. An intricate stylist who has adopted many innovative forms, Vargas Llosa has adhered to the distinct Latin American tradition of inculcating social and political criticism in his writing. This was evident from his first novel *La ciudad de los perros* (*The Time of the Hero*), in which he attacked Peru's military education system. Some of Vargas Llosa's most highly regarded novels are *The Green House* (1968), *Conversation in the Cathedral* (1975), and *The War of the End of the World* (1984). The novelist was a candidate for president in 1990 and lost to Alberto Fujimori. He took Spanish citizenship in 1994.

Juan Velasco Alvarado. Army General and head of the self-styled Revolutionary Government of the Armed Forces from October 1968 to when he was deposed in August 1975. Genuinely committed to reforming Peruvian society to help the poor and also prevent revolutionary violence, Velasco was a fiery leader who never fully gained the complete support of the nation or the armed forces for his government's programs. Still, the Velasco era was remarkable for the changes wrought from above.

Selected Bibliography

Because this is intended to be an introductory study of Peru, I have included only English-language sources in this bibliography, with one exception, Jorge Basadre Grohman's seminal multivolume history of Peru. I have tried to include the best and most recent scholarship with a further intent to include the most accessible studies for younger students. Detailed attention to the notes will reveal Spanish-language sources of particular pertinence. I have presented a greater number of entries for the 20th century and organized the entries thematically rather than chronologically. This is done in recognition of the extensive 20th-century historical literature and the high interest in contemporary topics.

GENERAL HISTORIES AND ANTHOLOGIES

Basadre, Jorge. *Historia de la republica del Perú, 1822–1933*. 10 vols. 7th ed. Lima: Editorial Universitaria, 1983.

Hunefeldt, Christine. *Peru: A Brief History*. New York: Facts on File, 2004.

Klarén, Peter F. *Peru: Society and Nationhood in the Andes*. New York: Oxford University Press, 2000.

Starn, Orin, Carlos Iván Degregori, and Robin Kirk. *The Peru Reader: History, Culture and Politics*. 2nd ed. Durham: Duke University Press, 2005.

ANCIENT PERU

Anton, F. *Ancient Peruvian Textiles*. London: Thames and Hudson, 1987.
Bauer, Brian. *The Development of the Inca State*. Austin: University of Texas Press, 1992.
Bawden, Garth. "The Structural Paradox: Moche Culture as Political Ideology." *Latin American Antiquity* 6, no. 3 (1995): 255–273.
Betanzos, Juan de. *Narratives of the Incas*. Austin: University of Texas Press, 1996.
Billman, Brian R. "Irrigation and the Origins of the Southern Moche State in Northern Peru." *Latin American Antiquity* 13, no. 4 (2000): 371–400.
Cobo, Bernabe. *History of the Inca Empire*. Translated by Roland D. Buchanan. Austin: University of Texas Press, 1979.
Davies, Nigel. *The Incas*. Boulder: University Press of Colorado, 1995.
Hadingham, Evan. *Lines in the Mountain God: Nazca and the Mysteries of Peru*. Norman: University of Oklahoma Press, 1988.
Hyslop, John. *Inka Settlement Planning*. Austin: University of Texas Press, 1990.
Isbell, W., and G. McEwan, editors. *Huari Administrative Structures: Pre-Historical Monumental Architecture and State Government*. Washington, DC: Dumbarton Oaks, 1991.
Kolata, Alan. *Tiwanaku and its Hinterland: Archaeology and Paleocology of an Andean Civilization*. Washington, DC: Smithsonian Books, 1996.
LeVine, Terry. *Inca Storage Systems*. Norman: University of Oklahoma Press, 1992.
McEwan, Gordon F. "Some Formal Correspondences between the Formal Architecture of the Wari and the Chimu Cultures of Ancient Peru," *Latin American Antiquity*, 1, no. 2 (1990): 97–116.
Mann, Charles C. *1491: Revelations of the Americas Before Columbus*. New York: Knopf, 2006.
Morris, Craig, and Andrea Von Hagen. *The Inca Empire and its Origins*. Washington, DC: The American Museum of Natural History, 1993.
Moseley, Michael. *The Incas and their Ancestors: The Archeology of Peru*. London: Thames and Hudson, 2001.
Murra, John. "Cloth and its Functions in the Inca State." *American Anthropologist* 64, no. 4 (1962): 710–728.
Murra, John. *The Economic Organization of the Inka State*. Greenwich, CT: JAI Press, 1988.
Rostworoski de Diez Canseco, Maria, with Harry Iceland. *History of the Inca Realm*. Cambridge: University of Cambridge Press, 1999.
Silverblatt, Irene. *Moon, Sun and Witches: Gender, Ideology and Class in Inca and Colonial Peru*. Princeton: Princeton University Press, 1987.
Stone-Miller, Rebecca. *Art of the Andes: From Chavín to Inca*. London: Thames and Hudson, 1995.
Urton, Gary. *The History of Myth: Pacaritambo and the Origins of the Inkas*. Austin: University of Texas Press, 1990.
Urton, Gary. *Signs of the Inka Khipu: Binary Coding in the Inka Knot String Records*. Austin: University of Texas Press, 2003.
Zuidema, R. Tom. *Inca Civilization in Cuzco*. Austin: University of Texas Press, 1990.

THE ENCOUNTER AND ITS CONSEQUENCES

Cook, Noble David. *Demographic Collapse: Indian Peru, 1520–1620*. Cambridge: Cambridge University Press, 1981.
Lockhart, James. *The Men of Cajamarca*. Austin: University of Texas Press, 1972.

MacCormack, Sabine. *Religion in the Andes: Vision and Imagination in Early Colonial Peru.* Princeton: Princeton University Press, 1991.

Ramirez, Susan. *The World Upside Down: Cross Cultural Contact and Conflict in Sixteenth Century Peru.* Stanford: Stanford University Press, 1996.

Restall, Matthew. *Seven Myths of the Spanish Conquest.* Oxford: Oxford University Press, 2003.

Stern, Steve J. *Peru's Indian Peoples and the Challenge of the Conquest: Humanga to 1640.* Madison: University of Wisconsin Press, 1982.

Wachtel, Nathan. *The Vision of the Vanquished: The Spanish Conquest of Peru through Indian Eyes.* New York: Barnes and Nobel, 1977.

SPANISH COLONIAL

Adorno, Rolena. "The Depiction of Self and Other in Spanish Colonial Peru." *Art Journal* 49, no. 2 (1990): 110–118.

Andrien, Kenneth J. *Andean Worlds: Indigenous History, Culture and Consciousness Under Spanish Rule, 1532–1825.* Albuquerque: University of New Mexico Press, 2001.

Andrien, Kenneth J. *Crisis and Decline: The Viceroyalty of Peru in the Seventeenth Century.* Albuquerque: University of New Mexico Press, 1985.

Bowser, Frederick. *The African Slave Trade in Colonial Peru, 1524–1650.* Stanford: Stanford University Press, 1974.

Bradley, Peter T. *Hapsburg Peru: Images, Imagination and Memory.* Edited by David Cahill. Liverpool: Liverpool University Press, 2000.

Campbell, Leon G. *The Military and Society in Colonial Peru.* Philadelphia: American Philosophical Society, 1978.

Campbell, Leon G. "The Social Structure of the Tupac Amaru Army." *Hispanic American Historical Review* 61, no. 4 (1981): 675–693.

Clayton, Lawrence. *Caulkers and Carpenters in the New World: Shipyards of Colonial Guayaquil.* Athens: Ohio University Press, 1980.

Clayton, Lawrence. "Trade and Navigation in the Seventeenth Century Viceroyalty of Peru." *Journal of Latin American Studies* 7 (1975): 1–21.

Fisher, John R. *Bourbon Peru, 1750–1824.* Liverpool: Liverpool University Press, 2003.

Fisher, John R. *Silver Mines and Silver Miners in Colonial Peru.* Liverpool: Center for Latin American Studies, University of Liverpool, 1977.

Gade, Daniel W., and Mario Escobar. "Village Settlement and the Colonial Legacy in Southern Peru." *Geographical Review* 72, no. 4 (1982): 430–439.

Gibson, Charles. *Spain in America.* New York: Harper and Row, 1966.

Jacobsen, Nils. *Mirages of Transition: The Peruvian Altiplano, 1780–1930.* Berkeley: University of California Press, 1993.

Klein, Herbert. *The American Finances of the Spanish Empire: Royal Expenditures in Colonial Mexico, Peru and Bolivia, 1680–1809.* Albuquerque: University of Mexico Press, 1999.

Lockhart, James. *Spanish Peru: A Colonial Society.* Madison: University of Wisconsin Press, 1994.

Martin, Luis. *Daughters of the Conquistadores: Women of the Viceroyalty of Peru.* Albuquerque: University of New Mexico Press, 1983.

Ramirez, Susan. *Provincial Patriarchs: Land Tenure and the Economics of Power in Colonial Peru.* Albuquerque: University of New Mexico Press, 1986.

Silverblatt, Irene. "New Christians and New World Fears in Seventeenth Century Peru." *Comparative Studies in Society and History* 42, no. 3 (2000): 524–546.

Spaulding, Karen. *Huarichiri: An Andean Society under Inca and Spanish Rule.* Stanford: Stanford University Press, 1984.

Stern, Steve, ed. *Resistance, Rebellion and Consciousness in the Andean Peasant World: 18th to 20th Centuries.* Madison: University of Wisconsin Press, 1987.

INDEPENDENCE ERA

Andrews, George Reid. "Spanish American Independence: A Structural Analysis." *Latin American Perspectives* 12, no. 1 (1985): 105–132.

Anna, Timothy E. *The Fall of the Royal Government in Peru.* Lincoln: University of Nebraska Press, 1979.

Brading, Celia Wu. *Generals and Diplomats: Great Britain and Peru, 1820–1840.* Cambridge: Cambridge University Press, 1991.

Campbell, Leon. "Recent Research on Andean Peasant Revolts, 1750–1820." *Latin American Research Review* 14, no. 1 (1977): 3–49.

Fisher, John. "Royalism, Regionalism and Rebellion in Colonial Peru, 1808–1815." *Hispanic American Historical Review* 59, no. 2 (1979): 232–257.

Flores Galindo, Aberto. "In Search of an Inca." In Stern, *Resistance, Rebellion and Consciousness*, 93–112.

Salomon, Frank. "Ancestor Cults and Resistance to the State in Arequipa." In Stern, *Resistance, Rebellion and Consciousness*, 148–165.

Stavig, Ward. *The World of Tupac Amaru: Conflict, Community and Identity in Colonial Peru.* Lincoln: University of Nebraska Press, 1999.

Walker, Charles F. *Smoldering Ashes: Cuzco and the Creation of Republican Peru, 1780–1840.* Durham: Duke University Press, 1999.

19TH-CENTURY PERU

Blanchard, Peter. *Slavery and Abolition in Early Republican Peru.* Austin: University of Texas Press, 1992.

Bonilla, Heraclio. "The Indian Peasantry and Peru during the War with Chile." In Stern, *Resistance, Rebellion and Consciousness*, 219–231.

Clayton, Lawrence. *W. R. Grace and Company: The Formative Year, 1850–1930.* Ottawa, IL: Jameson, 1986.

Duesta, Jose R. *The Bewitchment of Silver: The Social Economy of Mining in Nineteenth-Century Peru.* Athens: Ohio University Press, 1999.

Gilbert, Denis. *The Oligarchy and the Old Regime in Peru.* Ithaca: Cornell University Press, 1977.

Gonzales, Michael J., *Plantation Agriculture and Social Control in Northern Peru.* Austin: University of Texas Press, 1985.

Gonzalez, Michael J. "Planters and Politics in Peru, 1895–1919." *Journal of Latin American Studies* 23, no. 3 (1991): 515–542.

Gootenberg, Paul. *Between Silver and Guano: Commercial Policy and the State in Postindependence Peru.* Princeton: Princeton University Press, 1989.

Hunefeldt, Christine. *Paying the Price of Freedom: Family and Labor among Lima's Slaves, 1800–1854.* Berkeley: University of California Press, 1994.

Jacobsen, Nils. "Liberalism and Indian Communities in Peru, 1821–1920." In *Liberals the Church and Indian Peasants*, edited by Robert H. Jackson, 123–170. Albuquerque: University of New Mexico Press, 1997.

Klaiber, Jeffrey. *The Catholic Church in Peru, 1821–1985.* Washington, DC: Catholic University of America Press, 1992.

Klaiber, Jeffrey. *The Catholic Church, Religion and Revolution in Peru, 1824–1976.* Notre Dame: University of Notre Dame Press, 1977.

Lofstrom, William L. Paita: *The Outpost of Empire: The Impact of the New England Whaling Fleet on the Socio-Economic Development of Northern Peru, 1832–1865.* Mystic, CT: Mystic Seaport Press, 1977.

Mallon, Florencia. *The Defense of Community in Peru's Central Highlands: Peasant Struggle and Capitalist Transition, 1860–1940.* Princeton: Princeton University Press, 1983.

Nugent, David. *Modernity at the Edge of Empire: Individual and Nation in the Northern Peruvian Andes, 1881–1935.* Stanford: Stanford University Press, 1997.

Peloso, Vincent, and Barbara Tannenbaum, Editors. *Liberals, Politics and Power, State Formation in Nineteenth-Century Latin America.* Athens: University of Georgia Press, 1996. See especially chapter "The Politics of Emergency Finance in Peru, 1820–1845."

Sater, William. *Andean Tragedy: Fighting the War of the Pacific.* Lincoln: University of Nebraska Press, 2007.

Sater, William. *Chile and the War of the Pacific.* Lincoln: University of Nebraska Press, 1986.

Stewart, Watt. *Chinese Bondage in Peru: A History of the Chinese Coolie Trade in Peru, 1849–1874.* Durham: Duke University Press, 1952.

Stewart, Watt. *Henry Meiggs: Yankee Pizarro.* Durham: Duke University Press, 1946.

St. John, Ronald Bruce. *The Foreign Policy of Peru.* Boulder, CO: Westview Press, 1992.

Thorp, Rosemary, and Geoff Bertram. *Peru 1890–1977: Growth and Policy in an Open Economy.* New York: Columbia University Press, 1978.

20TH-CENTURY PERU

Economic

Becker, David C. *The Bourgeoisie and the Limits of Dependency: Mining, Class and Power in "Revolutionary" Peru.* Princeton: Princeton University Press, 1983.

Blanchard, Peter. *The Origins of the Peruvian Labor Movement, 1883–1919.* Pittsburgh: University of Pittsburgh Press, 1982.

Crabtree, John, and James Thomas. *Fujimori's Peru: The Political Economy.* Washington, DC: The Brookings Institution, 1998.

Dore, Elizabeth. *The Peruvian Mining Industry: Growth, Stagnation and Crisis.* Boulder: Westview Press, 1988.

Drake, Paul. *The Money Doctor in the Andes: The Kemmerer Missions, 1923–1933.* Durham: Duke University Press, 1989.

Fisher, John, ed. *Social and Economic Change in Modern Peru.* Liverpool: Liverpool University Press, 1976.

Gonzales, Michael J. "Chinese Plantation Workers and Social Control in Peru in the Late Nineteenth Century," *Journal of Latin American Studies*, Vol XII. 3 (October 1989), 385–424.

Goodsell, Charles T. *American Corporations and Peruvian Politics.* Cambridge, MA: Harvard University Press, 1973.

Hunt, Shane. *Real Wages and Economic Growth in Peru.* Boston: Boston University Center for Latin American Development Studies, 1977.

Jacobsen, Nils. *Mirages of Transition.* Thorp and Bertram, Peru, 1890–1977.

Webb, Richard. *Government Policy and the Distribution of Income in Peru, 1963–1973.* Cambridge, MA: Harvard University Press, 1977.

Weeks, John. *The Limits of Capitalist Development: The Industrialization of Peru, 1950–1980.* Boulder: Westview Press, 1980.

Peasants and Immigrants

Allen, Catherine J. "The Hold Life Has." In Starn, Degregori, and Kirk. *The Peru Reader: History, Culture and Politics,* 388–400.

Flores-Ochoa, Jorge A. *Pastoralists of the Andes: The Alpaca Herders of Paratía.* Philadelphia: Institute for the Study of Human Issues, 1979.

Friedman, Max Paul. *Nazis and Good Neighbors: The United States Campaign Against the Germans of Latin America in World War II.* New York: Cambridge University Press, 2003.

Gardiner, C. Harvey. *The Japanese and Peru: 1873–1973.* Albuquerque: University of New Mexico Press, 1975.

Gardiner, C. Harvey. *Pawns in a Triangle of Hate: The Peruvian Japanese and the United States.* Seattle: University of Washington Press, 1981.

Gonzales, Michael J. "The Rise of Cotton Tenant Farming in Peru, 1890–1920." *Agricultural History* 65, no. 1 (1991): 51–71.

Handleman, Howard. *Struggle in the Andes: Peasant Political Mobilization in Peru.* Austin: University of Texas Press, 1975.

Higashide, Seiichi. *Adios to Tears: The Memoirs of a Japanese-Peruvian Internee in the U.S. Concentration Camps.* Seattle: University of Washington Press, 2001.

Isbell, Billie Jean. *To Defend Ourselves: Ecology and Ritual in an Andean Village.* Austin: University of Texas Press, 1978.

McClintock, Cynthia. *Peasant Cooperatives and Political Change in Peru.* Princeton: Princeton University Press, 1981.

Mallon. *The Defense of the Community* cited earlier as Florencia Mallon, *The Defense of the Community in Peru's Central Highlands: Peasant Struggle and Capitalist Transition, 1860–1940.* Princeton: Princeton University Press, 1983.

Masterson, Daniel M., and Sayaka Funada Classen. "The Japanese in Peru and Brazil: A Comparative Perspective." In *Mass Migration to Modern Latin America,* edited by Samuel L. Baily and Eduardo José Miguez, 113–136. Wilmington, DE: Scholarly Resources, 2003.

Masterson, Daniel M. with Sayaka Funada Classen. *The Japanese in Latin America.* Urbana: University of Illinois Press, 2004.

Meyerson, Julia. *Tambo: Life in an Andean Village.* Austin: University of Texas Press, 1990.

Nicario. "Memories of a Cadre." In Starn, Degregori, and Kirk. *The Peru Reader,* 328–335.

Peloso, Vincent C. *Peasants on Plantations: Subaltern Strategies of Labor and Resistance in the Pisco Valley Peru.* Durham: Duke University Press, 1999.

Roberts, Bryan. *Miners, Peasants and Entrepreneurs; and Peasant Cooperation and Capitalist Expansion in Central Peru.* Austin: University of Texas Press, 1978.

Seligman, Linda. *Between Reform and Revolution: Political Struggles in the Peruvian Andes, 1969–1991.* Stanford: Stanford University Press, 1995.

Taylor, Lewis. *Bandits and Politics in Peru: Landlord and Peasant Violence in Hualgayoc, 1900–1930.* Cambridge: Cambridge University Press, 1983.

Watters, Raymond F. *Poverty and the Peasantry in Peru's Southern Andes, 1963–1990.* Pittsburgh: Pittsburgh University Press, 1992.

Worral, Janet. "Growth and Assimilation of the Italian Colony in Peru, 1860–1914," *Studi Emigrazione* 13 (1976): 41–60.

Worral, Janet. "Italian Immigrants in the Peruvian Economy," *Italian Americana* 2 (1975): 50–63.

The Military

Del Campo Rodríguez, Juan. *An Illustrated History of the Peruvian Navy*. Lima: Dirección de Intereses Maritimos, 2000.

Kruijt, Dirk. *Revolution by Decree: Peru, 1968–1975*. Amsterdam: Thesis Publications, 1994.

Masterson, Daniel M. *Militarism and Politics in Latin America: Peru from Sánchez Cerro to Sendero Luminoso*. Westport, CT: Greenwood Press, 1991.

Masterson, Daniel M. "*Caudillismo* and Institutional Change: Manuel Odría and the Peruvian Armed Forces, 1948–1956." In *Ranks and Privilege: The Military and Society in Latin America*, edited by Linda A. Rodríquez, 143–155. Wilmington, DE: Scholarly Resources, 1994.

Maurceri, Philip. "Military Politics and Counter-Insurgency in Peru." *Journal of Inter-American Studies and World Affairs* 34, no. 4 (1991–1992): 83–109.

North, Liisa, and Tanya Korovkin. *The Peruvian Revolution and the Officers in Power, 1967–1976*. Montreal: Centre for Developing Area Studies, McGill University, 1978.

Nunn, Frederick. "Professional Militarism in Twentieth Century Peru: Historical and Theoretical Background to the *golpe de estado* of 1968." *Hispanic American Historical Review* 59, no. 3 (1979): 391–418.

Nunn, Frederick. *Time of the Generals: Latin American Professional Militarism in World Perspective*. Lincoln: University of Nebraska Press, 1992.

Obando, Enrique. "Civil Military Relations in Peru, 1980–1996: How to Control and Co-opt the Military (and the Consequences of Doing So)." In *Shining and Other Paths: War and Society in Peru, 1980–1995*, 385–410, edited by Steve J. Stern, Durham: Duke University Press, 1998.

Philip, George D. E. *The Rise and Fall of the Peruvian Military Radicals, 1968–1976*. London: Athlone Press, 1978.

Scheina, Robert L. *Latin America's Wars*. 2 vols. Washington, DC: Brasseys, 2003.

Intellectual/Biography

Becker, Mark. *Mariátegui and Latin American Marxist Theory*. Athens, Ohio: Ohio University Press, 1993.

Bronner, Fred. "José de Riva Agüero (1885–1944), Peruvian Historian." *Hispanic American Historical Review* 36, no. 4 (1956): 490–502.

Charrvarría, Jesús. "The Intellectuals and the Crisis of Modern Peruvian Nationalism, 1870–1919." *Hispanic American Historical Review* 50, no. 1 (1970): 257–278.

Henderson, Donald C., and Grace R. Peréz. *An Annotated Calendar of the Luis Alberto Sánchez Correspondence*. University Park: Penn State University Press, 1982.

Mariátegui, José Carlos. *Seven Interpretive Essays on Peruvian Reality*, Translated by Marjory Urquidi. Austin: University of Texas Press, 1971.

Nunn, Frederick. "Mendacius Inventions, Vercarius Perceptions: The Peruvian Reality of Vargas Llosa's *La ciudad y los perros*," *The Americas* 43, no. 4 (1987): 453–466.

Pike, Fredrick B. *The Politics of the Miraculous in Peru: Haya de la Torre and the Spiritualist Tradition*. Lincoln: University of Nebraska Press, 1986.

Vanden, Harry E. *National Marxism in Latin America: José Carlos Mariátegui's Thought and Politics*. Boulder, CO: Westview Press, 1986.

Vargas Llosa, Mario. *A Fish in the Water*. New York: Penguin Books, 1995.

Church and Religion

Fleet, Michael, and Brian H. Smith. *The Catholic Church and Democracy in Chile and Peru.* Notre Dame: University of Notre Dame Press, 1997.

Klaiber, Jeffrey. *The Catholic Church in Peru.* Washington, DC: Catholic University Press, 1992.

Klaiber, Jeffrey. *Religion and Revolution in Peru, 1824–1976.* Notre Dame: University of Notre Dame Press, 1977.

Klaiber, Jeffrey. "The Catholic Lay Movement in Peru." *The Americas* 40, no. 2, (1983): 149–170.

Minaya, Luis. "Is Peru Turning Protestant." In Starn, Degregori, and Kirk. *The Peru Reader,* 471–477.

Paerregaard, Karsten. *Peruvians Dispersed: A Global Ethnography of Migration.* Plymouth, England: Lexington Books, 2008.

Peña, Milagros. "Liberation Theology in Peru: An Analysis of the Role of Intellectuals in Social Movement." *Journal of the Scientific Study of Religion* 33, no. 1 (1994): 34–45.

Pike, Frederick B. "Church and State in Peru and Chile since 1840: A Study in Contrasts." *The American Historical Review* 73, no. 1 (1967): 30–50.

Sigmund, Paul. *Liberation Theology at the Crossroads.* New York: Oxford University Press, 1990.

Sociopolitical Movements

Alexander, Robert J. *Aprismo: The Ideas and Doctrines of Víctor Raúl Haya de la Torre.* Kent: Kent State University Press, 1973.

De la Cadena, Marisol. *Indigenous Mestizos: The Politics of Race and Culture in Cuzco Peru, 1919–1991.* Durham: Duke University Press, 2000.

Ciccarelli, Orazio A. "Fascism and Politics during the Benavides Regime, 1933–1939: The Italian Perspective." *Hispanic American Historical Review* 70 (1990): 405–432.

Ciccarelli, Orazio A. "Militarism, *Aprismo* and Violence in Peru: The Presidential Election of 1931." *Buffalo: SUNY at Buffalo Council on International Studies,* 45, (1973).

Davies, Thomas M. *Indian Integration in Peru: A Half Century of Experience, 1900–1948.* Lincoln: University of Nebraska Press, 1974.

Davies, Thomas M. "The *Indigenismo* of the Peruvian *Aprista* Party." *Hispanic American Historical Review* 51, no. 4 (1971): 626–645.

Degregori, Carlos Iván. "Why Peasants Rebel: The Case of Peru's *Sendero Luminoso.*" *World Politics* 37, no. 1 (1984): 48–84.

Gorriti, Gustavo. "The Quota." In Starn, Degregori, and Kirk. *The Peru Reader,* 316–328.

Heilman, Jaymie P. "By Other Means: Politics in Ayacucho before Peru's Shining Path War, 1879–1980." PhD diss., University of Wisconsin, 2006.

Jacobson, Nils. "Liberalism and Indian Communities in Peru, 1821–1920." In Jackson, *Liberals, The Church and Indian Peasants,* 123–170.

Kanter, Harry. *The Ideology and Program of the Peruvian Aprista Movement.* Berkeley: University of California Press, 1953.

Kirk, Robin. *Decade of Chaqwa: Peru's Internal Refuges.* Washington, DC: U.S. Committee for Refugees: 1991.

Klarén, Peter F. *Modernization, Dislocation and Aprismo: Origins of Peru's Aprista Party, 1880–1932.* Austin: University of Texas Press, 1973.

Klaiber, Jeffrey. "The Popular Universities and the Origins of *Aprismo,* 1921–1924." *Hispanic American Historical Review* 55, no. 4 (1975): 693–715.

McClintock, Cynthia. *Politics, Economics and Revolution: Explaining the Guerrilla Movements in Peru and El Salvador.* Washington, DC: U.S. Institute of Peace, 1998.

Masterson, Daniel M. "In the Shining Path of Mariátegui, Mao Tse-tung or Presidente Gonzalo: Peru's *Sendero Luminoso* in Historical Perspective," In *Revolution and Revolutionaries: Guerrilla Movements in Latin America*, edited by Daniel Castro, 171–191. Wilmington, DE: 1999.

Palmer, David Scott, editor. *The Shining Path of Peru.* New York: St. Martins Press, 1994.

Pancho. "Vietnam in the Andes." In Starn, Degregori, and Kirk., *The Peru Reader,* 342–348.

Smith, Michael L. "Shining Path's Urban Strategy: Ate Vitarte." In Palmer, *The Shining Path of Peru,* 127–148.

Stein, Steve. *Populism in Peru: The Emergence of the Masses and Politics of Social Control.* Madison: University of Wisconsin Press, 1980.

Stokes, Susan. *Cultures in Conflict: Social Movements and the State in Peru.* Berkeley: University of California Press, 1995.

Foreign Relations

Clayton, Lawrence. *Peru and the United States: The Condor and the Eagle.* Athens: University of Georgia Press, 1999.

McClintock, Cynthia. *The United States and Peru: Cooperation and Cost.* New York: Routledge, 2002.

Palmer, David Scott. "Peru-Ecuador Border Conflict: Missed Opportunities, Misplaced Nationalism and Multi-lateral Peacekeeping." *Journal of Inter American Studies and World Affairs* 39, no. 3 (1997): 109–148.

Parodi, Carlos. *The Politics of South American Boundaries.* New York: Praeger, 2002.

Pike, Frederick. *The United States and the Andean Republics: Peru, Bolivia and Ecuador.* Cambridge, MA: Harvard University Press, 1977.

St. John, Ronald Bruce, *The Foreign Policy of Peru.* Washington, DC: L. Reinner, 1992.

Wilson, Joe. *The United States, Chile and Peru in the Tacna Arica Plebiscite.* Washington, DC: University Press of America, 1979.

Wood, Bryce. *The United States and Latin American Wars, 1932–1942.* New York: Columbia University Press, 1966.

Urbanization

Anonymous. "Soup of the Day: Family Kitchen No 79." In Starn, Degregori, and Kirk. *The Peru Reader,* 422–424.

Collier, David. *Squatters and Oligarchs: Authoritarian Rule and Policy Change in Peru.* Baltimore: Johns Hopkins University Press, 1976.

Collier, David. "Squatter Settlements and Policy Innovation in Peru." In *The Peruvian Experiment: Continuity and Change Under Military Rule,* edited by Abraham Lowenthal, 79–128. Princeton: Princeton University Press, 1975.

DeSoto, Hernando. *The Other Path: The Invisible Revolution in the Third World.* New York: Harper and Row, 1989.

Dietz, Henry. *Poverty and Problem Solving Under Military Rule: The Urban Poor in Lima, Peru.* Austin: University of Texas Press, 1980.

Lobo, Susan, *A House of Our Own.* (Tucson: University of Arizona Press, 1981).

Mangin, William. "Latin American Squatter Settlements: A Problem and a Solution," *Latin American Research Review* 2, no. 3 (1967): 65–98.

Paerregaard, Karsten. *Linking Separate Worlds: Urban Migrants and Rural Lives in Peru.* Oxford: Berg, 1997.

The Fujimori Phenomenon

Cameron, Maxwell, and Philip Maurceri, editors. *The Peruvian Labyrinth: Polity, Society and Economy*. University Park: Penn State University Press, 1997.
Conaghan, Catherine. *Fujimori's Peru: Deception in the Public Sphere*. Pittsburgh: Pittsburgh University Press, 2005.
Crabtree, John, and James Thomas, editors. *Fujimori's Peru: The Political Economy*.
Mauceri, Philip. *State Under Siege: Development and Policy Making in Peru*. Boulder, CO: Westview Press, 1996.
Vargas Llosa, Alvaro. *The Madness of Things Peruvian: Democracy Under Siege*. New Brunswick: Rutgers University Press, 1994.
Vargas Llosa, Mario. *A Fish in the Water.*

Women

Andreas, Carol. *When Women Rebel: The Rise of Popular Feminism in Peru*. Westport, CT: Lawrence Hill, 1985.
Barriga, Maruja. "The Difficult Equilibrium Between Bread and Roses: Women's Organizations and the Transition from Dictatorship to Democracy in Peru." In *The Women's Movement in Latin America: Participation and Democracy*, edited by Jane S. Jacquette, 2nd ed. Boulder: Westview Press, 1994.
Moyano, María Elena. *The Autobiography of María Elena Moyano: The Life and Death of a Peruvian Activist*. Translated by Patricia S. Taylor Edmisten. Gainesville: University of Florida Press, 2000.
Rousseau, Stephanie. "Women's Citizenship and Neopopulism: Peru under the Fujimori Regime." *Latin American Politics and Society* 48, no. 1 (2006): 117–141.
Vargas, Virginia. "The Women's Movement in Peru: Streams, Spaces and Knots." *European Review of Latin American and Caribbean Studies* 50 (1991): 7–50.

Index

About the Author

DANIEL MASTERSON is Professor of History at the U.S. Naval Academy in Annapolis, MD.

Other Titles in the Greenwood Histories of the Modern Nations
Frank W. Thackeray and John E. Findling, Series Editors

The History of Afghanistan
Meredith L. Runion

The History of Argentina
Daniel K. Lewis

The History of Australia
Frank G. Clarke

The History of the Baltic States
Kevin O'Connor

The History of Brazil
Robert M. Levine

The History of Canada
Scott W. See

The History of Central America
Thomas Pearcy

The History of Chile
John L. Rector

The History of China
David C. Wright

The History of Congo
Didier Gondola

The History of Cuba
Clifford L. Staten

The History of Egypt
Glenn E. Perry

The History of El Salvador
Christopher M. White

The History of Ethiopia
Saheed Adejumobi

The History of Finland
Jason Lavery

The History of France
W. Scott Haine

The History of Germany
Eleanor L. Turk

The History of Ghana
Roger S. Gocking

The History of Great Britain
Anne Baltz Rodrick

The History of Haiti
Steeve Coupeau

The History of Holland
Mark T. Hooker

The History of India
John McLeod

The History of Indonesia
Steven Drakeley

The History of Iran
Elton L. Daniel

The History of Iraq
Courtney Hunt

The History of Ireland
Daniel Webster Hollis III

The History of Israel
Arnold Blumberg

The History of Italy
Charles L. Killinger

The History of Japan, Second Edition
Louis G. Perez

The History of Korea
Djun Kil Kim